RHETORIC AND COURTLINESS IN EARLY MODERN LITERATURE

Rhetoric and Courtliness in Early Modern England explores the early modern interest in conversation as a newly identified art. Conversation was widely accepted to have been inspired by the republican philosopher Cicero. Recognising his influence on courtesy literature – the main source for 'civil conversation' – Jennifer Richards uncovers new ways of thinking about humanism as a project of linguistic and social reform. She argues that humanists explored styles of conversation to reform the manner of association between male associates; teachers and students, buyers and sellers, and settlers and colonial others. They reconsidered the meaning of 'honesty' in social interchange in an attempt to represent the tension between self-interest and social duty. Richards explores the interest in civil conversation among mid-Tudor humanists, John Cheke, Thomas Smith and Roger Ascham, as well as their self-styled successors, Gabriel Harvey and Edmund Spenser.

JENNIFER RICHARDS is Lecturer in English at the University of Newcastle upon Tyne. She is the editor, with James Knowles of *Shakespeare's Late Plays: New Readings* (1999) and the author of articles in *Renaissance Quarterly* and *Criticism*.

RHETORIC AND COURTLINESS IN EARLY MODERN LITERATURE

JENNIFER RICHARDS
University of Newcastle upon Tyne

CAMBRIDGE UNIVERSITY PRESS

PUBLISHED BY THE PRESS SYNDICATE OF THE UNIVERSITY OF CAMBRIDGE
The Pitt Building, Trumpington Street, Cambridge CB2 1RP, United Kingdom

CAMBRIDGE UNIVERSITY PRESS
The Edinburgh Building, Cambridge, CB2 2RU, UK
40 West 20th Street, New York, NY 10011-4211, USA
477 Williamstown Road, Port Melbourne, VIC 3207, Australia
Ruiz de Alarcón 13, 28014 Madrid, Spain
Dock House, The Waterfront, Cape Town 8001, South Africa

http://www.cambridge.org

© Jennifer Richards 2003

This book is in copyright. Subject to statutory exception
and to the provisions of relevant collective licensing agreements,
no reproduction of any part may take place without
the written permission of Cambridge University Press.

First published 2003

Printed in the United Kingdom at the University Press, Cambridge

Typeface Adobe Garamond 11/12.5 pt.   *System* LaTeX 2_ε [TB]

A catalogue record for this book is available from the British Library

ISBN 0 521 82470 2 hardback

Contents

Acknowledgements	*page* vi
Introduction	1
1. Types of honesty: civil and domestical conversation	20
2. From rhetoric to conversation: reading for Cicero in *The Book of the Courtier*	43
3. Honest rivalries: Tudor humanism and linguistic and social reform	65
4. Honest speakers: sociable commerce and civil conversation	87
5. A commonwealth of letters: Harvey and Spenser in dialogue	113
6. A new poet, a new social economy: homosociality in *The Shepheardes Calender*	139
Conclusion	168
Notes	171
Bibliography	195
Index	208

Acknowledgements

Many conversations have helped to shape this book, especially those I have shared with Lorna Hutson, Andrew McRae, Markku Peltonen, Neil Rhodes and Alison Thorne, all of whom commented generously upon chapters. Paul Suttie and Ariel Meirav were supportive friends in the early stages of my research; I am also very grateful for the encouragement offered by Jonquil Bevan and Ian Donaldson at this time. Thanks are also owed to Kate Chedgzoy, James Knowles, Steve Milner, Ceri Sullivan and Katherine Wilson. I benefited greatly from the good company and wide knowledge of Cathy Shrank and Phil Withington who showed me how fruitful conversation can develop between early modern literary critics and historians. Penny Fielding listened patiently to my ideas in their different versions; she also kept a very good table. Beate Muller has been an invaluable friend throughout my career at Newcastle. Thanks go to my mother, Wendy Francis, who insisted that I shorten my sentences. My two readers at Cambridge University Press gave the manuscript scrupulous attention. I am grateful to my colleagues in the English department at the University of Newcastle, who encouraged me to write the book that I wanted, and, in particular, to Mike Pincombe, who read far too many drafts of most of the chapters. My most tireless of readers and most generous of friends, though, is Dermot Cavanagh and it is to him that this book is dedicated.

This project would not have been completed without an AHRB research award in 1998–9. My research was also supported by British Academy Overseas Conference Grants in 1997 and 1999, enabling me to meet with Spenser colleagues at Kalamazoo. Parts of chapter 2 appeared in *Criticism* (1999) and *Renaissance Quarterly* (2001); I would like to thank the editors of these journals for permission to reprint this material.

Introduction

Recent years have seen a shift in focus among early modern English and British social historians from the 'demographic, economic and institutional' aspects of every day life to the cultural values and *mentalité* of 'communities'.[1] An area of study receiving fresh attention is the courtesy literature of 1500–1800 which disseminated new codes of conduct. Mostly, research in this area has established that the preoccupation with manners is an eighteenth-century phenomenon. Social historians of this period have argued that an increasing emphasis on good manners is related to the development of a consumer society, or have found in this century's conduct books a precursor to the bourgeois etiquette books of the nineteenth. This orientation towards the eighteenth century has inhibited debate about manners and sociability in the earlier period.[2] Yet, as Norbert Elias reminds us in *The Civilising Process* (1939), and, more recently, Anna Bryson in *From Courtesy to Civility* (1998), the change in the advice on manners actually begins in the early sixteenth century, with treatises such as Baldassare Castiglione's *Il libro del cortegiano*, printed in 1528.

The new emphasis on cultural values has the potential to bring social historians into closer contact with literary critics. 'Literary specialists', Anna Bryson argues, have for some time 'been offering a challenge to historians by showing much concern with the cultural codes, value systems and conflicts of value which underlie the productions of high culture'. In response, she urges her colleagues to recognise how an understanding 'of the traffic between the two definitions of culture' – culture both in the sense of 'art' and in the 'broader and more anthropological sense of the ways in which a society or group orders and perceives itself' – is 'crucial in the study of the literature of manners'.[3] However, I would argue that literary critics have yet to provide a sustained analysis of the relationship between literary form and manners: that is, a study of how the structuring of courtesy literature might both reflect and inform a particular apprehension of social and political interaction. For, though early modern literary critics have long expressed an interest in the courtesy books, these texts are usually invoked to explain the emergence of a culture of jostling and competitive courtiership.[4] More problematically, their discursive style tends to be overlooked, so that dialogic books are discussed alongside didactic prose treatises as if their different form did not matter. When their form *is* taken into consideration, moreover, it is presumed to exemplify a departure from, or a corruption of, a classical republican culture. The courtesy books are seen to disseminate an effete, dissembling courtly rhetoric that performs the subordination of the male aristocrat to a despotic monarch.[5] In this respect, early modern critics of courtesy share with historians of eighteenth-century politeness the assumption that the discourse of manners engenders conformist and hierarchically sensitive behaviour and the view that the 'social' and 'political' realms function independently.[6] However, we need not only to address what is distinctive about an earlier discourse of civility (as opposed to eighteenth-century notions of politeness), but to consider what a recovery of a sixteenth-century conception of the 'social sphere' might mean for our understanding of the period's political idiom.

This study has two broad aims. First, it argues that we need to attend more carefully to the dialogue form of the courtesy books, especially those which introduce and explore a new mode of speech, civil conversation. This speech form is derived from that same classical republican culture: that is, from the philosophical writings of the orator Cicero.[7] Recognising this will allow us to recover a lost discourse. Courtesy books written as dialogues are often engaging in a formal exploration of Ciceronian 'honestas' or self-restraint. For Cicero, and the courtesy writers who follow his example, apparently dissembling conduct is also 'honest' when it facilitates negotiation between different and conflicting interests. Without 'honestas' – that is, without the self-restraint of potentially domineering speakers – there can be no conversation *or* critical reflection. Many of the courtesy writers and translators are engaging directly with this aspect of Cicero's philosophy; they aim to accommodate Roman 'honestas' to Italian 'onesto' or plain English 'honesty'.[8] This is one of the fascinating and forgotten achievements of the courtesy books: that they contribute to the definition of a key concept of civility at a time when its meaning was highly unstable. In so doing, they offer a re-examination of the complex, sometimes conflictual, relationship between the individual and society. As I will argue, they are less interested in advising on tactics of self-promotion at court than in exploring ways of managing the relationship between self-interest and social duty, self-restraint and freedom and competition and cooperation in both social communication *and* commercial exchange. Indeed, their focus is extended far beyond the narrow confines of the court. Some courtesy books are describing conversation which is as suitable for the market as it is for the court.

Secondly, this study reconstructs an English, protestant reading community for the Italianate courtesy books. It investigates how a network of friends, based in Cambridge, were responsible for the dissemination of this distinctive rhetorical culture: from the 1530s onwards, John Cheke, Thomas Smith and Roger Ascham and, in the 1570s, Gabriel Harvey and Edmund Spenser. What these readers share in common with the Italian courtesy writers is a commitment to understanding Cicero's philosophical writings, in particular *De amicitia* and *De officiis*, so as to re-shape social relations, inevitably to their advantage. This self-interested recovery of Cicero is well recognised.[9] In this study, though, I will question a common form of ideology critique which tends to reduce social interaction to its most obvious manifestation: materialistic self-interest. The Elizabethan writers I will be analysing are of course self-promoting. Smith, the son of an Essex farmer, served under the Protector Somerset during the reign of Edward VI, and then became Elizabeth's ambassador to France in the 1560s, while, notoriously, Spenser, whose father was probably a journeyman tailor, became a landowner in Ireland. Harvey, the son of a Saffron Walden ropemaker, was less successful, though no less ambitious. He was appointed Lecturer in Greek in 1573 and, later, University Praelector in Rhetoric; however, he retired to Saffron Waldon in the late 1590s where he died in 1631. Even so, I want to explore, not how the ambitions of these men took both obvious and indirect forms in their life and writings, but rather, how they engaged in a process of dialogue and negotiation with their own aspirations and, in inevitably partial but deliberated ways, the interests of others.

A key aim of this book, then, will be to analyse how a group of humanists experimented with the dialogue form to express their personal aspirations whilst simultaneously recognising alternative and competing interests. We need to allow for the possibility that this negotiation was genuinely meant even as we identify the ways in which it failed or was exploited. In different ways, Smith, Ascham and Cheke, and later Harvey and Spenser, offer a self-conscious departure from the so-called 'cultural revolution' of the mid-Tudor Protestant reformers.[10] They use civil conversation to challenge a moral argument that was central to the first wave of Reformation literature: that an individual should serve the commonwealth by restraining his or her appetite for social advancement and personal profit. They do so by engaging in different kinds of textual conversation in order to discover a form of social interaction between teacher and pupil, or male friends, or indeed, individuals of different estates, which is capable of nurturing shared aspirations *and* sociability. In making this claim I am not denying that, as many have argued, the early modern period, with its expanding markets, print technology and, as some believe, increasingly centralised government, made possible a more individualistic ethos and instrumental association. Rather, I am arguing that we need to recognise the ongoing cultural significance of ideas of community and the common good with which any defence of self-interest or personal aspiration must negotiate.[11] The emphasis on the individual in this period remains part of a debate about one's 'duty' or 'obligation' to the commonweal; this is a difficult and disputed concept which is making a return in current debates about society and trust.[12]

In the sixteenth century this debate was only partly successful. We will need to be sceptical of Ascham's and Smith's efforts; the conversations they conduct are usually stage-managed by a dominant figure who clearly represents his own interest in being rewarded for the skilful management of others. Harvey and Spenser, in contrast, are more experimental; in their textual conversations they tend to question the role of the leading speaker, offering 'friendly' criticism of the attempts of early humanists at social negotiation. However, in the 1590s Harvey's own style of civility was to be criticised by the next generation of Cambridge graduates, especially by Thomas Nashe and Robert Greene. For all of these writers, though, the project of improving manners was inseparable from the pursuit of self-interest; this is not the same as the argument that reform is undertaken for the sake of self-promotion.[13]

Why then did civil conversation fail? An obvious reason is that this idealistic discourse could not keep pace with the increasing opportunities made available by ever-expanding markets and by colonisation. In the 1570s Harvey and Spenser experiment with the dialogue form to imagine a more open style of social communication for the benefit of the commonwealth. As a settler in Ireland in the 1590s, however, Spenser's priorities change. More obviously coercive means are needed to achieve civility. Irenius, the leading speaker of *A View of the Present State of Ireland* (c. 1596), argues that civil conversation – both familiar discourse and trade – will only achieve a functioning commonwealth after the brutal military conquest of the wild Irish has been accomplished.[14] However, another reason is that the discourse is itself fraught with internal contradictions. Sixteenth-century humanists inherited an overlapping but distinct Socratic dialogue style which informed that rival genre to the courtesy book, the husbandry manual. The figures of the courtier and the husbandman offer different styles of social and commercial exchange and also different styles of 'honesty' which are not easily translated into a modern political idiom. To understand these traditions we will need to be more open in our thinking about where we locate 'subversive' or 'conservative' agendas. The representation of the courtier as dissembling in much modern criticism, for example, indicates the victory of the plain husbandman as a social and cultural authority. Yet, there are good reasons why such plain-speakers are not to be trusted, not least because there is no way of knowing whether the claim to be telling the truth, or the promise of transparency, however plainly put, is not also a rhetorical ploy which aims to occlude the interests of others.

Chapters 1 and 2 of this study involve a reappraisal of the dialogue form of the well-known courtesy books such as Castiglione's *Il cortegiano*, Englished as *The Book of the Courtier* by Thomas Hoby in 1561, and Stefano Guazzo's *La civil conversatione* (1574), the first three books of which were translated by George Pettie as *Civile Conversation* (1581) and book 4 by Bartholomew Young (1586). The question of how we should read a dialogue that purports to be a civil conversation is explored in detail in chapter 1, which considers the critical possibilities and rhetorical slipperiness of the form of *Civile Conversation* – the treatise that gave the phrase 'civil conversation' its 'European currency'.[15] This chapter studies the differences between the Roman (Ciceronian) and Greek (Socratic) dialogue forms, and considers what their confusion means for the debate about social duty and self-interest, especially for women. Chapter 2 explores Castiglione's challenging exploration in the *Courtier* of the potential of Ciceronian dialogue as a critical method, a means to put pressure on restrictive social conventions and assumptions about the political order. Chapter 3 addresses the difficult question of why a group of Cambridge-educated protestant reformers is so interested in this treatise. It argues that this community share with Castiglione a commitment to re-defining the meaning of honesty as part of a process of linguistic reform, and that this process is implicated in religious, political and social Reformation. It also recognises, though, that they compromise the apparent openness of Ciceronian conversation. In chapter 4 we will examine less familiar treatises, the anonymous *Cyvile and Uncyvile Life* (1579) and Lodowick Bryskett's *Discourse of Civill Life* (1606) (a courtesy book turned colonial tract which transforms the dissembling Italian courtier into a plain English husbandman). These books will help us to understand how the experimentation with the dialogue form in the period informs both a critique of dishonest or exploitative commercial exchange and the formulation of a discourse of self-improvement and colonial expansion. Chapters 5 and 6 consider the literary collaborations of Edmund

Spenser and Gabriel Harvey, which includes *The Shepheardes Calender*, as exemplary civil conversations that challenge the easy assumption of social authority by the earlier reformers. These final chapters aim also to recall what is innovative and distinctive about the attempt of early Elizabethan literary writing to achieve cultural influence and social and political change.

CIVILITY AND ITS DISCONTENTS

A potential danger with this attempt to recover the attachment to Ciceronian conversation in the sixteenth century is that it unravels the subtle critique of the 'civilising process' which has been so important to the development of theorised and ethical readings of literary texts in the last three decades. In *Practicing New Historicism* (2000), Catherine Gallagher and Stephen Greenblatt appeal to Johann Gottfried von Herder's 'principle of diversification' – that there are different truths for different cultures – to support their commitment to 'the abandonment of the project of charting the *translatio imperii*, the great westward trajectory of civilization from Athens to Rome to, say, London'.[16] In this study, however, I will be exploring the attempt of the dialogic courtesy books to explore formally a Greco-Roman idea of *societas* as an association of communicating or conversing individuals. Since such an emphasis promises a return to an abandoned project, I think I owe an explanation. For this idea of society – best expressed by the Roman republican philosopher Cicero – now appears disingenuous, even deceitful, thanks partly to the influential counter-argument of Sigmund Freud which underpins modern critiques of the 'civilising process': that civilisation necessitates the repression of the instinctive, often violent assertion of the super ego. Freud's *Civilization and its Discontents*, published in 1930, self-consciously turns Cicero's myth of *societas* – and the Enlightenment tradition it inspired – on its head. In contrast to Cicero, who argues that men are naturally social, Freud insists that:

> men are not gentle creatures who want to be loved... they are, on the contrary, creatures among whose instinctual endowments is to be reckoned a powerful share of aggressiveness. As a result, their neighbour is for them not only a potential helper or sexual object, but also someone who tempts them to satisfy their aggressiveness on him, to exploit his capacity for work without compensation, to use him sexually without his consent... *Homo homini lupus* [man is a wolf to man].[17]

Freud's influence is apparent in Norbert Elias's sociology of the courtesy books in *The Civilizing Process*, which explores the relationship between the rise of civility and state formation. Elias uses the language of Freudian psychoanalysis – ego, super-ego, repression – to assert the psychological dynamics of a civilising process that increases the thresholds of embarrassment and encourages self-surveillance.[18] More recently, Freud's insistence that 'it is impossible to overlook the extent to which civilization is built up upon a renunciation of instinct' has inspired the argument of Stephen Greenblatt in his ground-breaking *Renaissance Self-Fashioning* (1980) that the development of a courtesy tradition is homologous with colonial expansion.[19]

Against this insight, though, I will explore the critical possibilities which the discourse of civil conversation offered. In particular, I am interested in how the textual practice of civil conversation offered a method for demystifying commonplace ideas, while establishing new habits of thought. In *The Book of the Courtier* conversation is used to unmask the 'myth' of native nobility: nobility is exposed as a social practice rather than a birthright. Meanwhile, in the anonymous English *Cyvile and Uncyvile Life* it is used to demystify what its author sees as a form of 'false consciousness': a tradition of monologic, plain-speaking social complaint (represented, say, by the georgic idealism of Hugh Latimer in the 1550s). This tradition, which defended the need to suppress self-interest for the greater good of the community, is shown to be quietly self-interested. In all three books, though, there is an understanding that straight-talking is not adequately honest and a wish to expand the meaning of 'honesty' to include conduct which might be deemed ironic or dissembling.

This shift of focus from the disciplinary nature of the 'civilizing process' to the critical possibilities that civility offered particular social groupings – mainly, educated university men from relatively humble backgrounds – is not meant to be a 'whiggish' defence of the progressive democratisation of a civil society. I understand well the limits and, indeed, failure of this discourse, not least in relation to women. (It should be noted, though, that this failure is also often repeated by 'modern' critics of the civilising process, as Freud's persistent use of the male pronoun suggests.) The particular failure of civil conversation will be addressed in chapter 1 under the heading of 'domestic conversation'; in chapter 4, we will explore how the courtesy books, in conjunction with the husbandry manuals, did indeed inform colonial projects in Ireland. Meanwhile, my discussion of Harvey's and Spenser's collaboration in chapters 5 and 6 is not intended to herald the beginning of a sophisticated English literary culture, but to explore a moment of possibility revealed in the self-conscious conjoining of new styles of friendship and literary experiment in the 1570s.

My style of argument, however, was developed in negotiation with the critical practices which govern the so-called 'new historicism', to which I am indebted. In particular, I wish to avoid the impasse that characterised much early new historicist criticism. There is a need to understand civil conversation as a discourse – to explore it on its own terms – so as to avoid making the unmasking of ideology the special prerogative of the modern critic. This imperative remains an issue even as leading 'new historicists' review their critical practice. In *Practicing New Historicism* Gallagher and Greenblatt brilliantly respond to their critics. 'Our project', they strenuously argue, 'has never been about diminishing or belittling the power of artistic representations... but we never believe that our appreciation of this power necessitates either ignoring the cultural matrix out of which the representations emerge or uncritically endorsing the fantasies that the representations articulate'. The difficult question which might be posed of their critical work, though, is whether *its* form has always been adequate to the ambitious and thoughtful task they set themselves. In this most recent manifesto, for instance, they continue to defend the privilege of the modern critic who has the opportunity to recover 'something that the authors we study would not have had sufficient distance upon themselves and their own era to grasp'.[20] Yet, there remains a need to work into historicist practice an acceptance of the fact that this distance also means that there will be some things which *we* cannot grasp, and a need to recognise that in avoiding 'uncritically endorsing the fantasies that [past] representations articulate', we might easily mistake or misunderstand their strategies of critique. This is critical 'honesty'.

We can see the problem posed by suspicious reading if we attend to Greenblatt's use of Philibert de Vienne's French anti-court satire *Le Philosoph de Court* (1545) – *The Philosopher of the Court* – to demystify the courtly trope of *sprezzatura* (pretended ignorance) in *Renaissance Self-Fashioning* (1980), the formative example of new historicism. For Greenblatt, Philibert's treatise is invaluable because it exposes the subtle working of courtly ideology in sophisticated texts like Castiglione's *Courtier*. Philibert's argument is that sixteenth-century courtesy books disguise their departure from classical ethics – represented by Plato, Aristotle and Cicero – so as to appear ethical, when in fact all they recommend is a superficial and amoral behaviour. This is a reading which makes sense to us historically once the courtier is envisaged at the court of an autocratic ruler. In such a context, we presume, it is difficult, if not impossible, to speak frankly or to influence policy. The essential mode of operation becomes the winning of favour, an aim which it is supposed must be secured with sycophantic display.

The Philosopher of the Court is a spoof courtesy book which is modelled on Cicero's *De officiis*. The joke of this treatise is that *De officiis* is subjected to a biased courtly reading, presumably after the fashion of a courtesy book like the *Courtier*. For example, its narrator follows Cicero when suggesting that the courtier's philosophy is based on the four cardinal virtues of wisdom, justice, fortitude and temperance, but he proceeds to offer ironic re-definitions: the courtier is wise if he knows how to deceive, and he is temperate if he is willing to be pleasing. Philibert also invents a fifth virtue, 'Grace', which represents the *sprezzatura* of courtly display paradoxically, as an ethical deceitfulness. 'Philibert's interest is in the working of the court mind at such moments', remarks Greenblatt, and especially in 'the social accommodation of an ethical embarrassment'. To make manifest this accommodation Greenblatt follows the moves made by the narrator in the chapter on Grace. The narrator begins by noting that Socrates has taught us 'that we should not maske, or disguise our selves'. He pauses for a moment because, as he has argued throughout the book, dissimulation is 'of so great force in our Philosophie', but he quickly proceeds to explain away the conflict of interest. Dissembling to accommodate others is not 'evill', he remarks, and then adds that Socrates 'Himselfe doeth serve us for example, for although he was ever like unto himself, constant and not variable, and desirous not to be seene other than he seemed: yet was he the greatest dissembler in the worlde'.[21] Greenblatt's observation that 'Philibert has seen deeply into the mind he satirizes and cunningly mimics its forms of thought and expression' seems absolutely, perhaps *too* reassuringly, right.[22]

This insight into the dishonesty of courtly ideology does not seem to have been shared by Philibert's English translator, George North, who, as Daniel Javitch observes, apparently mistook *The Philosopher of the Court* for a straightforward courtesy book.[23] His misreading of Philibert raises interesting questions about the reception of sophisticated continental courtesy books at the Elizabethan court. Still, it is easy to underestimate the insights of our forebears who were probably better schooled in classical philosophy than ourselves. To proceed with care we should recognise the possibility that, if North did misread *The Philosopher of the Court*, then he may have done so because of the superficiality of Philibert's own reading of Cicero.

The prologue articulates the reasons for Philibert's rejection of court culture quite clearly. In North's translation Philibert's narrator begins with a rant against the courtly philosopher who, living in the world, has 'no other guide than that blinde beast of common and popular judgement' rather than the promptings of Nature (sig. B5v). He attacks the courtier's confusion of the distinction ancient philosophers made between 'first nature', given us at our birth by God, and a corrupted 'seconde Nature', synonymous with custom or habit, before going on to perform (ironically of course) just such a confusion (sigs. B7r–B8r). The narrator's early attack is meant to clarify the subject of the satire: the failure of courtly philosophers to distinguish between nature and custom, truth and lies, right and wrong. He wants to show us how courtly philosophers turn words inside out, wresting them from their true meaning for personal advantage. Yet, the joke is really on Philibert. The irony, as we will discover at more leisure in chapter 2, is that it is Philibert's misrepresentation of Cicero which actually approximates Cicero's interrogation of the ironic Socrates in *De oratore*: honesty for Cicero encompasses the kind of dissimulative – or accommodating – conduct which Philibert dismisses. Thus, a key speaker in this rhetorical manual admits that 'what impressed me most deeply about Plato [in his disguise as Socrates] was, that it was when making fun of orators that he himself seemed to me to be the consummate orator'.[24] Cicero and Castiglione understand that this kind of pretended ignorance is an important discursive tool. It helps them to expose the artificiality of the distinction between nature and custom or truth and lies insisted upon by some philosophers who, like Plato, are committed to the discovery of a universal Truth.

Readings of the courtesy books which emphasise their dishonesty are within the venerable tradition of Elizabethan anti-court satire, as Greenblatt's self-identification with Philibert suggests. But we should be wary of associating ourselves too readily with such truth-telling critics. Philibert's treatise offers a sophisticated study of the presumed ideology of courtliness, and yet his critical thinking relies on an overly simplified vocabulary of opposites drawn from the very Platonic tradition that Cicero is seeking to unmask: honesty versus dissimulation, the metaphysical philosopher versus the courtier deemed a slave to fickle opinion. These same terms are to be found in less sophisticated satires. The dialectic of Antonio de Guevara's *Libro Llamado Menosprecio de Corte y Alabança de Aldea* (1539), translated into English in 1548 by Sir Frances Bryant as *A Dispraise of the life of the Courtier, and a Commendacion of the life of the labouryng man*, is between the courtier who 'occupieth himselfe in nothyng but in eatyng, drinkyng, & sleapyng' and inventing 'shiftes' and the husbandman (really a landowner) who recreates himself pleasantly and honestly in the village, fishing, netting birds and hunting with dogs. Since the court is a fantastical place, Guevara concludes, we should, like Plato, abandon its 'clamor & cry' and dwell in a village, in fact an *Academica* or 'schole' where we will find 'a pore, an honest, and a peaceable life'.[25] We might remember here the advice of the critical theorist Hannah Arendt to all plain-speakers in her essay 'Truth and Politics', that the truth-telling favoured by Plato is a kind of despotism because it fails to take into account different opinions.[26]

Ironically, it is Freud who shows us how we might accommodate a more dialectical reading of the civilising process. *Civilization and its Discontents* – 'that remorselessly bleak treatise for which all civilization is ultimately self-marring', as Terry Eagleton describes it – is one of several studies by Freud on the antagonistic relationship between man and 'civilization'.[27] In 1927 he published an earlier essay, *The Future of an Illusion*, which offers a rather different process of argument both to discredit 'civilization' and to defend psychoanalysis as the means to fulfil the sense of hope and possibility which the concept also carries. This essay is close in spirit to the civilising courtesy books. Its style of argument is dialectical; that is, it prompts us repeatedly to return to, and to rethink, familiar terms and concepts. One of those familiar concepts is 'illusion', another is 'fact'.

The essay begins with the same premise as *Civilization and its Discontents*, that destructive and anti-social feelings are a 'psychological fact' (p. 7), and the reaffirmation of the 'fact that the regulations of civilization can only be maintained by a certain degree of coercion' (p. 8). Freud also establishes that religion is a necessary supplement, serving 'to reconcile a man to the sacrifices he has made on behalf of civilization' with the illusory promise of fulfilment in the next life (p. 14). However, in contrast to the monologic *Civilization and its Discontents*, *The Future of an Illusion* includes an imagined antagonist who defends religion. Consequently, the progress of Freud's argument is gradual and contradictory, yet it allows for the questioning of the recognised 'facts' of religion and civilisation.

The psychoanalyst shares the same aims as the religious zealot, 'namely', the increase of 'the love of man and the decrease of suffering' (p. 53). But he differs in his adherence to, and contrary apprehension of, the 'facts' of his discipline. Our narrator recognises that '[r]eligious ideas are teachings and assertions about facts and conditions of external (or internal reality) which tell one something one has not discovered for oneself and which lay claim to one's belief' (p. 25). One might easily say the same of the 'psychological fact' that civilisation depends on coercion and repression. And yet, our narrator seeks to destabilise this 'fact' even as he asserts it, signalling his difference from the religious zealot. In this essay we learn to distinguish between religion as a psychical delusion (rather than an illusion) because it can never fulfil our wishes in this life, and the science of psychoanalysis as 'illusory' in the sense that it holds out the possibility of self-fulfilment. When the antagonist argues that our narrator is contradictory (and therefore deluded) because he asserts that 'men... are so entirely governed by their instinctual wishes', and yet believes that 'civilization' might be achieved by rational rather than affective (and repressive) means, the narrator responds thus: 'It is true that men are like this; but have you asked yourself whether they *must* be like this, whether their innermost nature necessitates it?' (p. 47). Unlike the religious zealot, the psychoanalyst understands that 'facts' are not immutable or given, but the product of culture and education. The essay's method of argument aims to convey that the 'psychological fact' of the repressive nature of the civilising process is true only insofar as it is a stage in the way in which we think about ourselves.[28]

REREADING THE COURTESY BOOKS

My argument that the dialogue form of the courtesy books really matters may seem straightforward enough but it marks a significant departure from our accustomed way of reading them. Anna Bryson may recommend the innovative analysis of the courtesy books by literary critics to social historians, but in fact these same critics have tended to fit this genre to well-established historical paradigms such as the 'crisis of the aristocracy', or the shift from a 'lineage society' to a 'civil society' (where the term 'civil society' connotes a more atomised social grouping).[29] Thus, Frank Whigham argues that English interest in courtesy literature 'arose during what Lawrence Stone calls "the century of mobility, 1540–1640", during which "English society experienced a seismic upheaval of unprecedented magnitude"'.[30] Whigham bases his argument that the courtesy books defend aristocratic privilege on Stone's statistical analysis of the swelling of the upper ranks of society in this period. The treatises, he argues, were written to reassure the established aristocracy of their 'natural' authority, but they were also used by aspiring courtiers eager to gain access to the corridors of power at the Elizabethan court by aping the manners of their superiors.[31] To underscore their attractiveness to a jostling, competitive readership, however, Whigham ignores the dialogue form of some key texts, prompting a rather flat or literal reading of a frequently ironic and questioning body of writing. These books, he argues, 'formally invite...particulate consumption' by readers eager to become courtly. Such fragmented reading is typical of the period; 'established and mobile Elizabethans alike would deploy arguments on either side as need arose, without feeling either devious or conspiratorial – indeed, without sensing any contradiction at all'.[32]

Some courtesy books do invite 'particulate consumption', enabling young men to get on quickly in the world. Giovanni della Casa's *Galateo* – made popular by R. Peterson's translation in 1576 – gives explicit advice on

Introduction 13

how not to behave in public. On della Casa's advice we learn (among other things) not to inspect the contents of our handkerchiefs as if 'pearles and Rubies dropped from [our] braynes'.[33] More choice is offered by Simon Robson's pseudo-Italian courtesy book, *The court of civill courtesie* (1577), which claims to have been translated 'out of the Italian, by a Gentleman'.[34] However, even this text offers a rather rigid sense of correct social conduct. Robson claims on his title page that the text is 'Fitly furnished with a pleasant porte of stately phrases and pithie precepts' for young gentlemen who are 'desirous to frame their behaviour according to their estates, at all times, and in all companies'. This seems to be the strength of the book: that it gives practical sentences which enable young men to manage the tricky rules of deference which inform their social world. However, the complexity of this etiquette is perplexing to the modern reader. A gentleman who finds himself in the company of someone of lower rank than himself but yet highly esteemed is advised to give up his place at the table, though 'with sucth a modest audacitie, mingled with a smylyng grace, and curteous speeche, neither too lowde nor whisperyng, as the rest of the company may well perceive: it is the vertues, and not the man that is preferred, and that it is offered rather of a curteous disposition, then of a sheepishe simplicitie'. If this sounds too difficult a negotiation to achieve then we might employ one of Robson's ready-made phrases:

> I pray you goe, for I love to follow the steps of mine elders.
> You must needes goe, for I cannot a waye to goe formost.
> On, on I pray you, you bee the next the dore.
> If you goe not wee shall strive all day, for I will not.
> You make too mutch adoe for so smal a matter.   (B1r-B1v)

Not all texts, however, are prescriptive and not all invite 'particulate consumption'. Texts like *Civile Conversation* or *Cyvile and Uncyvile Life* are written as conversations rather than manuals, and their leading speakers ostentatiously pretend ignorance, or defer to the wisdom of their obviously junior or misguided interlocutors, for example, when the leading interlocutor of *Cyvile and Uncyvile Life*, the courtier Vallentine, generously admits to his friend, the country gentleman Vincent: 'I am very glad that my poore reasons have taken good effect, but therin I wil challenge no more to my selfe, then I deserve: which is, that I have put you in minde of that you either forgot, or else (for want of leysure) never considered: For I acknowledge you of much more wisdome and iudgement then I am'.[35] This style disseminates a practice of civility which may be assimilated by the careful reader, not the particulate consumers suggested by Whigham, but those educated Elizabethan men who, like Gabriel Harvey, were evidently willing to read a text over and over again.[36]

Recognising the reading practice these books encourage inevitably affects the way we should read them. Deference is not just a matter of doffing one's cap to a superior. As Gerald M. Sider explains, it also entails the 'diffuse or specific conscious adjustments people make to each other's claims in their lives *as a whole*', and it is integral to the constitution of 'oppositional social relations'.[37] *Sprezzatura* or feigned ignorance may look like a disdainful snub to 'untowardly asseheades' and suggest an unwillingness to clarify the rules which might allow outsiders entry into an aristocratic 'club'.[38] In some contexts it must have worked in just such a way to exclude outsiders. Yet, as the example of Vallentine in *Cyvile and Uncyvile Life* shows, it is also used in civil conversation 'ideally' to draw less assured interlocutors into social exchange, while requiring self-restraint in confident and dominant speakers. As we will see in chapter 4, in this particular treatise such self-restraint really matters; its author is also providing a critique of the 'honest' generosity of the traditional manorial lord which conceals his exploitation of tenants.

This study signals a shift away from the individualistic and competitive paradigm taken for granted by recent readers of the courtesy books, to an emphasis on negotiation.[39] It complements the recovery by some social and cultural historians of the importance of ideas of community to early modern culture.[40] The longstanding assumption that the early modern period marks a transition from one form of social organisation, the 'community', to another, 'society', argue Alexandra Shepard and Phil Withington, 'ignores the fact that medieval settlements were stratified, conflictual, demographically unstable, and integrated into national institutional structures'. It also ignores the polyvalence of the term 'community' in the sixteenth century. Recent work has stripped this term of its nostalgic association with a lost 'merry England', using it more loosely to connote simply '"small groups, bounded in one way or another".'[41] This definition allows in turn for studies of communities to focus on 'conflict and power', rather than just 'the processes of reconciliation'.[42] What a literary study of the early modern courtesy books and their readers can contribute to this burgeoning field is the recovery of a discourse of negotiation which is predicated on a particular paradigm, honest rivalry. Rivalry is 'honest' when it recognises and tries to manage 'conflict and power' in social relationships. This paradigm is employed by humanists to replace one ideal of community, the security of which rests on the preservation of the 'estates', with another, in which the play between the conflicting interests of men of similar and different estates is seen as productive *and* sociable. The phrase honest rivalry – which I derive from Cicero's study of friendship, *De amicitia* – is a more useful term than 'competition' because it forces us to recognise the importance attached to community in this period when the straightforward assertion of self-interest was deemed anti-social and unethical.[43]

With this emphasis on community in mind, this study also challenges the deep-rooted assumption that the courtesy books defend the privileges of an established elite by naturalising vertical relations. The style and content of these books would have been recognised by educated, aspirational men from a variety of backgrounds as having been written for them. Among many social historians there is an awareness of the need to question the gentrification of civility. Thus, Jonathan Barry reiterates a paradox of the courtesy books, that the manners such treatises recommend are 'in many cases, those practised by servants and tradesmen, as well as other inferiors, in their dealings with their masters, customers, and superiors'.[44] In his study of the civility – or 'bourgeois collectivism' – of urban freemen in early seventeenth-century London, Barry presents a challenge not just to the gentrification of civility, but also to a concept which defines much socio-economic study of the early modern period, the rise of 'possessive individualism'. The work ethic of 'thrift, respectability, and industry' associated with urban freemen is usually 'seen as the foundation of individualism', he argues, but success was assumed by them 'to depend on collective rather than individual action', and was 'accompanied by a set of overtly collective values, of sociability and good fellowship'. These values were learned in specific contexts rather than books, which included the private household as well as a variety of public settings: alehouses, inns, coffee houses and 'other places of entertainment'.[45]

Barry draws a distinction in his essay between courtesy books which taught gentlemen how to behave like tradesmen and the experience of associational life which taught urban freemen how to be civil. However, we need not only to resist seeing the dialogic courtesy books as representing theory rather than practice, but to expand our conception of their readership to include university men from humble, artisanal backgrounds as well as courtiers. Courtesy books written as dialogues already disseminate a practice of conversing; they may even have been read aloud in company as 'live' dialogues.[46] In England, they attracted the interest of educated male readers who were successfully engaged in forming practical friendships and networks in the service of the protestant Reformation. For example, Thomas Hoby began his translation of Castiglione's *Courtier* in the 1550s while travelling on the continent; it was printed in 1561, along with a letter from his former tutor, John Cheke. This translation is praised by another friend, Roger Ascham, in his influential *The Schoolmaster*.[47] It is true that these men all share in common some connection to the 'court': Cheke was tutor to prince Edward while Ascham was tutor to the princess Elizabeth, and later her Latin secretary. Another member of this group, Thomas Smith, was ambassador to France and also an advisor to the Privy Council. The primary connection between them, however, is that they are members of an informal network of friends designated 'the Athenian tribe' active in Cambridge in the 1540s, who later migrated to London.[48] The identity of this group lies in the attempt of Cheke and Smith to promote the Erasmian pronunciation of Greek in the 1540s, and in a commitment to the 'new learning' which encouraged a return to sources, both the Bible and classical texts. They are also committed to the recovery of classical forms of social and political organisation.[49] Their interest in Castiglione is inspired by a desire to develop the English vernacular through translation and, also, to understand Cicero: Hoby in particular understood that Castiglione had offered a brilliant new reading of *De oratore* and *De officiis* which would help to develop 'civyll condicions' among his compatriots.[50]

For these humanists the development of 'civyll condicions' was integral to the success of the Reformation. On the one hand, they are searching for a 'civil' speech form which might carry their challenge to the social and political order without seeming divisive and factional; on the other hand, they understand that the process of Reformation entails (in theory) an expansion of participation in both religious and political debate. One way in which political participation is expanded in the period is through the incorporation of towns and boroughs (and the second half of the sixteenth century saw a dramatic increase in this policy). Incorporation entails the extension of metropolitan institutions – magistracy, parliament, counsel, law – to local communities. It provides an infrastructure which facilitates different kinds of conversation, including the civil varieties favoured by the humanists.[51] Incorporation was often accompanied by debate about civic and republican idioms. John Barston, a graduate of St John's College, Cambridge and the new town clerk of Tewkesbury, notes Markku Peltonen, celebrated the incorporation of his town with the print publication of a prose treatise that explores Ciceronian ideas of society, sociability and honesty in *Safeguard of Societie* (1576). The courtesy books so eagerly translated in this period also support interest in civic culture. 'A sixteenth-century Englishman perusing George Pettie's translation of Guazzo's *The civile conversation*', writes Peltonen, 'could read of the importance of public debate', for 'commonwealthes, Cities, yea, small Townes, do they not assemble together to choose officers, & to establish orders by common consent?'[52]

One of the most committed humanist readers of the courtesy books, however, is undoubtedly a Cambridge fellow who belonged to the next generation of scholars, Gabriel Harvey. Harvey owned two copies of the *Courtier*, an Italian version and Hoby's translation (the latter is heavily annotated); he also owned Italian and English copies of Guazzo's *Civile Conversation*, and he transcribes several pages of dialogue concerning the boorishness of country gentlemen from *Cyvile and Uncyvile Life* into his commonplace book.[53] Meanwhile Harvey's *Letter-Book*, compiled between 1573 and 1579, explores the opportunities which the courtesy books offered for 'everyday' social and literary exchange. This manuscript collection identifies the courtesy books as the new reading of Cambridge students; it also includes a range of conversations: among them, petitioning letters to John Young, formal letters seeking advice from Smith, letters to his pupil Arthur Capel, friendly, jocular letters to Spenser, the correspondence of a woman to her lover (a miller), a 'garden communication', and a prose fiction in which Harvey recalls how, by intercepting a letter, he trumps a local nobleman attempting to seduce his sister.[54]

Though Harvey is loosely connected to the 'Athenian tribe' through acquaintance with Thomas Smith (his academic mentor and neighbour in Saffron Walden), he is eager to constitute a rival 'Ciceronian' community which would be seen to advance on the achievements of both Smith and Ascham. Harvey aims to make the English dialogue more conversational, taming the dominant 'teacherly' speakers of Smith's and Ascham's texts. As we will see in chapter 5, Harvey's familiar letters to Spenser – a 'civil conversation' *in absentia* – gently expose the failure of Ascham to understand fully and practise conversation in *The Schoolmaster*, a failure which inhibits the 'civilising' of the English vernacular and of male social interaction. They also aim to reform Smith's idea of the role of the university graduate. Instead of managing commerce between the different estates (as Smith aspires to do), the academic Harvey is eager to accommodate himself to the 'market'. Spenser and Harvey also rival another offshoot from the original 'Athenian tribe', a community of friends which emerged at the Inns of Court in the 1560s. In chapter 6 I will explore how Spenser's *The Shepheardes Calender* (1579) offers an alternative exercise in homosociality to the ideal of self-sacrificing male friendship explored by Barnabe Googe and George Turbeville in their poetry collections. That is, Spenser and Harvey propose a more flexible model of male social interaction which works through the dialectical tension between competition and cooperation so as to promote the 'sociability' of personal aspiration. This flexibility is reflected in the varied locations in which their 'actual' and 'fictional' conversations take place: the household of employers (like Robert Dudley, Earl of Leicester), a shared bed in Westminster, a garden.[55]

The example of Gabriel Harvey – the son of a Saffron Walden ropemaker – shows us how civil conversation might be used to trump bullying aristocratic superiors. The second half of the sixteenth century saw a great increase in admissions to both Oxford and Cambridge. A large number of these men came from non-aristocratic backgrounds. However, the universities also saw an increase in the number of aristocrats joining its student body, affecting the culture of the colleges.[56] In the early 1570s we find Harvey using civility as the standard against which he judged one aristocratic fellow of Pembroke Hall, Cambridge, Thomas Neville. In his letters to John Young, the London-based Master of Pembroke Hall, Harvey recounts how Neville attempted to block his progression to the Master of Arts on spurious grounds. The main problem seems to have been Harvey's unsociability rather than his academic ability. In the first letter, dated 21 March 1573, he explains that Neville 'laid against mi commun behaviur, that I was not familiar like a fellow, and that I did disdain everi mans cumpani'. His somewhat pettish response, that he often stayed up after dinner and that he 'was as fellowli as the best', as well as his insistence that 'What thai cale sociable I know not: this I am suer, I never avoidid cumpani: I have bene merri in cumpani: I have been ful hardly drawn out of cumpani', might help us to see what Neville means.[57] Harvey seems to be the serious, humourless scholar with a chip on his shoulder to the noble man Neville and his wassailing peers. He does not fit into the new aristocratic society of the colleges, perhaps partly because of his origins, and partly too because of his academism. Yet, the letters describe a culture clash not just between a lowly scholar and an aristocratic don, but between a civil gentleman and an unreformed, boorish nobleman. For Harvey's letter to Young also reveals a different conception of sociability as civility which is contrasted with Neville's unruly camaraderie. Harvey does not just record the vindictive behaviour of his aristocratic peers; he also describes Neville's refusal to be sociable on his terms. 'I have not shoun mi self so surli towards mi inferiors', writes Harvey, 'as M. Nevil hath shoun him self disdainly towards his œquals and superiors too.' Neville, complains Harvey, refuses to return salutations. For example, he 'hath lookd awri an another wai, nether afording me a word, nor a cap', showing 'a lusti contempt of so silli a frend' (pp. 4–5). Neville's snobbish disdain for the lowly Harvey is an instance of his own failure to behave with the familiarity of a civil gentleman. When

Harvey complains of Neville's incivility it is likely that he has in mind the complaint of Anniball in Guazzo's *Civile Conversation* that 'I knowe some so haughtie and uncivill, that they disdaine to salute those whiche salute them, which is a signe of a barbarous minde' (2. 156).

Harvey's preoccupation with the niceties of salutation in the 1570s is not indicative of a petty mind nurtured on the reading of conduct books. Indeed, it is time to ditch the commonplace argument that these books represent a departure from serious political debate. In general, neither the courtesy books nor the English dialogues we will be exploring deal with matters of 'high' politics. That is, they tend not to offer counsel to monarchs. This is true even of the experienced counsellor Thomas Smith, whose dialogue on the reform of Greek pronunciation uses a classical political idiom to critique the tyranny of colleagues in the early 1540s, but no obvious interest is shown in the wider court politics of Henry VIII. This is where an emphasis on 'community' can help, by discovering, as Patrick Collinson explains, 'signs of political life at levels where it was not previously thought to have existed'. The emphasis on community, he notes, can 'disclose the horizontal connections of political life at those lower levels as coexistent with the vertical connections which depended upon monarchy and lordship and which have been the ordinary concerns of political history'. Indeed, early modern England is best understood as 'a series of overlapping, superimposed communities which are also semi-autonomous, self-governing political cultures' or '"republics"'.[58] Intimate, social relationships are imbued with a political significance. Smith, Ascham and Harvey are all concerned with issues of good government, but the dialogues they write are usually located in their immediate environs, especially Cambridge. Thus, Smith describes himself and his friends as 'cives' or citizens of the University.[59] Harvey's criticism of Neville's incivility is in this tradition. Neville is not just failing to greet Harvey nicely; he is also failing as a citizen of the commonwealth (or corporation) of Cambridge to which both men equally belong.

CHAPTER I

Types of honesty: civil and domestical conversation

Advice on conduct had been given for centuries. 'Social prescriptions concerning cleanliness, sobriety of dress and demeanour, ritual at table, and respectful conduct to superiors', writes Anna Bryson, 'were written into monastic Rules' from the twelfth century. More detailed lists, she adds, survive in vernacular treatises in England from at least the fifteenth century.[1] Treatises such as *Urbanitatis* (c. 1460) advise their readers to keep themselves 'Fro spettying & snetyng' and to 'Be privy of voydance' (or discreet when farting).[2] Much of this advice found its way into sixteenth-century Italian treatises, for example, Giovanni della Casa's *Galateo*. Some sixteenth-century English books of manners are clearly modelled on medieval conduct books, suggesting, as Bryson argues, that there was 'no sharp chronological break'.[3] Thus, Hugh Rhodes, a Gentleman of the Chapel under Edward VI – and a 'regular sobersides' according to his Victorian editor – is the author of the compilation *The Boke of Nurture, or Schoole of Good Maners: for Men, Servants, and Children, with Stans puer ad mensam*.[4] Its first text is reminiscent of John Russell's *Boke of Nurture* (c. 1450); it also expands the popular *Stans puer ad mensam*, attributed to John Lydgate. Rhodes's treatise is of uncertain date; it was probably written as early as 1530, and it was reprinted several times, including in 1577. In it, Rhodes predictably reminds the reader not to scratch his head at the table, not to spit across the table and to 'Belche thou neare to no mans face / with a corrupt fumosytye'.[5]

Even so, Rhodes's treatise is uncharacteristic of sixteenth-century conduct books. It is distinctly 'medieval' in conception; it offers young pages advice on the table manners and rituals of dining in the great hall. Sixteenth-century conduct books, in contrast, 'tend to be more varied, more ambitious, and more discursive'.[6] They describe the conduct proper to a variety of situations and interlocutors. More importantly, several of the influential texts were written in dialogue form, thereby signalling a new preoccupation with polite conversation. The page boy is advised in *Stans puer ad mensam* to 'kepe honestly silence'.[7] In the *Boke of Nurture* Rhodes also advises him to be circumspect in speaking, and always to recognise his lord's precedence:

> Talke not to thy soveraygne deare
> no tyme when he doth drinke;
> When he speaketh, give audyence,
> and from him doe not shrynke...
>
> To prate in thy maysters presence,
> it is no humanitye;
> But to speake when he talketh to thee
> is good curtesye.[8]

Stefano Guazzo's *Civile Conversation* could not be more different. This treatise signals a shift in emphasis from the honest silence of the page in the company of his lord in the great hall, to the chatty conviviality of friends in a more private and intimate space.[9] Indeed, Guazzo is very specific about the location of his 'civil conversation'; it takes place in a 'little closet' in his house (1. 15).

Social historians have drawn our attention to the changing uses of space in the country houses of the gentry in this period as attitudes to public entertainment shifted. Felicity Heal, for example, discovers in noble households of the fourteenth and fifteenth centuries a gradual 'growth of individual chambers' which 'witness an impulse towards privacy'.[10] This impulse would be gradually realised in the sixteenth century. Thus, Alice T. Friedman describes as typical of Tudor aristocratic house-planning an 'increase in the size and number of spaces (rooms, terraces, gardens) provided for socialising and polite entertainment', the gradual isolation of the manor house from the village community and the provision for 'diversification of private spaces and service areas – including private studies, muniment rooms, and storage rooms'. Many of these architectural changes, she suggests, were prompted by 'improvements in business technique'. Thus, small rooms became repositories for the documents needed for 'increased control of both property and tenants'.[11] This archival function is true also of that one room which has attracted critical interest in recent years, the 'closet', a space set aside for private devotion and study. The closet has much to tell us about attitudes to privacy in the sixteenth century. As Alan Stewart argues, the closet is not only a place for the solitary reader; it is also 'a secret non-public transactive space between two men behind a locked door', a space, that is, where companions might engage in the open secret of plotting their careers or making business plans. John Dee mapped the north-west passage with companions in his closet. Sir William More's closet at Losely

Hall was also used for business. Its contents include classical treatises, recent poets, chronicles, books of geometry, almanacs, dictionaries, books of proverbs and prognostications. These are '*working* papers', argues Stewart, 'a resource of useful reference information with which to cross-reference and to plan'.[12]

Guazzo's 'little closet' is a meeting place for two friends and, in this sense, it confirms Stewart's description of the room as a 'nonpublic transactive space'. Yet, if we are to understand what is going on in Guazzo's imaginary closet we will need to adapt Stewart's model. Like the actual closets which Stewart describes, this fictive space contains 'a fewe small bookes'; however, as Guazzo explains, they are 'rather for a shewe then for studie' (1. 15). Later, in book I, the leading speaker Anniball notices that the closet is decorated with 'diverse pleasant pictures' which 'doth mervellously recreate our mindes, and ministreth occasion of witty talke' (1. 55). These details suggest a different use of this space. Guazzo's closet is not a place for secret negotiations, but a transitional space in which a negotiation between solitary and public selves takes place. It is also a space in which classical learning is practised rather than discussed. That is, this closet is a place for 'witty talke' or conversation after the fashion suggested in Cicero's *De officiis*, an activity which is represented by Guazzo as a remedy for the ills of solitary study.

Civile Conversation opens with Guazzo telling us how he discovered that his brother William 'was become so weake, leane, and falne away, by the harde handling of a very long quartane Ague' (1. 14). William is visited by a neighbour, the physician Anniball, who discovers that the young man is suffering from an excess of scholarly seclusion. He has cut himself off from the world, partly from a distaste for company, but partly, too, because he aspires to the 'name of a simple scholler, [rather] then of an ignorant Courtier' (1. 38). This is because William believes that scholars 'are favoured and honoured amongst other learned men, who take for plainnesse of manners and gentlenesse of minde, that which the common sorte calleth foolishnesse' (1. 37). In the course of their conversation Anniball enables William to experience how (as Cicero also argues), 'man, being a compagnable creature, loveth naturally the conversation of other men', and he persuades him of the need for the skills of an 'ignorant Courtier' (1. 20).[13] In its final book, William is deemed skilled enough to proceed into a larger group, and Anniball describes the conduct proper to a banquet. This treatise could not be further from Rhodes's *The Boke of Nurture*. The public behaviour of William is determined in an intimate friendship with another man, a relationship which is built on – and maintained by – conversation.

Guazzo clearly attributes to conversation the power of self-transformation. Not only do we watch William becoming sociable (and more tolerant) as he converses with Anniball, but in the course of this dialogue, conventional ideas about social interaction are tested and modified.

One idea which is examined closely is the virtue of 'honesty', a virtue which serves as a glue to all social relationships. In the course of his conversation with Anniball, William will learn to appreciate the greater honesty of the dissimulative courtier rather than the anti-social simplicity of the 'scholler'. For the scholar only maintains his simple lifestyle by removing himself from the rough and tumble of daily social interaction, whereas the courtier attempts to balance honestly – or decorously – personal aspirations with social duty. In this chapter I want to explore how the character Anniball makes William honest and sociable in *Civile Conversation*, and also how, in the attempt, the concept of 'honesty' is defined in such a way as to make plain the potential of others. I will also explore, however, how seemingly honest conversation can equally disguise the power dynamic of intimate relationships, especially between a husband and wife. 'Honesty' remains the crucial term here: how we define it will affect profoundly the way in which we imagine people should relate to one another.

Conversation is a difficult speech form to analyse. Until recently, linguists have tended to focus on the isolated 'speech act' rather than the notoriously unruly, interactive process of conversing.[14] For early modern critics, however, there is another problem: how do you analyse a speech act which does not survive in textual form? Or, as Peter Burke argues in *The Art of Conversation*: how do you reconstruct 'speech from writing'?[15] One way around this problem is to apply to literary dialogues or letters models developed by recent conversation analysts. Burke explores the correspondence between the advice on conversation in the courtesy books and the theory of conversation developed by the philosopher H. P. Grice.[16] Meanwhile, in her fascinating study of *Shakespeare and Social Dialogue* Lynne Magnusson applies the universal rules of politeness developed by the linguist Stephen Levinson and the anthropologist Penelope Brown from their analysis of modern English, Tamil and Tzeltal to early modern familiar letters.[17]

However, there are problems with this approach, as Burke recognises.[18] First, the desire to develop rules for conversation shifts attention away from this speech-form's resistance to rule-making. Cicero, the main source for early modern reflections on the art of conversation, is very cautious about providing rules. As we will see in chapter 2, his rhetorical manual *De oratore* explores the relationship between the arts of conversation and oratory, and yet no exposition of conversation is offered. We understand it only in the experience of the form of the text itself. The later *De officiis* offers nine rules, and these are worth quoting in full because they will provide our most formal guide to the speech form:

Conversation, then, in which the Socratics are the best models, should have these qualities. (1) It should be easy and not in the least dogmatic; (2) it should have the spice of wit. (3) And the one who engages in conversation should not debar others from participating in it, as if he were entering upon a private monopoly; but, as in other things, so in a general conversation he should think it not unfair for each to have his turn. (4) He should observe, first and foremost, what the subject of conversation is. If it is grave, he should treat it with seriousness; if humorous, with wit. (5) And above all, he should be on the watch that his conversation shall not betray some defect in his character... The subjects of conversation are usually affairs of the home or politics or the practice of the professions and learning. (6) Accordingly, if the talk begins to drift off to other channels, pains should be taken to bring it back again to the matter in hand – but with due consideration for the company present; for we are not all interested in the same things at all times or in the same degree. (7) We must observe, too, how far the conversation is agreeable and, as it had a reason for beginning, so there must be a point at which to close it tactfully.

(8) But as we have a most excellent rule for every phase of life, to avoid exhibitions of passion, that is, mental excitement that is excessive and uncontrolled by reason; so our conversation ought to be free from such emotions: let there be no exhibition of anger or inordinate desire, of indolence or indifference, or anything of the kind. (9) We must also take the greatest care to show courtesy and consideration toward those with whom we converse. (1. 134–36)

Cicero offers this curtailed advice in compensation for the scarcity of manuals dealing with conversation. There are 'none who make conversation a subject of study', he complains, 'whereas pupils throng about the rhetoricians everywhere. And yet the same rules that we have for words and sentences in rhetoric will apply also to conversation' (1. 132). Although Cicero claims not to know why this is the case, several of the rules he isolates do offer some kind of explanation. The emphasis is on the need to be tactful, to be easy and familiar, to accommodate oneself to others, and to avoid being prescriptive. Conversation requires the exercise of a decorum which is not readily explained.

Secondly, recent models make it more difficult for us to understand what was perceived to be the social use of conversation in the late sixteenth century. Brown and Levinson enable Magnusson to expose the complex interplay between 'positionality' and style in early modern letters and to demonstrate what we have long suspected, that 'discourse inscribes power relations'.[19] However, they do not help us to understand the attempt to reconceive 'society' which underpins interest in conversation in the period or, indeed, how the emphasis on familiarity in early modern conversation theory is used to challenge the confident assertion of social difference. Linguistic gestures of self-deprecation on Brown and Levinson's model function as examples of 'negative politeness' in the style of the 'cringing' servility often attributed by Westerners to '"oriental" politeness'.[20] Negative politeness typically includes speech acts which seek to please the hearer ('May it please you'), verbs of 'weak force' ('beseech', 'pray', 'entreat'), indirection and self-deprecation, and it seeks to reproduce 'existing hierarchical arrangements'.[21] In literary representations of conversation, though, gestures which might appear 'negative' and distancing can create a levelling familiarity. What is important about the self-deprecating gesture of pretending ignorance in the courtesy books is that it is often employed 'ideally' by a senior interlocutor who understands the limits of his social authority and who wants to bring out the potential of a junior companion. When it is used by a junior interlocutor (for example, by a courtier to his prince as we will see in chapter 2) it is imagined to offer an affective means of tempering a potentially tyrannical companion.

In the sixteenth century the dialogue form might follow one of several models: Socratic, Ciceronian or Lucianic. The two forms which influence the writing of the courtesy books, the Socratic (or Platonic) and Ciceronian, are documentary; they depict real people in real settings. As Virginia Cox explains, in the Socratic dialogue the speakers are 'midwives' to the truth, whereas the Ciceronian dialogue is concerned with 'the individual, the concrete, the historically verifiable'.[22] The Socratic dialogues – as recorded by Plato – usually involve a process of cross-examination to refute the argument of an opponent by drawing out its contradictions. The method is described brilliantly by Mary Margaret McCabe:

Socrates insistently questions his interlocutors about what they are doing and why. He asks because he wants to know and because he claims to be ignorant himself. Ironically he commends his interlocutor's expertise and then, by careful analysis, shows his interlocutors to be in an even worse cognitive case. For when the interlocutor defines some ethical notion Socrates elicits from him a whole collection of sincere beliefs and assumptions, and then shows that those beliefs are inconsistent with the proposed definition. This, famously, results in dismay, irritation, even apoplectic horror on the part of the interlocutor.

You may see why they gave Socrates hemlock. His methods are not only maddening for his victims; they also seem pretty destructive.[23]

By contrast, the Ciceronian form involves discussion between equals and, as several critics note, it feels much more like a conversation than the Socratic dialogue.[24]

Plato's dialogues are conversational. As McCabe argues, they proceed 'by question and answer, person to person, live and face to face'. However, they are also confrontational; Socrates aims to unravel, even to destroy, the beliefs of an opponent.[25] This is in contrast to the relaxed style of Ciceronian conversation. In this form speakers tend to recognise that an opponent has something useful to say. One way of illustrating the difference between the two styles is to consider the way in which Cicero's speakers use Socratic irony, the 'pretended ignorance' named in *De oratore* as *dissimulatio* and employed by Antonius, one of two leading speakers in this dialogue about the ideal orator. As we will see in chapter 2, Antonius does not feign ignorance in a round-about attempt to destroy the beliefs of his audience. Rather, this rhetorical gesture prompts his auditors to recognise a truism of which Cicero is sure they are already vaguely aware: that an orator must practise his skills, and that there is no better form of practice than by engaging in everyday talk or conversation, just as Antonius is doing at that very moment.

Cicero's preoccupation with conversation surfaces again in *De officiis*, his late philosophical treatise which explores the relationship between the apparently antithetical concepts of moral goodness (*honestas*) and profit (*utilitas*); his argument is that nothing is profitable or expedient that is not also honest. 'Honestas' has four categories or virtues: wisdom, justice, fortitude and decorum or propriety (which includes temperance) (1. 93).[26] It is closely related to decorum: 'what is proper is morally right', Cicero explains, 'and what is morally right is proper' (1. 94).[27] This relationship, though, is hard to grasp partly because Cicero's idea of decorum proves rather slippery. By way of explanation Cicero argues that poets observe decorum 'when every word or action is in accord with each individual character'; he then explains that the philosopher is concerned with what is decorous or proper for humanity. '[T]o us', he explains, 'Nature has assigned the rôles of steadfastness, temperance, self-control, and considerateness of others; Nature also teaches us not to be careless in our behaviour towards our fellow men' (1. 97–8). On this definition, decorum includes a show of 'reverence' to others, 'considerateness', self-control of the passions *and* attention to one's dress and deportment (1. 99, 102, 126–7). It also includes conversation.

Conversation is discussed under this fourth category. There is a clear correspondence between Cicero's description of decorum and the practice of conversation described at 1. 34–6; several rules (especially 1, 4, 7, and 9) correspond to his conception of decorum as pleasing behaviour. For him – and, as we will see, the courtesy authors who follow his example – conversation is honest when it conforms to these rules. But it is also honest *and* profitable in a broader sense because it enables a 'man' to fulfil the role 'he' has been assigned by 'Nature': to be sociable. It is not difficult to recognise how the polite refusal to teach an auditor how to speak is 'honest' or morally right because it creates the conditions for conversation. That is, such a gesture invites an auditor to become a speaker; once engaged in conversation 'he' can realise his capacity to be social (a capacity that remains buried while 'he' remains in the role of auditor).

This discussion may seem academic to us because Cicero's idea of 'honestas' or moral goodness does not fit with our own notion of honesty. How readily would we define 'honestie' with the Tudor scholar Thomas Wilson as 'to set furthe the body with handsome apparell'?[28] Any standard modern English dictionary will explain the term 'honest' as 'sincere, truthful, candid', not lying or stealing, and trustworthy. According to the *Oxford English Dictionary*, this is a meaning it has carried since at least the fifteenth century.[29] Recent social historians have emphasised the importance of this sense of honesty to the creation of successful social relationships. In *A Social History of Truth* (1994) Steven Shapin explains how a 'world-known-in-common is built up through acts of trust, and its properties are decided through the civil conversations of trusting individuals'. Civility and good manners, he explains, rest on the assumption that our conversation is 'reliably oriented towards and about the realities upon which we report'.[30]

However, it is easy to forget, as William Empson so painstakingly demonstrated in *The Structure of Complex Words* half a century ago, that 'honest' is also one of the most muddled of words. The *Oxford English Dictionary* records a variety of early meanings from 'Held in honour' (1a) to 'a vague epithet of appreciation or praise, especially as used in a patronising way to an inferior' (1c). As Empson reminds us, its meaning of 'telling the truth', which acquired prominence in the sixteenth century, co-existed alongside a quite different, slang meaning, 'hearty'.[31] Its meaning was yet further complicated in the sixteenth century by attempts to translate and understand Cicero's 'honestas'. In 1538 Thomas Elyot's Latin-English dictionary explained Latin 'honestas' with a single word, 'honestie'. By 1565, however, Thomas Cooper distinguishes between the noun and adjective (honestus); the latter he translates in various ways, including 'of good reputation', 'good', 'beautiful' and 'comely'. He also offers almost two columns of Latin examples, some of which are drawn from *De officiis*.[32] Cooper's translation of 'honestus' as 'comely' (the Elizabethan term for decorous) is consonant with Cicero's definition. However, it would take a number of courtesy books to explore the fullness of its meaning. What these books make apparent is that it is sometimes also 'honest' *not* to tell the truth in order to sustain mutual trust between interlocutors; they do so by exploring 'honesty' in its aspect as decorum – the concept which Cicero understood in *De officiis* was in some sense unteachable. This is why the form of the conversational courtesy books matters. This meaning of 'honesty' as decorous self-restraint and accommodation only emerges *in* conversation. Treatises which discuss the term straightforwardly lose its association with 'decorum'; this association is also lost to those critics who approach the dialogic courtesy books as straightforward didactic treatises rather than as literary texts. In such readings we arrive too quickly at the modern definition of 'honesty' as truth-telling or straight-talking, and so overlook a discourse which was alert to the process of negotiation.

Attending to the way in which the meaning of 'honesty' is produced in conversation will also make apparent how the process of negotiation envisaged accepts that the expression of disagreement or dissenting views is civil rather than uncivil. That is, the style of argument of treatises like the *Courtier*, and (to a lesser degree) *Civile Conversation*, offers a model of interaction predicated on the honest rivalry described by Cicero in *De amicitia*, a treatise written in the same year as *De officiis* (44 BC). *De amicitia* contributed many commonplaces to the debate about male friendship in the sixteenth century, several of which we will meet later in this book; these include the argument that 'friendship cannot exist except among good men' (5. 18) and that friendship 'springs rather from nature than from need' (8. 27).[33] *De amicitia* also introduced the idea that true friends 'vie' with each other 'in a rivalry of virtue [honesta certatio]' (9. 32). Cicero supposes that friendship exists between men of the same degree, but the argument of *De amicitia* recognises its existence between men at different stages in their life and education. What is important about this idea in the sixteenth century is that it provides a clear counter-argument to that of *Stans puer ad mensam* which advises only that the page boy 'kepe honestly silence' and speaks circumspectly in his lord's presence. As we will see in chapter 3, in the context of the English debates about 'honesty' from the 1540s, this idea of virtuous or honest rivalry provides a model of interaction between individuals of different estates.

In the following section I will explore what Guazzo means when he describes civil conversation as 'an honest commendable and vertuous kinde of living in the world' in *Civile Conversation* (1. 56), and also how he explores the difficult concept of decorum. That is, I want to show how the meaning of honesty as decorous self-restraint emerges gradually in the course of the conversation, enabling William to abandon his attachment to the unsociable and unchallenged authority of the 'simple' scholar. I also want to show how William's conversation with Anniball exemplifies an honest rivalry between friends. Anniball's self-restraint, represented in his refusal to teach William, draws his younger friend into conversation, and thus enables him to realise his 'honesty' or virtue; in effect, William is being encouraged to be more tolerant within a wider social mix. It is important, though, that we also recognise the gendering of honesty in Guazzo's treatise. The honesty of Rhodes's page survives as proper conduct for wives: silence, obedience and chastity. In the final section of this chapter, I will explore a source for this type of honesty, Xenophon's *Oeconomicus*. I will also consider the overlap between these distinct definitions so as to understand the way in which Guazzo's aspirations for conversation between closeted men is compromised by the conversations which take place in the larger domestic sphere of the household.

CIVIL CONVERSATION

There are many kinds of dialogue in the sixteenth century and, obviously, not all of them are civil conversations. In this book the term 'civil conversation' describes texts written as dialogues which engage with some aspect of Cicero's theory and practice of conversation.[34] Of the several courtesy books only Castiglione's the *Courtier* is strictly in imitation of Cicero's dialogue style. Guazzo's *Civile Conversation* is more typical in adopting the Socratic form. It involves only two disputants: a leading interlocutor Anniball Magnocavalli, and a straw man, Guazzo's younger brother, William. However, *Civile Conversation* disseminates Cicero's idea of conversation explicitly – Anniball both quotes from and paraphrases passages from *De officiis* – and implicitly, by exploring a conversation in action.

Not all books interested in civil conversation are written as dialogues. For example, Richard Pritchard's *The schoole of honest and vertuous lyfe* (1579) provides 'pettie Scholars' (boys at the 'petty' or junior grammar school) with a summary of book 1 of *De officiis*, and a straightforward list of precepts for conversation. 'If a man be spurred to speake', Pritchard tells his pupils, 'let him have speeche of things fit for the place, time and company'. The speaker is to 'interrupt none in their talke, nor correct it', and he is 'to kepe that which is a meane and measurable order in our talke'. In the chapter entitled 'Observations in mutuall talke or communication', four further rules are given: 'Carpe not', 'Bee not an oppen accuser of the common people, or coyner of lyes', 'Search not after the secreates of other men', and give 'salutation fittinge' to a superior. Pritchard adds advice suitable to the socially awkward young male audience his book addresses:

> frame the state of thy body, that you stand upright, not reelinge this way nor that way, not ytching, nor rubbinge, nor favouringe on legge, more one than another, not bytinge or smacking thy lippes, not scratching thy head, nor pickinge thy eares, not lowringe thy lookes, nor glauncinge thine eyes too and fro, not sad nor fierce, but meeke and merry, showinge good disposition and nature, to bee habitant and graciously grafted in thee.[35]

Treatises aimed at adult aristocratic readers follow much the same format. Book 5 of *Institution of a Noble Man* (1607) by the Scot James Cleland offers advice on 'Civil Conversation', much of which is already familiar to us: 'take diligently heede not to make your selves slaves or subject unto any certaine particulare humors'; it 'is great wisdom for a man to accommodate himselfe and to frame his manners apt and meete for al honest companie'; 'Salutation is the first point of curtesie in our private conversation'.[36] Cleland's text does experiment with form. Some chapters are arranged in parallel columns so that the reader may (with some difficulty) contrast opposites, 'virtue' and 'vice' (pp. 164–6) and 'friend' and 'flatterer' (pp. 193–6). But it does not attempt to show us how a civil conversation might work, with the result that the critical potential of this speech form is unexplored.

Civile Conversation is quite different, for it allows the rules of conversation to emerge from its representation of the speech form. In this treatise, meaning is produced *in* conversation so, for example, familiar concepts like 'honesty' gradually take on a different resonance as the dialogue progresses. Once Anniball has persuaded William that conversation is beneficial, it falls to him to explain the manner it should take. William worries that there are too many kinds of conversation to study, whereupon Anniball reassuringly explains that he intends to 'set a part al other sorts, and propose for this purpose the civile conversation'. When William then asks 'What meane you by that woord, Civile?' we fall upon our only definition of civil conversation. Anniball explains that the term 'Civile' applies to those who live in the country as well towns:

> so I will that civile conversation appertaine not onely to men inhabiting cities, but to all sortes of persons of what place, or of what calling soever they be.
> Too bee shorte, my meaning is, that civile conversation is an honest commendable and vertuous kinde of living in the world. (1. 56)

This definition, however, is too general to be really useful. Part of the problem lies with the word 'honest'. We may think that we know what

Anniball means. Indeed, later in book 1 he will define an 'honest man' as someone who 'plainly telleth the trueth' (1. 96). No surprises here. But no definition is ever as straightforward as it seems in this meandering text. A moment later Anniball admits that 'I denie not, but that it is commendable to coyne a lye at some time, and in some place, so that it tende to some honest ende' (1. 97). And we will find that his account of civil conversation is full of such honest lies, for example, when he advises 'that wee ought not to interrupt him which speaketh, but rather with a certaine modestie to take sometime that which he saieth, for newes, though everie one knewe it before' (2. 150–1). Indeed, Anniball also uses the word 'honest' in more than one sense. In the example below, where he is explaining to William how he behaved when placed in the company of unfamiliar people from whom he could not withdraw for fear of being accused of 'too muche gravitie, or too litle courtesie', 'honesty' is equivalent to humouring others.

And though at the first I was in my dumpes, yet afterwarde I went away well pleased and joyful: seeing that I had so well framed my selfe to the humours of others, and that I had got my selfe honestly away being verie well thought of by the companie when I was gone. (1. 22)

That is, Guazzo is adapting Cicero's idea of 'honestas'. For Anniball, a man is honest when he humours his companions. By the same token, 'civile conversation is an honest commendable and vertuous kinde of living' because it requires a man to 'submit' himself 'to the common opinion of al men' (2. 115), and to refrain from mocking others less fortunate than himself (2. 160). 'Honesty' also encompasses the governing trope of civil conversation, the feigned ignorance (*sprezzatura*) which Anniball employs to draw William into a conversation. This pretence is honest because it prompts William to be 'true' to himself, realising his talent for sociability. Thus, when Anniball explains that he 'make[s] account to speake to persons of weake capacitie', endeavouring in conversation 'to present them with such things as are not out of their reach', William modestly imagines himself included and his self-deprecating response reveals his capacity to engage in civil conversation: 'Your discourses shall so much the better content mee', he offers, 'by how much the more they shalbe familiar, and suche as are meete for the weakenesse of my understanding' (2. 116).

Anniball pretends ignorance because he is teaching William something he already knows. Despite his ostentatious hostility to the dissembling tactics of the 'ignorant Courtier', William unknowingly deploys the same rhetorical gesture at the beginning of the dialogue. 'Thinke not, I beseech you, that I enter into the lystes against you, like a subtile Logician', he offers at the beginning of book 1, 'for I never learned the places from whence argumentes are drawn, and that which I say, is rather of mine owne opinion, then by any judgement or learning: but my desire is to give you occasion to give me some light of your knowledge, being willing rather to understande, then to withstande' (1. 23). Anniball, however, recognises William's capacity to be a civil gentleman. 'You have swarved nothing at all in this discourse from the dutie of a perfect Courtier', he responds, 'whose propertie it is to do all things with carefull diligence, and skilfull art: mary yet so that the art is hidden, and the whole seemeth to be doone by chaunce, that he may thereby be had in more admiration' (1. 27). In the course of the dialogue William is being taught to recognise both his ready possession of the skills of a conversationalist, and the value of behaving like an 'ignorant Courtier'.

This is, of course, why Guazzo dramatises a civil conversation (rather than providing a list of rules). He wants the reader to appreciate the dynamic, constitutive property of conversing, as well as 'his' own talent for sociability. It is not only the meaning of 'honesty' which is being shaped in the course of the conversation. William's sense of his own (and others) aspirations is also being fashioned in this rivalrous interaction with Anniball. Recognising this aim should influence the way we read *Civile Conversation*, which holds out all kinds of possibilities for the socially aspiring male reader. There has been a tendency to describe *Civile Conversation* as an elitist text which mystifies the source of nobility. Indeed, in book 2, which explores the appropriate forms of interaction between a variety of different men, there is also a much stronger emphasis on social difference. For example, when Anniball declares that 'wee are so much the more esteemed of, by howe muche our Civilitie differeth from the nature and fashions of the vulgar sorte'. Even so, Anniball is challenged by William, who notes that his friend has contradicted himself. Anniball then explains that he means his friend 'to proceede in common talke simply and plainly, according as the truth of the matter shal require', and offers this unexpected proof:

if you consider how in Villages, Hamlets, and fields, you shall finde many men, who though they leade their life farre distant from the graces and the Muses (as the proverb is) and come stamping in with their high clouted shooes, yet are of good understanding, whereof they give sufficient testimonie by their wise and discreete talke: you cannot denie, but that nature hath given and sowed in us certaine seedes of Rhetorike and Philosophie. (2. 123)

Anniball *is* contradictory. In book 1 he happily declares that he is 'verie glad our discourses are rather familiar and pleasaunt, then affected and grave' and he warns William that he will use many proverbs 'which verie Artificers have in their mouth, and comptes, which are used to bee told by the fire side' (1. 24). This interest in the speech of artificers or artisans is not lost in book 2, despite the new-found attachment to linguistic decorum. When Anniball advises William to build up a store of delightful phrases in book 2, he identifies one useful source, common talk. Thus, William is asked to remember 'that there is not any so fond, or so barren in his speach, but that sometime he saith something worthie of memorie'. As he adds, 'flowers of speache growe up chiefly in the learned, yet you see that nature maketh some of them to florish even amongst the common sort, unknowing unto them: and you shall see artificers, and others of low estate, to apply fitly to their purpose in due time and place, Sentences, pleasant Jestes, Fables, Allegories, Similitudes, Proverbes, Comptes, and other delightfull speache' (2. 136). In fact, in book 2 Anniball will define 'nobility' in such a way as not to preclude social advancement.[37]

This contradictory manner of argument signals an author who is not so much divided in his attitude to 'nobility', but rather struggling to find a style which can adequately demonstrate how the nobility of a speaker might be realised in the act of conversing civilly.[38] Because of its form, this treatise can 'honestly' uphold contradictory arguments: Anniball's insistence that a gentleman should distinguish his speech from that of country clowns does not negate his later argument that a clown can be a gentleman, or conversely, that a gentleman can be a clown (2. 175). This emphasis is in contrast to Cleland's monologic discussion of the same topic in the early seventeenth century (he advises the nobleman to be 'plyable to al sorts of people', but also that to 'converse with inferiours, as your conversation breedeth contempt, so it argueth a base mind'). Indeed, Cleland's argument – that a nobleman should 'put a distinction betweene [his] discourses and a *Scythians*, a *Barbarians*, or a *Gothes*. For it is a pitty when a Noble man is better distinguished from a Clowne by his golden laces, then by his good language' – is never challenged or modified in the progress of the book.[39] Cleland's treatise fully deserves the designation 'elitist', Guazzo's does not.

DOMESTICAL CONVERSATION

I do not want to suggest, however, that this courtesy book is successful in its provision of an 'honest' critique, that is, a critique which makes transparent power within social exchange. Or to argue that it expresses genuine rivalry. One of the paradoxes of mid-century courtesy books like Guazzo's is that civil conversation is discussed as a means of breaking down traditional social barriers and of reinforcing difference. This paradoxical opening and closing of the possibility for interaction seems to be repeated in the form of the treatise itself. Written as a dialogue, Guazzo's treatise aims to illustrate the opportunities civil conversation offers for self-improvement. But, this intention is thwarted. Its dialogue can seem laboured and artificial. This is partly because it explores the Ciceronian idea of conversation in the form of a Socratic dialogue. William is evidently a straw man. He merely draws out the authoritative views of Anniball (Guazzo) so that his teaching can be delivered in a non-didactic and engaging fashion.

This is perhaps the price to be paid for using the dialogue form more inclusively as a pedagogic tool. The *Courtier* is an 'elitist' treatise in one sense; it is set in the small Urbino court and its nobly born interlocutors describe the behaviour suitable for aristocrats in other Italian courts. All the same, Castiglione's dialogue feels more inclusive. One of its finest contributions to the informal Ciceronian dialogue form, as Virginia Cox notes, is the 'elimination of any divide between older and younger speakers'. This is facilitated by the character of Gaspare Pallavicino, the Urbino court's perpetual sceptic and its youngest speaker. The social world of *Civile Conversation* may be broader. William is being taught a sociability suitable for the 'market' of the world; he is expected to be able to speak civilly with other men from a range of different social backgrounds and in a variety of contexts. Yet, *Civile Conversation* illustrates the appetite for the more conservative Socratic form, in which a young pupil (William) is enlightened gradually by his venerable master (Anniball), that characterises the Italian dialogue after the Council of Trent in the 1560s *and* the English use of dialogue more generally. 'In a culture which was turning, increasingly, towards "monological" modes of argumentation', writes Cox of mid-sixteenth century Italy, 'Plato supplied a stylishly oblique but still markedly hierarchical model for the dialogue, more in keeping with the spirit of the times than a Ciceronian debate between equals.'[40]

This does not mean, though, that Guazzo, or the English courtesy writers who use the same form did not have laudable aspirations. In Guazzo's treatise Anniball sets out to make William, a solitary and rather arrogant young man, sensitive to the feelings of others. Its dialogue form enables a searching exploration of the principles of sociability: how to live with others in such a way as to maximise the benefits for all. The fact that Guazzo cannot answer this question reassuringly should not preclude a study of his attempt. But we would do well, all the same, to understand the limits of this dialogue. Why does it feel so coercive? Or rather, why does it feel so intent on what we might now call the 'interpellation' of the reader?[41]

Types of honesty: civil and domestical conversation

This is a difficult question to answer because the discussion in *Civile Conversation* in particular is relatively inclusive. Castiglione pays little attention to men of rank lower than the aristocratic Urbino courtiers in the *Courtier*, aside from advising that a nobleman shouldn't wrestle with them if he thinks there's any chance he might lose. In contrast, Guazzo excludes from civil conversation only those at the bottom of the social estates, labourers (2. 174–5). Elsewhere in this dialogue he positively includes that ill-defined social category of 'clowns' and he mentions approvingly the king who saluted a common prostitute.[42] Like Castiglione, Guazzo includes women, a detail which, as Helen Hackett notes, modern commentators of the courtesy books often overlook.[43] In book 4, where Anniball recalls a conversation which took place in mixed company at a banquet, the gentlewomen take a leading role: one of them is elected as the convenor of the discussion in place of the visiting prince. However, *Civile Conversation* also explores the kind of conversation which should take place between a husband and wife in book 3, and in so doing, it follows the example of Xenophon's study of household duties, *Oeconomicus*, which offers a rather different response to the question, what makes a good and honest man?[44] In this influential treatise, the 'honesty' of a gentleman is defined as the proper ordering of his conduct and speech which aims to secure the 'honesty' – or chastity, obedience *and* silence – of his wife.

Guazzo's attention to domestical conversation in book 3 starts promisingly enough. After the uncertain opening up of this topic at the end of book 2 (William misunderstands Anniball's reference to conversation between the two sexes as an allusion to sexual intercourse (2. 234)), Guazzo proceeds in the third book to develop a defence of the humane treatment of wives. Indeed, the family is integral to the safekeeping of a civil society. Men who beat their wives, or treat them like 'kitchinstuffes' or slaves are roundly berated while the praises of a loving husband are sung (3. 6; 3. 23). The first half of the book explains how one should choose and then 'love' a wife. Or rather, how a young wife should 'be framed to the pleasure of her husbande' (3. 20). This sounds much like the treatment which William receives in books 1 and 2, but, as we will see, it is not.

It is impossible to read such defences of women generously. In 1977 Kathleen M. Davies made a stand against those social historians who were arguing for a new ideal of family life in the seventeenth century in which marriage was based 'for the first time... on mutual respect and love'. The suggestion that books on domestic relations such as Richard Whytforde's *A Werke for Housholders* (?1531), William Gouge's *Of Domestical Duties* (1622) or John Dod and Robert Cleaver's *A Godlie Forme of Household*

Government (1612) represent a new departure in the conception of family life is misleading, she argues, because they are mostly concerned with the subordination of the wife to the husband.[45] In this respect they represent a reworking of ideas found in pre-Reformation moral literature, not a new development. More recently, Lorna Hutson has contributed to this argument in a different way, finding novelty in the emerging perception of the domestic sphere as an arena for the development of a skill crucial to the acquisition of a distinctive, elite 'masculinity', the art of persuasion. Treatises like the popular *Oeconomicus*, translated in 1532 by Gentian Hervet as *Xenophons treatise of house holde*, taught aspiring governors how, as Cicero argues in *De officiis*, to 'win the affectionate co-operation of our fellows and enlist it in our service' (2. 20).[46]

Xenophon's *Oeconomicus*, as Hutson notes, was to provide the basis for a defence of commercial activity in the sixteenth century, although it has long been neglected by economic historians because it offers an 'art of husbandry' or housekeeping, rather than a study of the economy *per se*. Yet, such indifference overlooks the important contribution that this text made, along with *De officiis*, to the defence of profit making as desirable in a period suspicious of usurious activity. *Oeconomicus* can be credited as a source for the division of labour in the household literature of sixteenth- and seventeenth-century England. As Hutson advises, however, it can also be credited with helping to redefine elite masculinity as a skill in 'the economics of using and ordering a discourse', a skill which might be used literally to one's profit at home and in the public sphere. Its further usefulness, she suggests, lies in its ability to displace the ethical dilemma integral to profit seeking into the domestic sphere through a fiction of willing cooperation.[47]

There is already an interesting relationship between *De officiis* and *Oeconomicus*, as Hutson notes.[48] Not only did Cicero translate *Oeconomicus* from Greek to Latin when he was a schoolboy, as he reminds us at the end of book 2, but he also refers the reader to this text as a source for the ethics of enterprise. It 'is a duty', observes Cicero, 'to make money, but only by honourable means; it is a duty also to save it and increase it by care and thrift'. 'These principles', he explains, 'Xenophon, a pupil of Socrates, has set forth most happily in his book entitled "Oeconomicus"' (2. 87). *Oeconomicus* was written in the 4th century BC, in part, its modern translator Sarah B. Pomeroy suggests, to tackle the problem of reduced Athenian agricultural production following the Peloponnesian War.[49] Xenophon aims to persuade landowners that farming is both a public service and a means to personal profit. To do so he invents a series of fictional dialogues. The first and main dialogue about *oikonomia* – the art of household management – is between Socrates and a gentleman companion named Critobulus. Socrates claims not to be able to teach this skill because he does not own a household, and therefore does not practise it. Instead, he reports a conversation he had with a gentleman landowner and householder called Ischomachus (the second dialogue). Ischomachus in turn teaches Socrates about *oikonomia* by reporting a conversation he had with his unnamed wife about her household duties (the third dialogue). As Hutson's careful reading of Hervet's 1532 translation makes apparent, the teaching of *oikonomia* is embodied in a series of displacements or sideways moves enacted in the various conversations. That is, *oikonomia* is never really defined. Instead, as the dialogue moves forwards so the signifying possibilities of this term seem to expand. It is the art of ordering one's household (or managing one's wife to order one's household); it is also an art of farming, and an art of military strategy and imperial government. These displacements enable us to understand that *oikonomia*, which begins modestly at home, underpins the art of government.[50] They also alert us to its rhetorical dimension: its use of displacement – represented in Socrates' original refusal to teach Ischomachus – to make others feel as if they are becoming independent agents even as they are being enlisted to serve one's interests.

Xenophon's *Oeconomicus* is used by Hutson to unmask such strategies of apparent kindness or civility which, according to Cicero in *De officiis*, should underpin the pleasant and courteous communication between individuals in society. However, Xenophon and Cicero are very different thinkers, and domestic and civil conversation are opposing as well as contiguous discourses. It is inevitable that Cicero and Xenophon were elided in the minds of many Elizabethans; it is also true that Cicero translated and wrote admiringly of Xenophon. Yet, these 'Socratic' thinkers are also writing in distinct cultures almost four hundred years apart. Civil and domestic discourses *are* different, insists Lena Cowen Orlin: 'the Renaissance concept of domestic virtue which succeeds the moral philosophy of friendship and benefice' in the seventeenth century, 'is one lodged in the realization of its philosophical opposite, individual oeconomic interest'.[51] This difference can be located in the conflicting, though overlapping, accounts of honest, elite masculine conduct which Xenophon and Cicero provide. This double legacy is present (unconsciously) in *Civile Conversation* as well as in Thomas Pritchard's *The schoole of honest and vertuous lyfe*. The latter advises that there are two ways to become wise according to Socrates: 'the one to huysht rather than to speake: the other, for to learne how to speake'.[52] It is visibly in contestation in the battle waged over the meaning of 'honesty' between the sixteenth-century courtesy books and the husbandry books inspired by *Oeconomicus*: when the landowner 'Cono' defends the 'honesty' of his lifestyle in Barnabe Googe's translation of Conrad Heresbach's *Foure Bookes of Husbandry*, he is explicitly favouring the orderly gentleman-husband of *Oeconomicus* over Castiglione's or Guazzo's Ciceronian courtier.[53]

The uneasy conversation between the 'honest' courtier and the 'honest' husbandman is explored in chapter 4. In this chapter, however, I want to describe the distinctive 'honesty' or decorum of Xenophon's landowner Ischomachus as he appears in Hervet's translation. *Oeconomicus* is a study of 'the duetie, and the propre office, of the ordrynge of an house' (sig. A2r). This topic is explored, though, in a conversation which answers the question: what makes 'a good and honest man' (Hervet's translation of Xenophon's *kalos te kagathos*, a true or decent gentleman). This translation of *kalos* as 'honest' is not surprising. The Greek adjective means decent, beautiful and good. As Helen North notes, it was translated by the Romans as *honestas* (decorum). It is in fact a source for Cicero's conception of decorum as affable speech and behaviour *and* comely appearance.[54] In *Oeconomicus*, however, Xenophon defines *kalos* as a moral quality only. Socrates tells Critobulus that he searched unsuccessfully for 'a good and honest man' in the company of handsome men. Frustrated in his search, he seeks one who is reputed to be 'good and honest' by reputation only, and discovers Ischomachus. In the reported conversation between Ischomachus and Socrates that follows we discover that the adjective *kalos* applies to the landowner who has persuaded his wife and slaves (servants in Hervet) to serve his interests.

One of the paradoxes of Ischomachus's lifestyle is that he is a rich and busy man who still has the time to sit around chatting to Socrates in the stoa (the church porch in Hervet). This freedom to converse with one's friends 'man-to-man' is a marker of Ischomachus's gentility *and* moral goodness; he has ordered his affairs well enough to create time for such conversations. More importantly, his orderly conversation with Socrates is the key to his success, for it allows him to demonstrate the rhetorical skill which enables him to govern others – wife and slaves or servants – by persuading them to manage his affairs willingly and so free his time. Ischomachus is 'a good and honest man' because he has taught his wife by conversing with her 'to have a good wyll towarde us, and to love us... [and] to sette her good wyll and her good mynde to encrease our house' (sig. E1r). This process is illustrated in the reported dialogue between the newly married husband, Ischomachus, and his wife. The dialogue is Socratic in style; Ischomachus poses questions to his wife rather than simply telling her what is right and wrong. Yet, he also discreetly reverses the role of questioner and answerer, employing a form of questioning familiar to the Elizabethans as *rogatio*: to 'ask questions, or... enquire of others and set forth our own opinion'.[55] Ischomachus tells us that when his wife was domesticated sufficiently to hold a conversation he questioned her thus:

Tell me good bedfelowe, did ye ever cast in your mi[n]de, for what cause I have taken you, and your father and mother delivered you unto me? I trowe ye knowe well inoughe, that I toke you not for nede, that I had of a bedfelowe to lye with me, for I myghte have had inowe at my commandment. But when I had considered in my mynde... that hit were well done, to fynde out a good one to be parte taker both of our house, and of our childre[n] I chose you afore all other, and your father and mother like wise chose me. (sigs. C6r-C6v)

He then explains that his wife 'answered here unto after this maner. Wherein can I helpe you?' (sig. D7r).[56] And so the conversation proceeds. Only when the wife is finally able to answer a question on her own can she be said to be conversant *and* domesticated.[57] The lesson is completed when Ischomachus asks her how she would feel about tending to sick slaves or servants: 'By my feyth, sayde my wyfe, hit is a verye gratious and a kynde dede. For whan they be ones holpen, and eased they wyll cunne us very good thanke, and be the more lovynge and feythfull unto us'. In this answer the wife expresses both obedience to her husband and knowledge of how to cultivate obedience in her husband's servants through the exercise of kindness. She has learned her lesson well. Ischomachus is satisfied: 'me thoughte... that hit was an answere of a good and an honeste wyfe' (sig. D2r).

Some readers of book 3 of *Civil Conversation* may be initially impressed by Guazzo's inclusion of women.[58] '[A]s the cheefe conversation commeth by meane of mariage, for that Cities cannot be without families, nor families without Husband and Wife', he writes encouragingly at the opening of this book, 'there is no conversation more agreeable to nature, than that of the male and the female' (3. 3). Yet, Guazzo is not exactly extending the benefits of civility to women in the same way that he does to men of 'ungentle' birth in book 2. The conversation Guazzo anticipates between husband and wife is really a dialogue of the male *to* the female, or of a husband *to* his wife. The casual banter between men and women in Castiglione's treatise has no place in book 3 (although Guazzo does approximate it in the banquet scene of book 4). The limits of domestical conversation are soon apparent when Anniball alludes to the Pauline injunction that women should be silent and obedient (3. 25). This creates a real dilemma: how can a wife be 'civilised' if she cannot engage in conversation. But, of course, Guazzo's interests lie elsewhere. What he is really concerned with is the bringing of a young wife into domestic conversation, and through this, to an acceptance of the role of servant or subordinate to her husband.[59] This intention is apparent in the different meaning attributed to 'honesty' in book 3. Honesty in speech and deportment should still be pleasing, but only in so far as it accords with the feminine virtues of chastity and obedience. Women – and wives in particular – should not be too attractive. It is 'sieldome seene', argues Anniball, 'that those two great enemies, bewty and honesty agree togither' (3. 10). He also praises the 'honest Matrone' who refuses to wear cosmetics (3. 12) and advises that 'it behoveth an honest woman to shew her selfe so sober and chast in countenance, that no man may be so hardie to assayle her' (3. 38). A woman is not to invite conversation, which carries the secondary meaning of sexual intercourse. William observes that 'a grave looke, a demure countenance, modest gestures, and behaviour [are] meete for an honest woman' (3. 33).

Courtesy writers will have inherited from *De officiis* the idea that the capacity for people to live together in workable social groupings depends on a network of intimate relations between (in descending order) compatriots, citizens, neighbours, friends, and husbands and wives. For this reason women are often seen as central to the civilising process. Thus, in the *Courtier* Cicero's rules of conversation are relayed to us, with some modification, in book 3, which is dedicated to the description of the ideal female courtier.[60] Castiglione's list of noble women underscores his commitment to the idea that affectionate ties first acquired in the family help to build and preserve cities and restrain the enemies of civility (the despotic husband, the self-seeking citizen and the tyrant). But the sixteenth century also translated and assimilated treatises like *Oeconomicus* which make the management of a wife and servants the secret of masculine civility.

The crucial question is whether domestic conversation is the only foundation for the practice of civil conversation? This is a difficult question to answer. Guazzo clearly imagines that domestic and civil conversation *are* interdependent: the home is the training ground for a young man's public role. However, it is easy to overlook the extent to which the domestic conversation described in book 3 fosters the very values and attitudes which Anniball's description of conversation between men seeks to undermine. '[W]ee are to reproove the abuse of men, who in choosing a Wife, use no other order then they doe in buying a Horse', argues Anniball reassuringly. Less reassuring, though, is his explanation that 'we must use a more certayne and commodious way' (3. 14). Anniball reinforces, rather than dismisses, the animal analogy: 'men seeke diligently for Asses, Oxen, and Horse, of a good race, but a man careth not though his wife bee ill brought up, and worse borne, so that she be rich ynough' (3. 15). When choosing a wife one should use one's ears rather than eyes. It is important to discover a bride's pedigree as well as admire her looks, just as when buying a horse. The bridegroom needs to discover what 'the life and conversation of her parentes is, and hath bene, remembring the saying, that the Eagle breedeth not the Pigeon, but that Cat will after kynde' (3. 15).

William is alert to the difficulties raised by Anniball's argument. He tries to correct his new friend's narrow use of the term 'lineage', perhaps remembering the content of their conversation about nobility in book 2. Yet, he meets with a different response in book 3. '[I]f you search the auncient histories', he ventures in response to Anniball's emphasis on the importance of lineage, 'you will in a manner say that nature doth not her parte, for you shall finde that many vertuous men have been begotten by vyle and foolishe fathers: and contrariwise, that many good and wise fathers have gotten foolish and naughty children' (3. 15). Anniball refuses to change his mind. '[N]ature alway tendeth to the best', he argues, 'so that of good parentes, ought naturally to come good children: and if it fall out sometyme otherwise, the fault is not to be imputed to nature' (3. 16). 'I would have Gentlemen especially take heede', he argues, 'that they match only with those that come of Gentle blood: for the cavilling of Sophists against gentrie, is vayn, who having no regarde to things common, and knowne to every man, to wit, that to have a good race, men buy horse and dogges whiche come of a good kinde, of fruites also they make choise of the best sortes' (3. 18). And yet Anniball was one of those 'cavilling' sophists in book 2!

In book 3 the possibility for dialogue *is* closed both for wives and junior male friends. In books 1 and 2 we see William courteously modifying Anniball's argument. The usefulness of this method is noted at the opening of book 3: 'If it be so that your vertue receive increase by my discourses', observes Anniball, 'it is also that my discourses are much bettered by your witty demaundes' (3. 2). In book 3, however, no such negotiation is possible. Anniball's advice is explicit and unambiguous: one *must* be a loving rather than a punitive husband; one *must* select one's wife from a 'good' family, and so on. Anniball is no longer conversing with William to instil in him – or bring out of him – the principles of civil conversation. Rather, he is telling him how to domesticate a future wife.

This study explores how a model of familiar conversation between men derived from Cicero provided the basis for distinctive ways of thinking about social relations between aspirational men in early modern England.

The inspiration for this interest in conversation (certainly for Guazzo) is Castiglione's *The Book of the Courtier*, first printed in 1528. As we will see in chapter 2, this treatise offers a consideration of Cicero's ideas about conversation so as to present a critique of social and political hierarchies. However, we must bear in mind throughout this study that civil conversation is a compromised discourse; it is vulnerable to the dishonest affectation of sociability and the concealment of economic self-interest. The extent to which it is compromised might be registered not only in the reformers' attachment to dominant male speakers in their dialogues but also, more broadly, in that perceived bifurcation in the late seventeenth century between the public and private spheres, between a sphere which encouraged negotiation among free, prudential and self-interested individuals, and a sphere regarded as sentimental, feminine and outside public discourse. In the sixteenth century the domestic sphere of male homosociality – the closet, the dinner table, the garden, the bed or bedchamber, even the collaborative literary text – provides an arena for rethinking social relations between men. However, the failure in the philosophical texts of this period to make the 'highly charged intimate relationships' of that other domestic sphere, the household, the basis for the continued reassessment of these relations meant, as Jean Bethke Elshstain has argued, that the possibility for developing 'mutual recognition and intersubjective understanding' in social *and* political discourse was lost, to the detriment of men as well as women.[61]

CHAPTER 2

From rhetoric to conversation: reading for Cicero in The Book of the Courtier

Baldassare Castiglione's *Il libro del cortegiano* (1528) – *The Book of the Courtier* – is one of the most influential texts in Renaissance European culture. The book is a reported dialogue which supposedly took place in the palace of Urbino several decades prior to its recording, and it is permeated throughout by the nostalgia of its narrator, Castiglione, who is attempting to capture an idyllic moment in the life of that court. The dialogue takes place over four nights (each night is reported in one of its four books), and despite its seemingly serious topic – the definition of the ideal courtier – it has the spirit of a party game.

The importance of this book in late Renaissance Italian culture is well understood. Most often, it seems to signal the cultural bias towards the despotic court identified as a mark of late Italian humanism. 'If early humanism was a glorification of civic life', writes Eugenio Garin, then 'the last part of the fifteenth century was characterized by an orientation towards contemplation and an escape from the world'. Garin sees this as a development of an ascetic Platonism in the late fifteenth century which is 'determined by the pressure of the political development of Italy', specifically, the rise of princely power and the decline of the republican city-states. The republican citizen is superseded by the courtier, an individual 'whom it is impossible to imagine capable of clear political thinking'.[1] As he explains elsewhere, the 'courtier is no longer a free citizen of a free republic, still granted sovereign rights'. Rather, 'he is a man of the court, in the service of the sovereign, a man close to the prince and his collaborator'.[2]

Arguably, Castiglione's nostalgic and playful tone in the *Courtier* cannot quite conceal the despotic character of even the small Urbino court. As Thomas Greene observes, Federico Fregoso's proposal to describe the ideal courtier may assume a 'capacity for mature self-criticism as well as a firm, stable society capable of questioning its own foundation', but this game always retreats at the moment at which any insight into the true condition of the courtier – in service to a despotic prince – is about to be gained. It is a game which 'risks' the same 'ambiguity' as the prince who disguises himself as a prince in a masquerade; it threatens to 'subvert play and reality alike'.[3] Indeed, it is often difficult to know what reality Castiglione is remembering. In book 4, he predicts (retrospectively) the virtue of Urbino's future duke, Francesco della Rovere. Yet, the real personage, as Castiglione must have known full well, was as wilful and manipulative as any of Italy's despots. This prince, Lauro Martines notes, knew no bounds: 'Francesco Maria della Rovere, when seventeen years old, killed his sister's lover; later, as duke of Urbino and again with his own hands, he killed a cardinal – and got away with it – for alleged abuse to his honor.'[4]

Such commentary on the complex political world of cinquecento Italy is interesting not simply for the light it sheds on the evasiveness of the *Courtier*, but for the way in which it has informed our thinking about this treatise's reception in late sixteenth-century England. The *Courtier* was available in England shortly after the first edition appeared in Italy in 1528. It was known by Thomas Cromwell, and may have influenced the writing of Thomas Elyot's *The Boke Named the Governour* (1531).[5] However, it was not until Thomas Hoby's translation, printed in 1561, that Castiglione became influential in England.[6] It is notoriously difficult to account for this apparent cultural delay. One credible suggestion is that it was only at the autocratic Elizabethan court that the relevance of the *Courtier* was felt.[7]

This suspicion of the *Courtier* is not surprising. Hoby's translation captures for English readers the surreptitious practice and optimistic ends of an Italian courtier who aims to 'allure' his prince to him, and to 'distille' (*infondere*) into his mind 'goodnesse' and 'continencie' and 'temperance' (pp. 299/291).[8] In its fourth and final book its principal speaker Ottaviano promises to defend the courtier from the charge that his 'precise facions' and 'meerie talke' described in books 1–3 will make him 'womannish' (*effeminare*), and susceptible 'to a most wanton trade of livinge' (pp. 294–5/287). Yet, he appears naively (or disingenuously) to believe that a virtuous end justifies covert 'womannish' means. He argues that the courtier aims, by means of his 'honeste qualities', to leade his prince 'throughe the roughe way of vertue... deckynge yt about with boowes to shadowe yt and strawinge it over wyth sightlye flouers, to ease (*temperare*) the greefe of the peinfull journey in hym that is but of a weake force'. With the help of 'musike', 'armes', 'horses', 'rymes and meeter' and 'otherwhyle wyth communication of love', the courtier keeps his prince 'occupyed in honest pleasure', using 'flickeringe provocations' to bring him to 'some vertuous condicion', 'beeguilinge him with a holsome craft, as the warie phistiens do, ... whan they minister to yonge and tender children' (pp. 299–300). Ottaviano's courtly pedagogic method seems to offer only an elaborate form of flattery which promises to turn the prince into a tyrant and to dissolve the courtier's manly will.

Suspicion of this treatise is voiced by some contemporaries, including Philibert de Vienne who exposes the rhetorical manoeuvres of the *Courtier* as a kind of false consciousness. However, this suspicion was not shared by all. Recent critics have been quick to speculate about the kind of readers the *Courtier* might have attracted, but slow to explore the evidence we do possess of those who did read and approve of it.[9] Hoby's 1561 translation offers some unexpected insights. The prefatory material to his translation locates a reading community for Castiglione squarely among those university men involved in the Elizabethan settlement of 1559. The translation is dedicated to the protestant nobleman Henry Hastings, third Earl of Huntington, who was related to both Robert Dudley, Earl of Leicester and Henry Sidney by marriage. It is also prefaced by a letter from John Cheke, dated 16 July, 1557, and a sonnet from Thomas Sackville, the co-author with the radical protestant lawyer Thomas Norton of the first English classical drama in blank verse, *Gorboduc* (1561/2). Sackville also wrote an epistle for Batholomew Clerke's Latin translation of 1571. Meanwhile, both the *Courtier* and Hoby's translation of it are praised by Roger Ascham in *The Schoolmaster* (1570), the treatise which is supposedly inspired by a conversation with Richard Sackville (d. 1566), Thomas Sackville's father. The diplomat Thomas Smith was also a likely owner of the *Courtier*.[10] These readers were Cambridge graduates; several of them were members of a network of friends created at this university in the 1530s, the so-called 'Athenian tribe', which, under the leadership of Cheke and Smith in 1535–42, re-introduced the 'correct' pronunciation of classical Greek.

None of these Cambridge protestants fits our conception of the imagined courtly reader of the *Courtier*. Indeed, it is difficult to see what an Italian book on manners might have to say to a group committed to religious reform, although attempts have been made. David Norbrook, for instance, advises that it included 'enough didactic matter to attract mid-century humanists', and that its 'anti-ecclesiastical satire' in book 2 increased its attractiveness to protestants.[11] The apparently eclectic tastes of this group of readers, however, remains unaccounted for. Hoby's only other printed text is a translation of *The Gratulation of M. Bucer... into the churche of Englande for the restitucion of Christes religion* (1549).[12] Another admirer of Castiglione, Ascham, is notoriously Italophobic. Modern Italian cultural achievements, he worries in *The Schoolmaster* (1570), threaten to corrupt

English protestant youth. Why, then, is an exception made for the *Courtier*? The interest seems less bizarre when we remember that the link between the reform of religion and manners starts early in the century. 'Many of the writers who advocated "civilized" behaviour in the early modern period', observes Euan Cameron, 'wrote in an overtly religious spirit.' For example, the humanist Erasmus, one of the early catholic reformers, is also the author of *De civilitate morum puerilium* (*On the civility of the manners of children*) (?1526), which saw thirty editions by 1536.[13] But this insight still doesn't explain why there was interest in the 1560s in an Italian courtesy book printed in 1528.

To answer this carefully it is necessary to begin with a different question: why is it so difficult to identify the *Courtier* as reading material for reform-minded English humanists? One reason is the longstanding conception of humanism, specifically Italian humanism, as a civic and rhetorical movement. The free speech associated with the quattrocento city-republics is enshrined in their disputational culture.[14] The supposition that rhetorical debate serves a civic agenda would not matter so much had not the *Courtier* been repeatedly recognised by several influential critics as an anti-humanist and court-centred treatise which is preoccupied with 'aesthetic' rather than 'rhetorical' display, so representing the impossibility of ideology critique.[15] It is my view that this debate has seriously skewed our reading of the *Courtier* by introducing anachronistically the modern conception of 'aesthetics' which obscures its rhetorical and political form.

Sixteenth-century English readers were interested in the *Courtier* as a conversational treatise. Thomas Hoby's English and Bartholomew Clerke's Latin translations both attempt to capture the idiomatic style of the *Courtier*, accepting the importance attached by Castiglione to the adoption of 'everyday' speech. In his prefatory letter to the 1561 edition, John Cheke advises that Hoby could have chosen still plainer English phrases. Meanwhile, Hoby's 1588 edition includes parallel texts in Italian and French, suggesting an interest in the *Courtier* as a general linguistic aid. That is, the basis of the *Courtier*'s popularity seems to rest in part on its provision of practice in idiomatic and conversational Italian, Latin, English and French. Gabriel Harvey, a proud owner of the English and Italian versions of the *Courtier*, strongly recommends the young Arthur Capel to become 'conversant and occupied' with Clerke's Latin translation, along with the *Mirror for Magistrates*, Roger Ascham's *The Schoolmaster* and 'ani pes of Osorius, Sturmius, or Ramus'. He praises these books 'esspecially' since he believes they offer scholars 'most use and practis, either for writing or speaking, eloquently or wittely, now or hereafter'.[16] Meanwhile, in his copy of the

1581 Venetian edition of *La civil conversatione*, he makes clear its value as a treasure trove or 'thesaurus' of idiomatic Italian: 'Thesoro della Lingua, discorso, & conversatione Italiana'.[17] This interest begins with the 'Athenian tribe' in the 1540s who inherited the commitment of the northern humanists to the reform of the linguistic values of the medieval scholastics. In the 1520s and 1530s Juan Luis Vives and Desiderius Erasmus sought to replace scholastic *oratio* with humanistic *sermo*, that is, an artificial language of logic with 'the conversation of actual speakers in social relationships'.[18] The reception of the conversational Castiglione, however, also coincided with the practical, rhetorical needs of the protestant reformers who were vulnerable to the accusation that they were imposing their form of worship on the people and encouraging disobedience and dissent. The popularity of this book, I will argue, is informed less by its dissemination of a behaviour appropriate to an autocratic court, than by its contribution to the ideology of consensus upon which the legitimation of the protestant Reformation depended.

The interest in Cicero shared by Cheke, Smith and Ascham, and its contribution to reform in the 1540s, will be explored in chapter 3. In this chapter, I will focus on the way in which Castiglione makes possible an unremarked emphasis on conversation in Cicero's *De oratore* and *De officiis*, and what that means for our reading of the *Courtier*. Cicero was a greatly admired orator, and his several treatises – *Brutus*, *Orator*, *De oratore*, *De inventione* – disseminate his commitment to this art. Yet, as his philosophical treatise *De officiis* reveals, when the practice of oratory became impossible in the declining years of the Roman republic, 'conversation' was deemed to provide some kind of substitute *and* a means to critique the dictator Julius Caesar. (Cicero sees Casear as the epitome of the anti-social interlocutor.) Cicero's interest in conversation, however, was longstanding. The earlier *De oratore* reveals his preoccupation with the relationship between conversation and rhetoric; it explores how conversation among friends provides rhetorical training in winning an audience's goodwill by enacting the very quality which strengthens social bonds, 'honestas'.

Castiglione tells us in the preface to the *Courtier* that he imitated Cicero's *De oratore*; this advice, however, is hardly ever taken seriously.[19] However, as I will argue, the *Courtier* offers its readers a practical introduction to Cicero's politics of *societas*. As soon as the speaker Canossa declares in book 1 that he can only show, not teach, us how to be courtiers, the conversational form of *De oratore* is recalled, and along with it, an attitude to 'easy' social relationships. Not only does Castiglione introduce us to a different Cicero, however, but Cicero in turn will help us to arrive at a different view of

Castiglione: for this reason they will be analysed side-by-side in this chapter. In particular, Cicero helps us to revise our conception of the master-trope of the dissembling courtier, *sprezzatura*. Instead of seeing *sprezzatura* as a mark of the courtier's disdain for 'untowardely asseheades' (p. 35), as its etymology (from *sprezzare*, 'to disdain') encourages, I advise that we view it instead as a conversational gesture which enables the 'outsider' to realise his native nobility. What the manner of argument in the text advises is that nobility is a social habit which is acquired by practice in conversation. Castiglione takes his interest in Cicero much further in book 4, where the question that worries modern critics – what is 'honest' about the courtier's 'flickeringe provocations' – *is* answered. The courtier's pleasing manners and conversation are the means by which he inspires in the prince the decorum/temperance or 'honestas' described by Cicero in *De officiis*, and thereby forces him to negotiate.

RECOVERING CICERO IN BOOK I OF THE *COURTIER*

Cicero's perceived contribution to Renaissance humanism is his insight that wisdom and eloquence are intimately connected. Proving this relationship appears to be the sole aim of *De oratore*. In the preface to book 1, for example, Cicero explains that the dialogue represents a dispute between himself and his brother Quintus: Cicero believes that 'eloquence is dependent upon the trained skill of highly educated men', while Quintus considers in contrast that it depends only 'on a sort of natural talent and on practice' (1. 5). We also soon learn that these conflicting perspectives are shared with the dialogue's two disputants: Crassus argues for the synthesis of eloquence and wisdom (1. 63), while Antonius insists that the orator is just 'a man who can use language agreeable to the ear, and arguments suited to convince, in law-court disputes and in debates of public business' (1. 213). For Antonius, the orator should reserve 'his philosophical books...for a restful holiday' (1. 224), and, when his turn to speak comes, he explains that he can discuss only his own 'practice [*consuetudine*]' not an 'art' which he 'never learned' (1. 208). Yet, as Cicero explains, his aim is to show that the skill of Crassus and Antonius 'could never have been realized without a knowledge of every matter that went to produce that wisdom and that power of oratory which were manifest in those two' (2. 6).

For many readers of *De oratore* Crassus seems to represent Cicero's views while Antonius is relegated to the role of a straw-man, a means to facilitate dialogue and to make the dry discussion of rhetoric more interesting. Such a reading, though, depends on a particular approach to Antonius's infamous change of position. Early in book 2 Antonius admits to Crassus that 'yesterday it was my design, if I should have succeeded in refuting your arguments, to steal these pupils from you; but, to-day... I think it my duty not so much to fight with you as to enunciate my own personal views' (2. 40). Most commentators suppose that a compromise is reached,[20] one which confirms Cicero's view that eloquence depends on the 'skill of highly educated men'.

There is good reason for this. At the end of the first day, Crassus accuses Antonius of having turned the orator into a 'mechanic' or *operarius*, but, he adds, 'I rather suspect that you are really of a different opinion, and are gratifying that singular liking of yours for contradiction.' Significantly, Crassus pauses over this. He notes that this exercise is the special preserve of the orator, 'though nowadays it is in regular use among philosophers, and chiefly those who make a practice of arguing at extreme length either for or against [*in utramque partem*] any proposition whatever laid before them' (1. 263). It is difficult to ignore the importance that Antonius's recantation has played in the defining of the philosophical method of the humanists as argument 'for and against'.

Renaissance scholars will be familiar with Paul Oskar Kristeller's account of the rise of humanism. The humanists, he argues, were 'professional rhetoricians', the 'heirs and successors to the medieval tradition' of the *dictatores*, but they were also commited to the '*studia humanitatis*', to the study of 'a clearly defined cycle of scholarly disciplines, namely grammar, rhetoric, history, poetry and moral philosophy'.[21] Cicero's own reference to *studia humanitatis* can be found in his defence of poetry, *Pro Archia Poeta*. However, the text which features most frequently in subsequent discussions is *De oratore*, mainly because we find in it a considered attempt to explain how disciplines like rhetoric and philosophy, long-considered antithethical, can accommodate each other.

One of the ways in which Cicero attempts to bring rhetoric and philosophy together is by noting their formal similarities, as when Crassus observes that Antonius's style of argument 'for and against' has always been the preserve of the orator, but recognises that 'nowadays it is in regular use among philosophers' (1. 263). But it is also with the discovery of a shared method that the problem begins. For it is not clear what argument 'for or against' means in the context of *De oratore* which pretends to be a conversation, not the kind of rigorous debate we might expect in the Roman forum.

De oratore is famously modelled on a Platonic dialogue, *Phaedrus*: the disputants sit on benches under a plane-tree in Crassus's garden which recalls the similar location of Plato's text. Only, their recreation is made more comfortable still by the use of cushions, a detail which Cicero is careful to record (1. 28–9). The casualness of this context seems to invite some rather lesiurely and unrigorous discussion. In contrast to Cicero's earlier treatise, *De inventione*, which describes the parts of a speech and the kinds of topics needed in argument straightforwardly, the discussion in *De oratore* sometimes seems meandering and unfocused, especially over the crucial question of whether oratory is an art which needs to be studied, or a native talent that does not. It is hard not to stumble over the articulation of these relationships in *De oratore*, and it has left more than one critic complaining that the treatise, as charming as it is, 'covers up some imprecision' and is 'entirely too much like a real conversation'.[22]

Little attention is paid to Cicero's interest in conversational tactics because so much hangs on the interpretation of the relationship between rhetoric and philosophy in *De oratore*. But the fact that this rhetorical manual is written as a conversation – something that Cicero seems especially keen to impress on us – is surely a matter of interest.[23] It is a matter of interest because we know from *De officiis* that Cicero had adopted the argument of the Stoic Panaetius that 'the civilized repartee of the Socratic dialogues as a model of *sermo*' is the true philosophical method because it constitutes 'one of the bonds connecting the *societas generis humani*'.[24] In *De oratore* conversation is integral to the teaching of oratory, which is a special kind of art. Whereas the 'subjects of the other arts are derived as a rule from hidden and remote sources', Cicero explains, 'the whole art of oratory lies open to the view, and is concerned in some measure with the common practice [*uso*], custom [*mores*], and speech [*sermo*] of mankind' (1. 12). The rules of rhetoric are immanent in the 'changeable matter' of everyday speech. The aim of the conversational *De oratore* is to make this obvious to us.

Once we recognise the importance of conversation to Cicero then we might read Antonius's recantation slightly differently. Antonius is not arguing both sides of the question; indeed, he does not recant. He continues to insist that he has never studied philosophy even as it becomes increasingly evident that the opposite is true. Only on one occasion does he lift the veil. Of the study of philosophy he admits at the close of book 2, 'I do not disapprove of such pursuits, if kept within limits, though I hold that a reputation for such pursuits, or any suggestion of artifice, is likely to prejudice an orator with the judiciary: for it weakens at once the credibility of the orator and the cogency of his oratory' (2. 156). He is exposed as a dissembler for the second time at the end of the book by his antagonist: 'I am delighted', Crassus declares, 'to see you at last known as a master of the theory [of rhetoric], finally unmasked and stripped of the veil of your pretended ignorance [*dissimulatio*]' (2. 350). It turns out that Antonius has been practising a jest defined by a minor speaker, Julius, in book 2 as *dissimulatio*: 'pretending not to understand what you understand perfectly'. *Dissimulatio* includes jokes which depend on a cultivated naivety (as 'when Pontidius, being asked his opinion of the man who is taken in adultery, replied: "He is a slowcoach"' (2. 275)), as well as an extended, feigned ignorance like that of Socrates.[25] *Dissimulatio* is deemed characteristic of the kind of oratory identified as conciliatory and mild (*lenis*) rather than emotive (*vehemens*), the kind, that is, that aims to win the goodwill of an audience and is most like conversation (2. 212).

Antonius's refusal to teach his audience how to become excellent orators calls attention to his conversational style, and thus, the source of his excellence: practice in conversation. His style of argument is heuristic. Ironically, this means that Antonius is often most helpful when he is being most oblique, for example, in the passage below where he compares his study of Greek history to walking in the sunshine:

it is not because I am on the look-out for aids to oratory, but just for pleasure, that I make a habit, when I have time, of reading the works of these authors and a few more. To what purpose then? Well, I will own to some benefit: just as, when walking in the sunshine, though perhaps taking the stroll for a different reason, the natural result is that I get sunburnt, even so, after perusing those books at Misenum [when on holiday]..., I find that under their influence my discourse takes on what I may call a new complexion.... (2. 59–60)

His sun simile serves a double function. On the one hand, it draws attention away from the fact that he has 'perused' Greek treatises closely. On the other hand, it conveys the extent to which he has practised, and so absorbed (or made natural to him), the precepts and skills he has learned. He discreetly indicates that the source of his excellence is study and the cultivation of *facilitas*, misleading us only in so far as he tactically omits the distinction between acting naturally and acting habitually.

Castiglione's *Courtier* makes possible this retrospective reading of Cicero by imitating the dialogue style in book 1, a book which is scattered with allusions to *De oratore*. Castiglione's interest in Cicero surfaces in two discussions, the first is the debate about nobility, the second – which I will look at first – is concerned with imitation. I want to explore both Castiglione's argument about imitation *and* his practice; the latter will tell us much about how we should read the *Courtier*. It will also show us how the figure of *sprezzatura* might serve as a means to critique, rather than reinforce, habits of thoughts, in particular the idea that 'nobilty' and 'courtliness' are the inherited gifts of the nobly born.

The debate about imitation focuses on one question: should the courtier imitate the literary greats, borrowing from them words already endowed with authority, or should he follow the promptings of his own talents, and employ the language of his contemporaries? Throughout the discussion, Canossa is committed to the idea that all we need is talent and a willingness to adopt the contemporary linguistic idiom, but he needs to defend his position against an interlocutor, Fregoso, who champions the need for imitation. Castiglione seems to set up an argument 'for and against', and yet the dialogue does not quite work like that. When Fregoso objects that Canossa's advice encourages the courtier to reproduce the solecisms of ignorant speakers, our speaker produces this confusing and conclusive explanation:

The good use of speache therefore I beleve ariseth of men that have wytte, and with learning and practise have gotten a good judgement, and with it consent and agree to receave the woordes that they think good, which are knowen by a certaine naturall judgement, and not be art or anye maner rule. (p. 68)

This sentence seems to epitomise Canossa's disdainful refusal to teach us; it looks like a deliberate obfuscation. However, he is in fact following the example of the dissimulating Antonius, and is showing us the artificial causes of 'natural' rhetorical skill. The *questione della lingua* is difficult to follow not just because it is meandering, contradictory and ambiguous, but because it offers a partial account of *De oratore* while relying on our knowledge of that text.

For example, Canossa invokes Cicero to support his thesis that talent and natural judgement alone produce eloquence. He recalls the observation of Cicero's Antonius that many orators become excellent without needing to imitate a model: 'Me thynke I remember also that Cicero in a place bringeth in Marcus Antonius to say unto Sulpitius that ther are many that folow no man, and yet clime they to a high degree of excellency' (p. 71). He is referring here to Antonius's explanation that we see there are 'many who copy no man, but gain their objects by natural aptitude, without resembling any model' (2. 98); he is also recalling his reputation as a self-made orator who is 'so completely furnished with the bounty of nature, as to seem of more than human birth, and to have been shaped by some divinity' (1. 115).

From this excerpt it would seem that Canossa is interested only in Antonius's reputation as a gifted, self-made orator, and has forgotten the strategy of *dissimulatio* which he employs in *De oratore* to expose his 'naturalness' as a studied gesture. This is odd because he has already called our attention to Antonius's use of *dissimulatio* in the earlier debate on nobility (p. 53). (On that occasion he explicitly recalls Antonius's advice to show in rhetorical display 'as little trace as possible of any artifice' (2. 152–3).) However, Canossa does not need to invoke this aspect of Antonius's style since he is *showing* us how it works. For example, his praise of natural aptitude, like that of Antonius in *De oratore*, is tactical: just like his role-model, he is describing naturalness as an effect the courtier should strive to attain, not the cause of his delightful expression.

If we return to Canossa's problematic judgement, we should be able to see more clearly how that paradoxical sentence tells us all we need to know about the natural art of the courtier. Just as in *De oratore* so in book 1 of the *Courtier* good judgement is acquired as a habit. Canossa's emphasis on the need to follow instinct and 'usage' (linguistic custom) temporarily conceals the quality of the relationship between these two distinct entities – that instinct can be shaped by usage or practice – so that we can better comprehend their combined effect.

Canossa's use of the term '*consuetudine*' is doubly meaningful. When he claims that earlier writers learned by practice (*consuetudine*) he is acknowledging not only their desire to be true to idiomatic speech (practice), but also their educational process which involves assimilation (practise). Indeed, Canossa follows his advice on the good use of speech by explaining that the courtier should follow contemporary practice (*consuetudine*) rather than a particular literary model, and he cites the example of the ancients who themselves learned – as the English translator Thomas Hoby aptly offers – 'by use and custome' ('*imparato dalla consuetudine*') (pp. 69/90). Although Canossa does not allude here to Cicero, we can almost hear Crassus emphasising the importance both of idiomatic practice and of rhetorical practise (*consuetudo*), or, for that matter, Antonius reminding us, by refusing to teach us, of the importance of practise (*consuetudo*), rather than the study of rules (1. 152; 1. 208). I suggest that we now apply these insights to Canossa's earlier discussion of native nobility and to his famous introduction of the trope which characterises courtly display: *sprezzatura*.

Canossa's odd style of argument, which enables his critique of 'naturalness' in his discussion of eloquence, is a core aspect of the rhetorical structure of book 1, and is integral to our experience of reading it. Whether we initially recognise it or not, the same style of argument informs Canossa's earlier inquiry into primogeniture, prompting us to intuit that nobility is a practised virtue. Indeed, once we attend to Canossa's conversational style, his defence of the importance of noble lineage does not look quite the same. For instance, Canossa is interrupted in mid-flow by the sceptical Gaspare Pallavicino who notes that nature does not share his subtle distinctions. Noble birth is not so important to the courtier, he argues, since men of low degree are often seen to possess the same gifts of nature. Pallavicino understands the notion of the 'seeds of virtue' in its Ciceronian, republican context, and thus exposes its aristocratic appropriation by Canossa (p. 40).[26] Unexpectedly, Canossa modifies his initial position: he now admits that noble birth is important to the courtier for social rather than natural reasons, and he allows that men of low birth may possess the same virtues as their aristocratic counterparts, although he concludes that noble birth is still important since it is highly esteemed in the popular imagination (pp. 40–1). He reveals that our 'habit' of thinking about nobility is changeable.

Importantly, this is not the first time that the defence of aristocratic natural right is qualified. Even before Pallavicino's interruption Canossa had already hinted at an alternative means to courtly gracefulness. He does not just defer to the common practice of favouring those of noble birth, he also emphasises the active process of acquiring nobility through practise. He may insist that noble birth prompts virtue, yet, he acknowledges simultaneously that even the nobly born need to make a habit of courtly skills. He also adds that even if the courtier is not perfect by nature, he can improve himself with study and effort (p. 39).

In drawing attention to these modulations I do not mean to suggest that the argument of book 1 is contradictory, or that an initial defence of primogeniture is replaced with a tenet often seen as intrinsic to humanist education: that a good student depends on a combination of native wit, practice and study. Rather, it is the nature of Castiglione's indirection, and its contribution to our experience of reading book 1 which interests me. For Canossa clings to the idea that some courtiers are graceful by nature, despite acknowledging that gracefulness can be achieved with study and effort, as one of his listeners reminds us. This participant requests that Canossa clarify exactly how gracefulness is to be achieved (p. 51). Curiously, Canossa responds by refusing to teach us how to become graceful, telling us he is obliged only to show us the ideal (p. 52). He also reminds us of the proverb that grace cannot be learned, before proceeding to explain that a courtly aspirant can acquire gracefulness by imitating the example of excellent men, so long as he has the ability to do so (p. 52). As he explains, the court aspirant should steal gracefulness from men who seem to possess it in whole or part (p. 53). His choice of the verb 'to steal' suggests that gracefulness is a quality that is redistributable, not just a birthright, and that it must be acquired surreptitiously.

Canossa's attempt to resolve some of the difficulties his discussion of courtly gracefulness creates is to introduce a new concept, *sprezzatura*. Thus, he follows his account of imitative theft by recognising that gracefulness derives either from heaven or from a universal rule which he identifies as *sprezzatura*. To obtain gracefulness, he explains, the courtier must use a carelessness or 'Reckelesness' to conceal his art, and a few lines later he recalls the example of Crassus and Antonius (and especially the advice of Antonius) to show in rhetorical display 'as little trace as possible of any artifice' (2. 152–3).

And I remember that I have reade in my dayes, that there were some most excellent Oratours, which among other their cares, enforced themselves to make every man beleve that they had no sight in letters, and dissemblinge their conning, made semblant their orations to be made very simply, and rather as nature and trueth lead them, then study and arte. (p. 53)

Canossa's invocation of courtly *sprezzatura* is commonplace to us now, perhaps too commonplace, for it is easy to ignore the context in which this strategy is unveiled, that is, a debate concerning nobility and the lineal source of courtly gracefulness. Reading this passage in context enables us to see, first, that *sprezzatura* is not dissimulative in any simple sense, and, secondly, that its deployment by Canossa impinges on his discussion of native nobility. To understand *sprezzatura* we need to remember that Cicero's Antonius, whose example Canossa here follows, chose to hide his art partly by making it natural or habitual to him. Canossa incorporates Antonius's discreet advice on assimilation not only in his discussion of literary imitation later in book 1 (as we have just seen), but also in his description here of the acquisition of courtly gracefulness. Although his suggestion that the courtier should 'steal' his gracefulness from others implies that its acquisition is underhand, it also emphasises the naturalness of the process.

HONEST RIVALRY: TEMPERANCE IN BOOK 4

The *Courtier* does not reaffirm aristocratic difference, as is so often claimed, but rather tests our conception of what it means to be noble. We might still wonder, though, of what use is this heuristic style of argument if it only contributes to the teasing out of fine distinctions. To explore Castiglione's broader appeal, I want to tackle that other criticism levelled against the

Courtier: that it provides only for an education in ingratiation. There is good reason for this anxiety. Fregoso, the leading speaker of book 2, seems unduly preoccupied with sartorial taste. On one occasion he gives a detailed account of his preference for the colour black, which, he explains, has 'a better grace in garmentes then any other'. Almost immediately, though, he modifies this view: 'not throughly blacke', he explains, 'yet somwhat darke', and then quickly adds 'I meane for [the courtier's] ordinary apparaile'. He then proceeds to explain, 'upon armour it is more meete to have sightly and meery coulours, and also garmentes for pleasure, cut, pompous and riche. Likewise in open showes about triumphes, games, maskeries, and suche other matters, because so appointed there is in them a certein livelinesse and mirthe' (p. 131).

This preoccupation with aesthetic decorum – reflected in the compromising and obsessive style in book 2 just cited – appears destined only to educate in the art of pleasing. This becomes all the more apparent when we recognise that Fregoso's attention to dress has allowed him to circumvent a more difficult topic, the nature of the courtier's 'daily conversation' with his prince (p. 119). As he explains, the courtier must learn to 'turne al his thoughtes and force of minde to love, and (as it were) to reverence the Prince he serveth above al other thinges, and in his wil, maners and facions, to be altogether pliable to please him' (p. 120). Yet, when challenged by an interlocutor who accuses him of creating a 'joly flatterer' he is unable to offer a satisfactory answer (p. 120). He concludes this discussion by recalling the example of the tyrant Mucianus who killed his engineer because 'in steede of obeying him, he would have counsailed him' and turns to matters more pressing: a description of what the courtier should wear (p. 129).[27] This frivolity is underscored in the organisation of book 2 itself, which ends with a discussion of the courtier's use of witticisms drawn almost entirely from book 2 of Cicero's *De oratore*, but divested of its place in a much broader discussion of the importance of winning goodwill in judicial oratory. How, then, can we trust the defence of the courtier's conversation with his prince in book 4 when it is conducted in the same frivolous terms? We can do so, I want to argue, with the help of Cicero's *De officiis*, which makes temperance an aspect of manly decorum. That is, Cicero can help us to understand how, for Castiglione, the accommodating friendship of a pleasing courtier offers less an act of submission to a despotic overlord than a form of honest rivalry which entails a restraining – a tempering – of hubristic manliness.[28]

Recent attention to temperance, the virtue of self-restraint and moderation, has aimed to disclose its contribution to the repressive and exploitative aspects of the modernising or civilising process. In particular, Michel Foucault, in his history of sexuality, has drawn upon Aristotle's distinction in book 7 of *The Nicomachean Ethics* between the continent man who 'has evil desires' and who experiences 'pleasure' 'but does not yield to it', and the temperate man who 'is so constituted as to take no pleasure in things that are contrary to principle'.[29] As Foucault suggests, continence is a manly activity; it 'is characterized by an active form of self-mastery', 'by the fact that the subject deliberately chooses reasonable principles of action, that he is capable of following and applying'; indeed, it initiates a ' "polemical" ' attitude towards the self. In contrast, temperance seems more closely related to the absolute renunciation of desire so important to Christian ethics. Such an idea has been developed in terms of specific sixteenth-century colonising projects in several later studies. In a discussion of Edmund Spenser's Legend of Temperance in book 2 of *The Faerie Queene*, Greenblatt examines the association between the self-colonising violence of temperance and English attempts at plantation in Ireland in the 1590s. Meanwhile, Lorna Hutson explores 'moderation' as an art of timing or opportunism in the context of English economic ventures in the New World which becomes a 'model for the moral legitimation of conquest and colonization'.[30]

Temperance is of course a complex political virtue, as the studies of Helen F. North seek to show us. As an *arete politike*, temperance seeks to restrain the aggressiveness of citizens towards one another in a classical democracy; it is also the self-divided virtue of Roman imperialism, embodied, on the one hand, in the ideal of the shrewd, restrained ruler, and, on the other, in the model of the obedient subject.[31] It is in this second form, Quentin Skinner argues, that it appears in the new 'mirrors-for-princes' treatises of the cinquecento, a genre which adapted the political language of the earlier republican dialogues. Commenting on the princely mirror, *De regno et regis institutione* (*The Kingdom and the Education of a King*), Skinner observes that its author Francesco Patrizi 'concedes that "citizens ought to strive to acquire *virtus*"', but he makes it plain that he regards this as a relatively passive quality, one which includes the cultivation of "obedience and goodwill" and of "gratitude for the benefits they receive from their kings"'.[32]

One aspect of the new dimension to late fifteenth-century Italian political culture, Skinner recognises, is that advice is divided between the mirrors-for-princes and its sister-genre, the courtier's handbook. One example of this second type of treatise is Diomede Carafa's *Dello optimo cortesano* (*The Perfect Courtier*), which its author wrote while in service at the Neapolitan court in the 1480s. However, the 'most celebrated and influential work', he argues, is the *Courtier*.³³ Critics tend to concur that Castiglione's treatise describes exactly the kind of conduct needed at a despotic court. Books 1 and 2 outline the delightful accomplishments of a male courtier skilled in the art of dissimulation, while book 3 is dedicated rather to the arts of the more restricted female courtier. Book 4, which treats these frivolous issues in a more serious manner, was written later, and added at the last moment to the final redaction. Particularly disconcerting is Ottaviano's insistence in book 4 that the prince's virtues make him most dearly beloved of God, 'throughe whose grace he shall atteine unto that heroicall and noble vertue, that shall make him passe the boundes of the nature of manne, and shall rather be called a Demy God, then a manne mortall' (p. 312). Indeed, such a doctrine relegates the courtier to the role of a good-tempered and accommodating prince-pleaser.

As if to accommodate this role, book 4 emphasises the importance of temperance to the ideal courtier. Thus, quite early in the discussion, Ottaviano recalls Aristotle's comparison of temperance with continence in book 7 of *The Nicomachean Ethics*, arguing that the courtier should prefer the former because it ensures the subjection of unruly passions. Ottaviano proceeds to defend temperance against the criticism of one interlocutor that the tempered mind has no 'will' (*volontà*) to desire by calling attention to the fact that it defeats all grounds of 'greedie desire'; it overcomes one's internal enemies with absolute certainty. '[C]ontinencie', as Ottaviano explains in Hoby's careful translation:

may be compared to a Capitain that fighteth manlie [*virilmente*], and though his ennemies be stronge and well appointed, yet geveth he them the overthrowe, but for al that not without much a do and daunger. But temperance free from all disquietinge, is like the Capitain that without resistance overcommeth and reigneth. And havinge in the mynde where she is, not onlie assuaged, but clene quenched the fire of gredie desire [*cupidità*], even as a good Prince in civill warr dispatcheth the sedicious inward ennemies, and giveth the scepter and wholl rule to reason, so in like case this vertue not enforcing the mind, but powringe [*infondere*] therinto through most quiet waies a vehement persuasion that may incline him to honestie, maketh him quiet and full of rest, in everie part equall and of good proportion: and on everie side framed of a certein agreement with him self, that filleth him with such a cleare caulmenesse, that he is never out of pacience: and becommeth full and wholy most obedient to reason, and readie to tourn unto her all his motions, and folow her where she lust to leade him, without anie resistance. (pp. 306–7/425–6)

Our worst fears may be confirmed on reading this passage. Indeed, Ottaviano replaces an educational method based on polemic with a process of subjection through a surreptitious means which recalls the effects – alluring, distilling, easing, beguiling – of the courtier's own display. He unfolds a frightening view of the courtier as a mere lackey serving an absolute and despotic monarch.

Such a reading, though, while it may seem obvious to us, neglects two important aspects of Ottaviano's defence of the courtier's tempering style: first, that the surreptitious means employed by the courtier imply the interior subjection of the 'greedie desires' of the prince, and, secondly, that temperance is understood as tractability, a flowering of innate civility, not blind obedience. A quick reading of Ottaviano's military metaphor might suggest that the courtier's pleasing manners encourage the prince to establish unrestricted power over his subjects and neighbours. Yet, Ottaviano is describing a psychomachia in which the enemies – or 'greedie desires' – are internal to the prince himself.

Ottaviano's wish to advise on the restraint of the princely will is brought out a little later when he offers a straightforward condemnation of expansionist militaristic cultures. Commenting on the practice of raising obelisks, Ottaviano notes disapprovingly that 'these things and many mo, were invented to make men warlike, onlye to bring others in subjection'. This is 'not very reasonable', he adds, 'according to the lawe of nature which will not have, that in others the thinge should please us, whiche in ourselves is a greef to us', concluding that princes ought 'to make their people warlyke', so they can defend themselves 'from whoso woulde attempt to bringe them in bondage' (p. 317).

Castiglione aims not just to bind the will of the prince, but also to make it subject to (or accommodating of) external influence. To this end, he distinguishes between two kinds of rule. The first kind is 'Lordlye and forsyble, as maisters over slaves', and is analogous to a state in which 'doeth the soule commaunde the bodye', while the second kind is 'more milde and tractable, as good Princis by waye of lawes over their Subjectes, and in this reason commaundeth greedie desire' (p. 311). In a move typical of the dialogue, Ottaviano's original support for monarchical government (p. 309) is modified when he advises the prince to create a 'Counsell of the nobilitie', another of 'the people of a baser degree'. Adding a republican twist to the idea of the body politic, he imagines how the state might function as 'one bodie alone knitt together, the governance wherof should cheeflie depende upon the Prince, yet shoulde the rest beare a stroke also in it: and so shoulde this state have the fourme and maner of the three good governmentes, which is, a kingdome, men of the best sorte, and the people' (pp. 320–1).

Renewed attention to the Aristotelian virtue of temperance is advised by Michael C. Schoenfeldt, who observes that its misconception in new historicist work has inhibited discussion of the early modern politics of self-discipline. In this period, he explains, it is often 'self-control that authorises individuality'. Temperance 'is about how to fortify a self, not police a state. Its focus is a regime of self-discipline which an earlier culture imagined as a necessary step towards any prospect of liberation'.[34] The reader of the *Courtier*, however, cannot employ Aristotelian temperance quite so easily. This is because it is not so much what Ottaviano wants that is at stake in critical readings, but how he proposes to achieve it. Ottaviano wants us to believe that the courtier's 'beguiling' manner will make the prince tractable. He asks us to accept that the courtier's method of 'distilling' (*infondere*) temperance into the prince is equivalent to the action of temperance itself, the virtue which 'not enforcing the mind, but powringe [*infondere*] therinto through most quiet waies a vehement persuasion that may incline [its subject] to honestie, maketh him quiet and full of rest'. But how can we allow that the courtier's decorous conduct constitutes the action of temperance, let alone recognise as 'manly' – that is, as critical – a form of persuasion which depends on easing rather than debating, deliberating, polemicising or acting *upon* others? Indeed, how can we accept that such a discreet method 'may incline [the prince] to *honestie*'? To understand this we will need to spread our net a little wider than Aristotle's *Nichomachean Ethics*, and consider Cicero's aestheticisation of the Greek virtue of *sophrosyne* in *De officiis*.

Although Ottaviano tells us that the courtier's 'precise facions' inculcate in the prince temperance, not its opposing vice, *lascivia* or *luxoria*, we do not believe him. His claims are more readily taken as evidence of Castiglione's retreat into aesthetics, and his unwillingness to address the real situation confronting a much diminished nobility in Italy in the early 1500s.[35] Yet, for Castiglione, 'aesthetics' is not a transcendent category. Rather, it is informed by the politico-ethical decorum explored under the topic of 'temperance' as the fourth part of *honestas* or 'moral goodness' in book 1 of *De officiis*. In this text, Cicero discusses temperance as a virtue of moderation, restraint and an art of timing. In this last sense, though, he also explores it as an art of social decorum (1. 93). For Cicero, decorum has two aspects; in its general sense it involves 'moral goodness as a whole', but in its secondary sense it 'embraces temperance and self-control, together with a certain deportment such as becomes a gentleman' (1. 96).

Temperance is the knowledge of how to employ speech and manners decorously, that is, with consideration to one's social context and audience.

It is a flexible, political virtue of accommodation. According to Helen North, Cicero's aestheticisation of the Greek *sophrosyne* in *De officiis* places 'a new emphasis on what Cicero translates as *approbatio* ('approval')': 'Just as physical beauty combined with harmony gives pleasure (*delectat*), so *decorum* wins approval – *movet approbatinem*'.[36] Or, in Cicero's words: just 'as physical beauty with harmonious symmetry of the limbs engages the attention and delights the eye, for the very reason that all the parts combine in harmony and grace, so this propriety (*decorum*), which shines out in our conduct, engages the approbation (*approbatio*) of our fellow-men by the order, consistency, and self-control it imposes upon every word and deed' (1. 98). Temperance is the virtue of the 'genial conversationalist' (1. 108); it cultivates *verecundia* (shamefastness or modesty), 'the virtue that causes us to avoid offending fellow men', and prompts us to show consideration towards those with whom we speak (1. 136). It is tied to the ideal of a society organised on principles of mutual benefit and sustained by 'conversation'.

Recognising this type of 'honesty' will affect how we read the courtier's decorative display. We must take seriously Ottaviano's claim that the 'frute' of courtly conduct – 'musike, sportes, pastimes, and other pleasaunt facions' – is 'the traininge and the helping forward of the Prince to goodnesse' (p. 296), and that the enjoyment of 'precise facions' leads to the practice of the virtue of temperance. As Ottaviano argues, it is the very 'art' of the courtier which will make the prince 'moste wise, moste continent, moste temperate, moste manlye [*fortissimo*]' (pp. 312/432), because he understands from philosophy that in education 'the bodye [must] be cherished beefore the soule' (p. 319). An individual must cultivate and make habitual virtuous conduct, a process which depends on making the body 'handsome, towardlie, and livelie' (p. 320). Only then can he be said to be honest – or to possess 'moral goodness'. This helps to explain why for Castiglione 'honestie' is manifested in the courtier's appearance and conversation.

The qualities of affability and accommodation praised by Ottaviano structure the conversational form of book 4 and contribute positively to a sceptical treatment of absolutism. Just as in book 1, so in this book we must be careful not to take Ottaviano's initial pronouncements at face value. In the course of his conversation, he not only accommodates the interruptions of his audience, modifying and developing his views according to their contributions, but he also independently tempers some of his original commitments, which are often only one part of a developing argument. Ottaviano's pro-monarchical stance, indicated in his conception of a prince as a 'Demy God', seems fairly uncompromising. Yet, he has already warned us of the dangers of intemperate princes who set themselves up as false gods, princes who refuse to obey their own reason and the reasonable laws of their realm, thinking it not lordly, and who manipulate their image in the vain hope that they might 'be counted (almost) Goddes' (pp. 297/414). He encourages a sceptical response to appeals to divine right, and hints at a broader enquiry into the 'natural' basis of authority. Ottaviano makes manifest the dependency of unelected rulers by exposing as pretentious any claim to authority that rests solely on the hereditary principle. He makes it extremely difficult for a prince to believe that he might 'passe the boundes of the nature of manne' with God's 'grace' (pp. 312/432) because he is acutely sensitive to the relationship between a social effect (the assumption of authority) and its rightful cause (an on-going cultivation of social virtues, and the 'feminisation' of hubristic manliness).

Castiglione's conception of 'honestie' also affects the relationship between the courtier and the prince in interesting ways. Rather than seeing the courtier's attention to dress and manners as ingratiating, we should recognise instead how it encourages him to engage in an honest rivalry with his prince. Although Ottaviano repeatedly asserts the subordination of the courtier to the prince, the 'naturalness' of his servile role is not self-evident. Just such a point is raised by Elisabetta Gonzaga, when she comments on Ottaviano's excellence: 'it may be said, that you are not onlie the perfect Courtier whom we seke for, and able to instruct your Prince well, but also (if fortune be so favourable on your side) ye maye be the good Prince your self' (p. 332). Ottaviano (who was to become Doge of Genoa!) laughs off this suggestion. But his attention is drawn to it again a moment later when Guliano de' Medici makes a similar point: 'needes must the Courtier, by whose instruction the prince must be of such excellencye, be more excellente then the prince: and in this wise shall he be also of more woorthinesse then the prince himselfe, which is most unsittinge' (p. 333). These objections are quickly answered by Ottaviano, who insists on two preconditions for the prince's education: first, that the prince be naturally apt for the study, and, secondly, that he be given the opportunity to practise and so develop his virtues. Because of his position as head of the realm, Ottaviano explains, the prince has the opportunity to practise those skills of government which the courtier can only know in theory (pp. 334–5). But Ottaviano's response is ambiguous. While he reaffirms the importance of inherited virtue he also draws attention to the importance of study, indicating that the courtier, if given the occasion to practise those skills he already understands, could prove a proper prince. In fact, as Ottaviano accepts with a shrug of the shoulders, 'nature hath not appointed suche narrowe boundes to the dignities of men, that one maye not come up from one to an other: therfore many times meane souldiers arrise to be Capitaines:

private men, kinges: priestes, Popes: and scolers, maisters: and so with there degree or dignitie they take their name accordinglye' (p. 336).

The association of the *Courtier* with monologic courtesy books such as della Casa's *Galateo* has tended to encourage us to read it as a straightforward conduct manual. Careful consideration of their form and content, however, makes it difficult to compare the one's homely, often comic, advice with the other's philosophical interests. The *Courtier* is not prescriptive; it does not yield up its meaning to a selective reader. Rather, it requires patient attention and the acquisition of a textual practice. The intriguing question, though, is whether Tudor readers were willing to give the *Courtier* their time.

Recent scholarship has understood the immense popularity of the *Courtier* in the newly centralised European courts as dependent on its status as a manual of court behaviour. Peter Burke observes how, in the course of its printing history, editors developed a paratext to facilitate the easy retrieval of information.[37] Thomas Hoby's English edition, for instance, includes marginal glosses for use as an index and an appended summary of the chief qualities desirable in the male courtier (one of the first requirements of which is that the English courtier should 'be well borne and of a good stocke' (p. 367)). Thus, the print history of this treatise seems to indicate its transformation into exactly the kind of prescriptive text Castiglione resisted writing.

Even so, it not too far-fetched to suppose that patience was exercised in its reading. Harvey's copy of Hoby's translation dates at least two readings, one in 1572, the other in 1580. Moreover, the copious annotations in its margins suggest that this book was read with care; words and phrases are underlined, possibly so that they can be more easily recalled for use in conversation, while the margins record maxims which sum up a section of the text. Harvey also uses the *Courtier* to collect or record jokes, no doubt to reproduce on social occasions.[38] That is, Harvey is practising civility in the margins of this book. He was also interested in the form of this dialogue. The dating of its reading coincides with the writing of his *Letter-Book* (1573–7), a manuscript collection of dialogues and communications. The organisation of this collection is not accidental. As we saw in my introduction, it opens with a letter in which Harvey rehearses a complaint against him of unsociability. In response, he claims not to understand the idea of sociability among his aristocratic peers; the rest of the *Letter-Book* is an exploration of many different styles of civil interaction, along with recommendations that the *Courtier* and other courtesy manuals should constitute reading for Cambridge undergraduates.

Hoby's edition also encourages careful reading, despite its cursory summary of the chief qualities of the courtier in an appendix. In the preface he indicates that he understands that Castiglione has created a more flexible conception of 'nobility'. Not only is he sensitive to Castiglione's playful use of the term *'consuetudine'* in book 1 (for which he offers the double translation 'use and custome'), but he also alerts us in the preface to Canossa's emphasis on nobility as a practised virtue. He adopts a similarly circuitous style of argument to that of book I, modifying his own apparently conservative conception of nobility. In his salute to Henry Hastings, 'sonne and heire apparent to the noble Erle of Huntyngton' (p. 3), Hoby appears to anticipate Canossa's own respect for the laws of primogeniture. He explains his choice of a patron on the grounds that 'none, but a noble yonge Gentleman, and trayned up all his life time in Court, and of worthie qualities, is meete to receive and enterteine so worthy a Courtier', and he reminds us also that it was Hastings's 'noble Auncestours' who played host to Castiglione on his visit to England in 1506 (p. 4).

Initially, such language might recall the typical pose adopted by writers in dedications to aristocratic superiors, on whom they could hardly impose themselves as teachers. But, like Canossa in the text itself, Hoby does not simply reinforce expected aristocratic values. He may compliment Hastings when he claims his translation will 'confirme with reason the Courtly facions, comely exercises, and noble vertues, that unawares have from time to time crept into you', but he does not go so far as to suggest that they are native to him. Thus, he continues this sentence by noting that his 'noble vertues' have 'with practise and learning taken custome in you' (p. 4). Hoby invokes the 'noble Auncestorus' of Hastings, only to indicate that his 'noble vertues' have been acquired with 'practise' (they have 'crept' into him). Such a reading is important because Hoby's translation is not intended to confirm the natural status of the old nobility, or to insist on the exclusion of certain kinds of individual, but to make Castiglione's treatise 'commune to a greate meany', and, more specifically, to bring about the ennoblement of his 'inferior' countrymen (pp. 4–5). As he optimistically explains, 'we [may] perchaunce in time become as famous in Englande, as the learned men of other nations have ben and presently are' (p. 7). This translation of the *Courtier* was not an isolated undertaking. Hoby, who graduated from St. John's College in 1545, was a friend of Cheke and Ascham, and his translation carries their approval. In the following chapter, I will try to understand why.

CHAPTER 3

Honest rivalries: Tudor humanism and linguistic and social reform

Like other concepts, 'self-interest' is also deemed to have a history. In the course of the seventeenth century, argues Albert O. Hirschman, there emerged the belief that countervailing passions or 'interests' – greed, avarice, love of money – might be invoked for the restraining of uncivil passions, ambition, glory-seeking or the lust for power.[1] This influential thesis has been used to explain the rise of manners and the social and commercial sphere in the eighteenth century. Yet it remains problematic in terms of understanding historical development. One of the problems is that, on this view, the debate about social duty and self-interest is split across two hundred years, when in fact the dynamic relationship between them is the subject of humanist dialogue from at least the mid-sixteenth century.

This chapter revises our conception of the social thought of sixteenth century humanism. It questions the deep-rooted association of humanism with social exclusivity, aristocratic service and self-serving careerism.[2] I do not dispute that these are often the effects of humanist debate, or that they represent the explicit motivation of some of the contributors, but I want to accommodate an agenda that had more complex and conflicted qualities. My aim is to communicate the varied nature of debate among those Cambridge humanists associated with John Cheke, who were committed to linguistic, social and religious reform, and who had a far-reaching and formative influence on the development of Elizabethan literary culture (an influence which is rarely recognised today in critical readings). Theirs is a far from homogeneous culture; it demands consideration of some neglected texts and forgotten debates, but whose influence often unconsciously informs more recent critical work. One such debate concerns the conflict between self-interest and social duty; in some texts we can witness an innovative attempt to express more 'honestly' the presence of self-interest in all negotiations (although this attempt is obviously self-serving). Without addressing this debate we cannot appreciate the simultaneous attempt and failure of Cheke and Thomas Smith to question the source and nature of authority and to create a mode of opposition which is deemed 'civil' rather than seditious and hurtful to the commonwealth.

My starting point for this topic, however, considers a different, but related, problem: the assumed opposition between the courtier and the humanist. Since G. K. Hunter's *John Lyly: The Humanist as Courtier*, the assumption has been that they belong to opposing camps. This stand-off has been recently revised by Mike Pincombe who reminds us of the equivalence of humanism and courtliness, apparent in Abraham Fleming's phrase 'courtly Humanists' (the first time we meet the word 'humanist'), or Thomas Cooper's definition of 'Humanitie' as 'mans nature: gentlenesse: courtesie: gentill behaviour: civilitie: pleasantnesse in maners: doctrine: learnyng: liberall knowledge'.[3] Humanism was both inclusive and exclusive: some authors depict country people as backward, while others refuse to identify courtliness as the 'unique possession of courtiers'.[4] I am interested in how we might extend our understanding of 'courtly Humanism' to accommodate the particular inclusivity recommended by Ascham in the 1540s and to answer the question raised in chapter 2: why were this protestant moralist and his friends so taken with the *Courtier*?

The common assumption that the *Courtier* represents a departure from the rhetorical commitment of the Italian humanists to practical reasoning reproduces the unease with this Italian treatise expressed by earlier historians of English humanism. There has been a tendency to compare the superficiality of Castiglione's treatise with the sober and more serious aims of Thomas Elyot's *The Boke Named the Governour* (1531). The title of Elyot's treatise, argues Fritz Caspari, indicates immediately 'the need for a man different from the Italian courtier, for an independent individual, capable of governing, able to act and decide on his own'.[5] Discussion of the reception of the *Courtier* has been prejudiced in two respects. First, the misleading concept of 'aesthetics' has been introduced into early modern critical debate when what is needed is more nuanced discussion of a difficult term in classical rhetoric, decorum. Secondly, Castiglione's English readers are usually assumed to be courtiers, a rather vague designation as Steven May has argued.[6] Perhaps the most influential early readers of this treatise were the members of the so-called 'Athenian tribe' in Cambridge in the 1540s, especially, Cheke, Smith and Ascham. These men served as courtiers in the sense advised by May, that is, they were close to the person of Edward VI and of Elizabeth I. However, their identity is also bound up with their status as protestant reformers and humanists committed to the recovery of classical learning. They share in common with Castiglione an interest in Ciceronian '*honestas*' and in relation to this, a commitment to

Honest rivalries: Tudor humanism and linguistic and social reform 67

the civilising of the vernacular. Linguistic reform is inextricably linked to social, political and religious reform in the mid-Tudor period. The accommodation of English 'honesty' and Cicero's '*honestas*' in *Toxophilus: the Schole of Shootinge* (1545) enables Ascham to redefine the relationship between different estates, and to suggest a new model for gentlemen to follow, the urban artisan. Meanwhile, Smith and Cheke enact a friendship based on honest rivalry in their debate about the pronunciation of Greek in such a way as to reflect on the process of reformation itself.

FROM PLAINNESS TO HONESTY, FROM ESTATES TO SORTS

There are different ways in which the vernacular might be valued and cultivated. Since speech is recognised in the sixteenth century as the basic building block of society, it is obvious that whichever route to linguistic reform is taken will determine a particular conception of social and political relations. One attempt at reform in the mid-sixteenth century rests on the recovery of native literary styles and diction occasioned by a new confidence in English as a language fit for biblical translation. Archbishop Cranmer's prologue to the 1539 Great Bible, John N. King observes, repeats the insistence of Erasmus 'that the Word be spoken in the language of the people in such a way as to level class distinctions'. Cranmer also 'identifies the biblical *sermo humilis* with the plain style of native English literature'.[7] The 1550s saw a flourishing of native literature which recalled the Lollard roots of Tudor protestantism; this includes Robert Crowley's edition of William Langland's fourteenth-century dream vision *The Vision of Pierce Plowman* which appeared in 1550. Much of Crowley's writing promises to represent the interests of the lower estates. Thus, in *The Way to Wealth* (1550) – a response to Kett's rebellion in Norfolk in 1549 – Crowley speaks sympathetically for the 'pore man of the countrey' to discover who was responsible for the recent uprising: 'I know his answere. He woulde tel me that the great fermares, the grasiers, the riche buthares, the men of lawe, the marchauntes, the gentlemen, the knightes, the lordes, and, I can not tell who.'[8] He identifies aristocratic greed as one of the economic causes of the uprising, which began on the 20 June 1549 when villagers in Attleborough, Norfolk, pulled down hedges enclosing the land of a local landowner.

Even so, the literature of the commonwealth man Crowley, like the manifesto of the rebel Kett, is nostalgic.[9] It is committed to a view of society organised in terms of three estates, the knights, the clergy and the lay people. Crowley resurrects medieval estates satire so as to assert its particular philosophy, 'the desirability of every man's being content with his degree and the folly of trying to change his estate',[10] but he does so more expansively and dogmatically than many of his predecessors. 'No medieval moralist ever preached the doctrine of estates more forcefully than Crowley', argues Ruth Mohl, 'particularly to those of low estate'. *The Voyce of the Last Trumpet* (1549) may expand the original scheme of three estates to twelve – beggars, servants, yeomen, priests, scholars, learned men, physicians, lawyers, merchants, gentlemen, magistrates and women – but it also advises those of low estate of the fate which will befall them if they become ambitious.[11] Similarly, *The Way to Wealth* may speak for the labouring poor, but it also finds them guilty of sedition, and advises that they practise obedience and patience in keeping with their estate.

We will return to Crowley in chapter 4, where the limits of his project of linguistic and social reform are considered. In this chapter, however, I am interested in the attempted reforms of a different group with whom commonwealth men like Crowley are usually contrasted, the 'Athenian tribe' of John Cheke. Cheke is perhaps best known as the author of *The hurt of sedition* (1549), another response to Kett's rebellion and further uprisings in the west country. From the beginning of this treatise Cheke distances himself from the rebels: God 'stayed us from your wyckednes', he thunders, 'that by beholdynge the filth of your faulte, we myghte justly for offence, abhore you lyke rebels' (sig. A2v). The rebels claim to be rising for the sake of the commonwealth but, argues Cheke, their actions will bring about its destruction. Like Crowley, he describes the obedience the poor owe to the king and nobility (sig. B1r). However, as John D. Cox has noted, Crowley was at least 'evenhanded' in his analysis, 'designating the covetousness of the rich and poor alike as the source of the rebellion', whereas Cheke is evidently not.[12]

Unsurprisingly, Cheke's commitment to hierarchy in *The hurt of sedition* is seen to govern the proposed linguistic reforms of the humanists more generally. Crowley, argues Cox, represents the survival into the sixteenth century of a medieval tradition of decorum inspired by St Augustine's levelling of the classical low, middle and high styles: no style is higher than biblical *sermo humilis*. Consequently, the lowly plowman makes an authoritative social critic. In contrast, the dedication of the humanists to the recovery of classical Greek and Latin is the means by which the idea of decorum as a stratification of styles that reflect social degree is introduced into English speech and society.[13] On this view the humanists replace the native plain style with the Ciceronian aureate or high style, so privileging its users, educated men like themselves. In so doing they displace the traditional moral authority of the literary type of the 'plowman'.

What this argument assumes is that the modernisation of English is implicated in the structural modernisation of English society, as the language is refined so as to accommodate ever more nuanced discriminations in terms of class.[14] 'The transition from a society of "estates", or "orders", to a "class society"', writes Keith Wrightson, 'is one of the commonplaces of historical sociology'. It is also a commonplace of historical linguistics.[15] Thus, Joseph M. Williams notes the dissemination in the sixteenth century of the assumption of a 'congruence between a person's language and his social status', so that John Cleland could unhesitatingly argue in *The Institution of a Young Noble Man* (1607) that a nobleman should 'put a distinction betweene [his] discourses and a *Scythians*, a *Barbarians*, or a *Gothes*. For it is a pitty when a Nobleman is better distinguished from a Clowne by his golden laces, then by his good language' (p. 186).[16] The sixteenth century, Wrightson explains, saw a gradual transition in terms of the conception of its 'functional' organisation as three estates to 'a single hierarchy of degrees'. In this period, we find a new 'concern with order and degree, with authority and subordination'.[17] This is reflected in the influential *The Boke Named the Governour* (1531), an early treatise of English humanism. Its author, the catholic Henrician counsellor Thomas Elyot, insists that 'without ordre may be nothing stable or permanent; and it may not be called ordre, excepte it do conteyne in it degrees'.[18] According to Wrightson, it is only with the dissemination of the idea of 'sorts' in the late sixteenth and early seventeenth centuries that there emerged a 'language pregnant with conflict, aligning the "richer" against the "poorer"' and the '"better" against the "meaner"', and expressing 'the plasticity of social identity'.[19]

One of the arguments of the *Governour* is that the commonwealth should be ruled by a king advised by governors or counsellors who have been schooled in the classics. At every turn, the *Governour* reveals Elyot's classical knowledge; he introduces into English many neologisms, or translates Latin concepts. One such translation is the Latin '*honestas*' as 'simplicity'.[20] For Elyot, as we will see in the next section, 'simplicity' acquires in English a new range of connotations which inform his conception of an ordered society, the harmony of which depends on clear communication and aristocratic impartiality.

Later humanists did not always share Elyot's penchant for neologisms, but his attachment to orderly speech and manners, and his tendency to promote the interests of the university-educated, is reciprocated. In *The Arte of Rhetorique* (1553), Thomas Wilson, a student of Cheke's, insists that plainness is one of the most important qualities to which an orator should aspire. Like Elyot's 'simplicity', Wilson's 'plainness' connotes orderliness.

Meaning is made plain, Wilson advises, in well-ordered speech in everyday English. The Tudor orator is advised to 'utter his mind in plain wordes, suche as are usually received' and to tell his tale 'orderly without going about the busshe' (p. 25). Unlike Elyot, Wilson may dislike the use of neologisms; however, like Elyot, he understands plain speech to mean the kind of idiom which he and other humanists speak. Notoriously, he rejects the native idiom of provincial compatriots. As Cox complains, 'when illustrating linguistic solecisms he took frequent opportunities to put them in the mouths of anonymous "country fellows" who blunder about awkwardly in his anecdotes before their social betters'. Such a conception of plainness expresses an 'innovative scorn for agricultural labor' which might be interpreted as 'an indication' of the anxiety of the humanists 'to define themselves as privileged by their economic dependence on literacy and intellectual labor'.[21]

There is undoubtedly a direct line of cultural transmission from Elyot to Wilson: both defend an idea of a hierarchical society, the organisation of which is reflected in its linguistic order. Nevertheless, there are also dangers in making Elyot or Wilson representative of English humanism, not least because it obscures the negotiations which took place among the humanists more generally and the complexity of the idea of the plain style in the period. The neoclassicist Cheke shares with the Oxford-educated, plain-speaking Crowley an interest in recovering the vernacular for the teaching of the word of God. Cheke was convinced, for example, that English was sufficient of itself for the translation of the Bible. He was thus critical of earlier translations such as Wyclif's (1380) and Tyndale's (1534) which borrowed words from Greek or Latin. For Cheke, argues James Goodwin, 'speaking a language but partially understood by the lower orders of people would fail of profiting them so largely as could be wished'.[22] He tends to avoid words of Latin and Greek derivation, the meaning of which might be unavailable to those without knowledge of these languages. Sometimes this end inspired interesting choices of diction: Cheke chose 'moond' in place of Wyclif's and Tyndale's 'lunatik', 'crossed' in place of 'crucified', 'biwordes' instead of 'parablis' or 'similitudes'.[23] This emphasis is also recorded in the letter he wrote to Hoby, praising the translation of the *Courtier* but suggesting that yet plainer English terms might have been chosen. It points to the need for a more flexible conception of the plain style in the period: the argument that the humanists introduced the high or aureate Ciceronian style is misleading. It is more useful to speak of a variety of plain styles which are equally rhetorical, and to recognise that these could include Ciceronian *sermo humilis*, a 'negligent carelessness' that could be inclusive as well as exclusive.[24]

Native diction often signals a writer's commitment to the plain style, but not always. The purist Cheke still borrows a few words even as he argues against doing so. Other writers point to the absurdity of a debate about plain speech which is preoccupied solely with neologisms. What is more plain than the word plain, or common than the word common, argues George Pettie in the preface to *Civile Conversation*; both are borrowed words which have been anglicised (p. 11). Similarly, commitment to the plain style is not necessarily an expression of sympathy for ordinary folk. The plain-speaking Crowley speaks on behalf of labourers while also advising them to remember their estate; meanwhile, some neoclassicists recognise that civil speech belongs to artisans as well as nobles, and uncover a broad-based potential for self-improvement: 'you shall see artificers, and others of low estate', argues Anniball in *Civile Conversation*, 'to apply fitly to their purpose in due time and place, Sentences, pleasant Jestes, Fables, Allegories, Similitudes, Proverbes, Comptes, and other delightfull speache' (2. 136).

One English humanist who shared Guazzo's view was Roger Ascham. An attempt to recommend the plain dealing and honest rivalry of artisans lies at the heart of his challenge in *Toxophilus* to the ordered social vision of both a commonwealth man like Crowley and a neoclassicist wedded to 'simplicity' like Elyot. Ironically, it is with this attempt that we might also begin to explain Ascham's interest in Castiglione. I am not suggesting that Ascham is imitating Castiglione in *Toxophilus*; he simply shares with him an interest in Cicero's 'honestas', which he discovers is exemplified by a different 'sort' of speaker. The model praised in *Toxophilus* is based, not on nobly born courtiers, but on English yeomen and honest labourers, the artisans and craftsmen who were newly recognised as a 'middling sort' in the period.[25]

The appeal to this group is not unique to Ascham. They are also the likely (and forgotten) addressees of Cheke's *The hurt of sedition*. In this treatise, Cheke is upholding the property rights of aristocratic landowners *and* rural labourers. The latter group are identified as the victims of the uprisings: 'what a griefe is it to an honest man to labour truelye in youth, and to gaine paynfully by labour, wherewith to live honestli in age, and to have this gotten in longe time to be sodainlye caught awaye by the violence of sedition' (sig. E3r). Cheke's appeal to honest men is undoubtedly opportunistic and misleading; many members of this group were the perpetrators of the uprising. What his appeal recalls, however, is the complexity of the social make-up of Elizabethan uprisings which might include and exclude gentlemen and labourers. For example, the rebel leader Richard Kett was a tanner by trade and a landowner. Villagers were persuaded by a local troublemaker to pull down the hedges surrounding land he had enclosed. However, instead of becoming a victim of the uprising, Kett became its leader, agreeing 'that the common land he had enclosed should be made public again and, though his own interest in the enclosure conflict clearly lay with the landlords, [he] said he would stand with the rioters until they had obtained their rights'. He did so until his execution later that year.[26] The complex make-up of this rebellion is perhaps also reflected in the intended readership of *The hurt of sedition*. Reproduced as a relatively inexpensive octavo, it is likely that this treatise found an attentive audience among urban artisans as well as government officials. Many guilds, like the Company of Drapers, were called upon to defend London against advancing rebels from the west country. Its records note that on 15 July 1549 they were charged 'to prepare "good and substantial harness for thirty able and talle men and good substantial wepons and habylyments of warre", that is to say, "bowes and sheffs of arrows, hagbutters or handgones [handguns] and bylls [bills]" '.[27]

Toxophilus reflects a truism of the period, that 'honesty' belongs to men of low rather than high estate. This truism is represented, both positively and negatively, by a range of literary characters: the 'honest husbandman' of farming manuals, the character 'Honesty' identified by a courtier as a 'Base Villain' in the public-theatre comedy, *A Knack to Know a Knave* (1594), and, of course, the 'honest' (and sometimes not so honest) shepherds of Sidney's *Arcadia* (c. 1580).[28] This adjective, however, also belonged to urban artisans. Thanks to the work of Christopher Brook we have a better understanding of how sixteenth- and seventeenth-century guilds served to indoctrinate their apprentices in two related virtues: Christian charity and honesty. 'On one level,' Brooks explains, honesty 'included notions of fair dealing, probity, and uprightness of character'. Thus, the guilds would punish dishonest conduct: apprentices to the London Carpenters might be 'whipped for embezzling goods'. On another level, though, it 'was also associated with a certain mode of behaviour and speaking, a certain dignity of deportment, which conformed to generally accepted conventions'. Thus, the 'members of the Draper's Company in London were supposed to go "honestly" in processions'.[29] This second conception of honesty is Roman in origin; as Brooks notes, it was 'summarized in the life-size statues on the entrance of the medieval guildhall in London, which depicted the civic virtues of Discipline, Justice, Fortitude, and Temperance'.[30]

DISPUTING HONESTY IN ROGER ASCHAM'S *TOXOPHILUS*

In 1614 Barnaby Rich, a self-educated soldier and veteran of the Elizabethan campaigns in the Netherlands and Ireland, printed a satirical treatise entitled *The Honestie of this Age*. Rich claims the voice of the bluff, plain-speaking soldier who does not care about the reproaches his victims will aim at him: 'I speake plainely', he says, '& I meane honestly'.[31] The book's title promises to demonstrate the honesty of the age. Its narrator argues 'that in former ages the worlde hath beene simple and plaine dealing, but never honest till now' (sig. B1v). However, Rich's supposedly straight-talking persona points obliquely not only to the dishonesty of his age, but also to the mistaken usage of the word 'honesty' by his compatriots which, wrested from its association with plainness and simplicity, has allowed deceitful conduct to increase unchecked. In this age, he argues, the adjective 'honest' is applied too loosely to a range of individuals who refuse to deal plainly. 'In former ages' a man who 'was rich in knowledge was called a wise man, but now there is no man wise, but he that hath wit to gather wealth, and it is a hard matter in this Age, for a man to rayse himselfe by honest principles, yet we doe all seeke to climbe, but not by *Jacobs Ladder*'. Nowadays '*Drunkennes*' passes for '*Good Fellowship*' while '*Good Husbandry*' is deemed 'wretched *Misery*' and '*Hypocrisie*' is called '*Sincerity*' (sig. B2r). What this book insists on, with the help of its ironic narrator, is that the words 'honest' and 'honesty' should be associated once again with the old-fashioned virtues of simplicity and plainness.

The Honestie of this Age records the success of courtesy books like the *Courtier* and *Civile Conversation* in redefining the term 'honesty' to include personal ambition and accommodating manners. It also reminds us, however, of the survival of a robust tradition of anti-court satire which valued so-called plain-dealing and humility above dissembling 'courtly' vices. Thus, Rich's treatise proved popular; it was reprinted twice in 1615 and in 1616. Above all, though, Rich demonstrates the instability of the word 'honesty' in early modern English. In the end, 'honesty' did come to mean sincerity and truthfulness, as he wished; however, the struggle for this definition was not assured.

The linguistic battle over the meaning of 'honesty' is also a battle for the reconception of social relations as part of a project of reform. Words, as Alexandra Shepard and Phil Withington observe, 'constitute nothing less than archaeological sites: layered pits full of the debris and traces of past battles, social configurations, and dominant and subordinate meanings'. Indeed, the transformations of meaning a word undergoes 'provides insight into the dynamics of broader socio-economic and cultural change'.[32] Among Tudor humanists, this battle begins in earnest in 1531 in *The Boke Named the Governour*. In the chapter 'Of Fraude and Disceyte' in book 3, Elyot chooses the word 'simplicity' – which carried a range of meanings in the sixteenth century, open, straightforward, humble, free from elaboration and homely – to translate Cicero's '*honestas*' in *De officiis*.[33] 'Trewely in every covenaunt, bargayne, or promise aught to be simplicitie', he writes, 'that is to saye, one playne understandinge or meaning betwene the parties' (p. 208). Elyot shares the desire of Rich a century later to fix the meaning of words because he believes that 'simplicity' or 'playne understanding' is essential to the constitution of a just and ordered society. If there is no common understanding of the meaning of words then there can be no agreement – and, therefore, no social bond – between the men and women who use them.

In the *Governour* Elyot aspires to fix and make natural to English borrowed words and concepts.[34] Thus, he opens the treatise with a simplified definition of the Latin word *respublica* as 'publike weale', not 'common weale' (p. 1). This definition betrays his attitude to power and power-sharing. He famously rejects the translation 'common weale' because he fears that it will encourage individuals mistakenly to believe that 'every thinge shulde be to all men in commune, without discrepance of any astate or condition', thereby leading to the breakdown of social order and aristocratic government (p. 2). Elyot is attempting to make plain, and thus incontestable, a social order for the government of England which is led by an elite drawn primarily from the ranks of the aristocracy and who have been given the humanist education he advises. For him 'simplicity' is a loaded term. It denotes not only plain-dealing and openness but also personal disinterestedness (just as it does for Rich). In the chapter on fraud, for instance, Elyot describes a dishonest man as someone 'of a covaytous or malicious minde [who] will digresse purposely from that simplicitie, takinge advauntage of a sentence or worde, whiche mought be ambiguous or doubtefull... where he certainly knoweth the trouthe to be otherwise' (pp. 208–9). The assumption is that the noble governor who wields power in the commonwealth is not 'interested' but is rather characterised by stoic self-possession.

The *Governour* highlights some of the problems with humanist cultural reform identified by a number of critics.[35] Typical is the argument of John D. Cox that Elyot 'is frankly self-serving' when he claims that education can make a man almost divine.[36] Awareness of these problems encourages a suspicious reading of the *Governour*, that is, a reading alert to the possibility that Elyot is concealing personal aspirations under cover of a moral defence of service to the commonwealth. In book 2, when describing male friendship, he turns to Boccaccio's tale of Titus and Gisippus (pp. 166–86). This tale promises to prove the importance of male friendships to society at large, but it serves only to demonstrate the efficacy with which friends might unite to deceive their families and neighbours into giving them what they want.[37] Elsewhere, he reveals a self-interested ambivalence towards 'simplicity'. In a dialogue printed three years after the *Governour* and two years after Elyot's fall from political grace, *Pasquil the Playne*, the plain-speaking counsellor Pasquil offers an admirable defence of the need to speak frankly and dispassionately at court, but his clever arguments come to nothing. His fellow 'interested' interlocutors, the flatterer Gnatho and the silent Harprocrisie, remain unpersuaded at the end.[38]

The *Governour* exemplifies the difficulty of resolving the tension between self-interest and social duty when the moral argument subordinates individual interests to those of the community. No matter how elegantly a moralist might insist that personal ambition must be denied for the good of a community, there will always exist the sneaking suspicion that this is truer for some than others. This insight was also understood in the period by careful readers of Cicero's *De officiis*. As we will see in chapter 4, the maxim 'we are not born for ourselves alone' was reiterated repeatedly (especially by the commonwealth men Crowley and Latimer in the 1550s). However, there was more than one reading of it. It might be cited to reinforce the philosophy of estates satire, or to signal an interest in unravelling the complex relationship between personal and communal interest in imitation of *De officiis*, so as to avoid subordinating one to another. We don't have to believe that Ascham, Cheke or Smith resolved this conflict; as I will argue, they did not. Nonetheless, interest in this problem provided for rival conceptions of social duty and some interesting debates. If Elyot uses Cicero to make simplicity – or disinterestedness – proper to a governing elite then other humanists like Ascham attempt to make the dynamic relationship between self-interest and social duty structure conversation between men of different estates.

Toxophilus is a dialogue in two books between two scholars: Toxophilus, who is as skilled in archery as he is in the classics, is the main disputant while Philologus is his erudite but sceptical companion. The treatise is a defence of the art of shooting, but, like the *Governour*, it is also concerned with the physical and academic education of noblemen's sons.[39] However, there are important differences in both form and content. The *Governour* recommends wrestling, swimming, running and hunting as useful sports for the nobleman (pp. 73–9). The 'most honourable exercise', though, is identified as horse-riding which, as Elyot explains, 'nat onely importeth a majestie and drede to inferiour persones, beholding him [the nobleman] above the common course of other men', but proves useful for vanquishing one's enemies in battle (p. 78). The emphasis in *Toxophilus* could not be more different. Its argument is that archery – the traditional art of the English yeoman – is a 'moost honest pastyme' for the nobility. Or, as Toxophilus explains, it is 'honest a thynge... for all men'.[40] Philologus frequently asks if Toxophilus really means *all* men, to which he receives the same reply, that everyone profits from the practice of this sport: 'I suppose there is none other degree of men, neither lowe nor hye, learned nor leude, yonge nor oulde' (sig. B4r). Archery is suitable for men of different 'degree'; it also makes apparent or plain the co-dependence of the estates. The noble archer is shown to be dependent on the skill of his craftsmen. Toxophilus summarises the technical knowledge about bows and arrows which a dedicated archer needs to know in book 2, but he also reminds Philologus that he 'muste be contente to put [his] trust in honest stringers' and 'bowyer[s]' (sigs. O1r, O3v). In contrast to Elyot and Wilson, who seem to set themselves apart from labourers, Ascham suggests that the English yeomen and craftsmen are 'honest' examples for the nobility to follow.

In contrast to Elyot, for whom 'simplicity' requires fixing the meaning of borrowed words, Ascham temporarily unfixes the meaning of plain English 'honesty'. In book 1 we learn that archery is 'honest' because it encourages plain manners: it takes place in the open and during daylight hours, in contrast to gaming and dicing which take place at night and in private chambers. Thus, Toxophilus offers, 'If shotinge faulte at any tyme, it hydes it not, it lurkes not in corners and huddermother: but openly accuseth and bewrayeth it selfe' (sig. B3v). It is 'Honeste' for the same reason, Ascham explains in the preface, for a Cambridge academic to write in English rather than Latin or Greek so that ideas are discussed in the open (that is, in front of a wider audience) (sig. ¶3r). Archery is honest, though, in other senses which are closer to Cicero's conception of '*honestas*'. It encourages honest rivalry, an idea which lies at the heart of Ascham's reconception of both social exchange and the English plain style.

In book 1 Philologus draws a distinction between defending a cause 'ernestly' and proving it 'playnly' (sig. C1r). As Toxophilus explains, a plain argument depends not so much on pleasing orderliness but on persuasive examples and comparisons. *Toxophilus* is full of examples drawn from classical texts which are used to support its argument, but its eponymous disputant also uses a variety of 'comparisons' to 'make playne matters' (sig. D4v): thus, archery is compared to husbandry and compared with gaming and dicing. There is also a social aspect to this rhetorical figure. As the dialogue proceeds, it becomes clear that 'comparison' includes personal rivalry between men. '[T]he chyefe mayntayner of use, in any thyng, is comparyson, and honest contention', Toxophilus explains, because 'whan a manne stryveth to be better than an other, he wyll gladly use that thing, though it be never so paynfull wherein he woulde excell' (sig. L2r). One of the reasons why Ascham commends archery, then, is that it encourages competition. This is why its location in an open space and during daylight hours is so important: anyone can see the faults of an individual archer who is spurred on as a result to amend them. More importantly, Toxophilus is encouraging rivalry between men of different estates. He offers to noblemen the example of urban craftsmen who 'by contending one honestly with an other, do encrease theyr cunnyng with theyr substance' (sig. L2v). In this instance, rivalry is seen to make men honest.

Rivalry is also recognised by Elyot as an educational tool. In book 1, when arguing that noblemen's sons should be allured rather than forced to study, he advises that 'there is no better allectyve... than to induce them in a contention with their inferiour companions: they sometyme purposely suffring the more noble children to vainquysshe, and, as it were, gyvying to them place and soveraintie, thoughe indede the inferiour chyldren have more lernyng' (p. 21). Such rivalry, in other words, is deliberately rigged to give the nobly born the experience of superiority, an experience which their education aims to make natural to them. Again Ascham differs from Elyot; he argues that urban craftsmen epitomise the virtue of honesty he is advising because they encourage one another's desire to profit. Ascham's definition of honesty tallies with Ciceronian '*honestas*', which is defined by its relationship with *utilitas* or profit. Urban craftsmen are 'honest' according to Toxophilus because they live in close proximity to one another, and so by 'honest stryving togyther, who shall do best, every one maye waxe bothe cunninger and rycher' (sig. L2v). That is, honesty is realised in the competitive conduct of artisans which is in turn inspired by a desire for self-improvement. This emphasis on rivalry is marked in the form of the treatise. In Ascham's text, the complicated meaning of 'honesty' emerges only gradually in the course of the dialogue which also represents an honest rivalry between two comparable, but contrasting, interlocutors. Echoing *De oratore*, the 'teacher' Toxophilus refuses to teach Philologus. When Philologus asks in book 3 to be taught how to handle his bow in a comely or decorous fashion he is told in no uncertain terms:

Trewlye Philologe as you prove verye well in other matters, the best shootynge, is alwayes the moost cumlye shootynge but thys you know as well as I that Crassus shewethe in Cicero that as cumlinesse is the chefe poynt, & most to be sought for in all thynges, so cumlynesse onlye, can never be taught by any Arte or crafte. But may be perceyved well when it is done, not described wel how it should be done. (sig. T2r)

Toxophilus can only teach Philologus to shoot beautifully by competing with him; as his refusal implies, the dialogue supposedly performs such a rivalry.

Of course, *Toxophilus* does not perform a genuine rivalry. Its ambition to encourage the reader to explore a Roman idea of 'honesty' is hampered by its Socratic dialogue form (the treatise opens with discussion of Plato's *Phaedrus* without any of the qualifying critique of Socrates we find in *De oratore*). This dialogue is dominated by Toxophilus who imposes his views on Philoxenes even as he refuses to teach him. The difficulty is that Ascham identifies the honest man as the most dominant member of any social group, and this identification is reinforced when Toxophilus praises archery as a weapon of warfare. Toxophilus always appears to be on the side of the victor in any contention; thus, he cites approvingly Aristotle as saying 'Where is comparison, there is victorie: where is victorie, there is pleasure' (sig. L2v). As I want to argue, the difficulty Ascham has giving up the paternal role also haunts other mid-Tudor humanist writings, even as they search for a civil style of opposition.

HONEST OPPOSITION: JOHN CHEKE, THOMAS SMITH AND STEPHEN GARDINER

Honesty also structures the representation of friendship among men of the same degree. Ascham's *Schoolmaster*, written in the mid 1560s, details the educational profits which his friendship with John Whitney – cultivated with the help of a shared reading of Cicero's *De amicitia* – produced.[41] Meanwhile, Ascham's surviving familiar letters to colleagues at St John's College during his travels on the continent in the early 1550s suggest the importance to him of performing Ciceronian *amicitia*. 'That honest company and quiet abiding I daily remember', he writes to his 'assured friends the fellows of St John's College' from Augsburg on 12 October 1551, 'I take pleasure in writing this letter, that is, in talking with you, in being at home for a while in St John's, from whence my heart can never be absent'.[42] Two other Cambridge humanists, Thomas Smith and John Cheke, also represented their friendship explicitly in Ciceronian terms, as an example of honest rivalry. Of his relationship with Cheke, Smith explains in *De Recta et Emendata Linguae Graecae Pronuntiatione* ('On the Correct and Improved Pronunciation of the Greek Language'), 'equal age, like rank, the same course of study, equal Royal patronage, and continual mental comparison and rivalry [*comparatio ingeniorum & aemulatio*] (which usually rouse hatred and dissension between others) have so far always brought us together and constrained us by brotherly love'.[43]

The cultivation of such friendships is pragmatic. William Cecil was to rely heavily on the Cambridge community when securing the Elizabethan settlement in 1559. Not only was Elizabeth's Privy Council in 1558 much smaller than Mary's, but its members were also tightly interconnected. Most of its members were either friends or kinsmen of Cecil and Elizabeth, and many of them were Cambridge men. Other friends from Cambridge – Ascham, Hoby, Smith – were active at the fringes of the court.[44] This group did not constitute a faction or party, Winthrop Hudson notes, but represented rather a 'cluster of informal relationships of trust among persons who had been or were to be near the centers of power'.[45] These friendships were integral to the protestant settlement in 1559; they enabled the passing of two acts which defined Christian worship in the following decades, the Act of Supremacy and the Act of Uniformity. They were also important to the ideology of the Reformation itself. The Ciceronian idea of honest rivalry offered a model of civil opposition in a period when protestants were vulnerable to the accusation of arousing dissent.[46] For example, the Act of Uniformity, which proposed to introduce the Edwardian prayer book in all services, was dogged by vituperative debate in the House of Lords. In resisting this act an old rival of Cheke's, Dr Feckenham, Abbot of Westminster, was to make an accusation which would have rankled with the reformers: that their lack of a common doctrine encouraged dissent and disobedience both between themselves and among the common people:

obedyence is gone, humilitie and mekeness cleare abolyshed, vertuous chast and straight livinge abandoned, . . . all degrees and kindes beynge desirous of fleshely and carnall libertie, whereby the springalls and children are degennerate from their naturall fathers, the servants contemptors of their masters commandments, the subjects disobedyent unto God and superior powers.[47]

This kind of accusation, however, had been prepared for almost two decades earlier. When Smith declares in *De Recta et Emendata Linguae Graecae Pronuntiatione* that the 'continual mental comparison and rivalry' between himself and Cheke, 'have so far always brought us together and constrained us by brotherly love', he exemplifies a manner of debate which apparently allows for the expression of different view-points without provoking 'hatred and dissension'. In the treatise on the pronunciation of Greek, Smith's friendship with Cheke is invoked in order to refute the accusation of Stephen Gardiner, then chancellor of the university, that Cheke had behaved autocratically, attempting to impose his system of pronunciation on the university community. This linguistic debate is implicated in the protestant Reformation, as contemporaries recognised, in its challenge to the authority of 'custom' (associated with the catholic church), in its concern with civil speech, and in its address to Stephen Gardiner, Bishop of Winchester, who was to play a crucial role in the Marian suppression of heretics.[48]

From the perspective of the protestant reformers Gardiner was an extremely conservative figure. He was an influential member of Henry VIII's council. Though he supported the Henrician Reformation (in 1535 he defended the Royal Supremacy in his treatise, *De vera obedienta*), he was also strongly opposed to protestantism.[49] As James Arthur Miller observes, he fought successfully on the council to retain episcopal power in the church and to reduce the influence of German protestants. In later years under Mary I he was responsible for securing the re-enactment of the heresy laws, and in January 1555 he presided over the trial which condemned Hooper, Rogers, Bradford, Saunders and Taylor to the stake.[50] He was also to become infamous for torturing Anne Askew during her examination. For some, the stance taken by Gardiner in the linguistic quarrel is an example of the stubbornness which characterises his adherence to religious custom. In the *Acts and Monuments* John Foxe wonders what 'moved [Gardiner] to be so sturdy against Cheke, and sir Thomas Smith, for the Greek pronunciation'; he concludes that it was his inclination to dislike novelty. 'Such was the disposition of that man... that of purpose he ever affected to seem to be a patron of old customs, though they were never so rotten with age'.[51] The linguistic debate of the 1540s does not just show up Gardiner's unthinking attachment to old customs, it also suggests a way of challenging the attribution of authority to custom in a culture which equated novelty and self-assertion with despotism. For, despite his involvement in the burning of heretics in the 1550s, Gardiner was as committed to protecting a community from such despotism – whether linguistic or religious – as Smith or Cheke claim to be. As he reasonably suggests in the pronunciation debate, it is surely more just to follow custom and tradition, however erroneous it may be, than to impose on a community an idea of 'truth' decided by a few men.[52]

Cheke and Smith began teaching their students the revised Erasmian pronunciation of Greek in 1535, when they were both just twenty-one years old. Cheke's early contribution, *De Pronuntiatione Graecae Linguae*, is a series of letters addressed to Gardiner; it was written in the early 1540s and printed in Basle in 1555. In 1542 Gardiner banned the project and introduced strict penalties for disobeying his decree (including expulsion from the university). One of the reasons for his dismay is that he believed Cheke had behaved wilfully, seeking single-handedly to replace a custom of pronunciation which carried the authority of the university community.[53] His complaint against the attempt to reform Greek is recorded and answered in a Latin treatise in three books, written by Smith and presented to Gardiner as a letter, *De Recta et Emendata Linguae Graecae Pronuntiatione*, dated 12 August 1542. The language of the dispute is highly politicised. On the one side, Smith believes he is defending free speech, on the other side, Gardiner believes he is resisting the autocratic overturning of the 'laws' of speech which carry common approval. If the system of Greek pronunciation is to be replaced, Gardiner argues, then it must be achieved with the consent of the whole university, not by one or two scholars acting independently. Gardiner's decree is described by Smith as an attack on free speech and the rights of Smith and Cheke as 'cives' or 'citizens' of the University of Cambridge (pp. 109–11). Smith makes this argument carefully, so as not to accuse Gardiner of tyranny. He argues in book 1 that Gardiner has dealt with the issue 'more severely and hardly than your kind disposition, or the nature of the case demands' (p. 17). He has listened to 'only one side', and has 'appoint[ed] heavy fines and new punishments' only because, as Smith complains, he thinks that the dipthongs αι and οι should be pronounced ε and ι (p. 19). The assumption is that if Gardiner listens to his reasons then he will understand immediately that he has been misled by ill-intentioned friends in Cambridge. However, the implication of Smith's argument is indeed that Gardiner has behaved like a tyrant. Until the decree, writes Smith, 'there was nothing to prevent zealous students from publishing freely, communicating whatever they found in the fine and liberal arts' (p. 99). He explains to Gardiner in his exaggerated way that:

when you attack us, not by reason but by threats and terror; not by the hands of learned men, but of those who know nothing of Greek; when you restrain our freedom of speech by laws and decrees, and other bugbears; you seem to have given an opening for those who talk somewhat boldy and freely to say that we seem to be oppressed. (p. 115)

Smith's treatise recovers not only classical Greek pronunciation but also a classical style of debate governed by 'brotherly love' (p. 201) which is exemplified by his friendship with Cheke. This style, he argues, enables disputants to arrive at the truth more easily. It also cements social relationships: 'if you agree in courtesy and grace, both learn from each other without bitterness; the matter is more thoroughly discussed, and friendship mightily grows and increases' (p. 109). Gardiner's complaint was that Cheke introduced the new system of pronunciation without the consensus of the university community. In response, Smith relates the history of the reform in such a way as to accommodate and cancel Gardiner's concerns. The new system, he explains, was not devised independently; rather, it grew up initially in conversation with continental humanists (pp. 25–35), and then with Cambridge friends, Cheke and John Ponet. It was practised for several years before being introduced accidentally in a public lecture when Smith let a few words in the new pronunciation slip into his speech. The argument is that the new system had already become customary to Smith, so much so that he had started to use it unknowingly in public. Thereafter, Smith offers, it was taken up voluntarily and enthusiastically by his students. At the end of book 3 Smith contrasts the method of these friends with Gardiner's own severe and autocratic style, turning the accusation of forcefulness against the accuser: 'we used no force, no compulsion, no fines. We took away no man's freedom of speech' (p. 181). Smith also demystifies the authority of custom itself, which is neither fixed nor absolute. For he reveals that he knows *how* customs are established: in the conversation of speech communities. His narration of the history of this new system of pronunciation in book 3 merely reiterates an earlier argument about the process of reform: 'we have shown the old ways to be ugly and wrong, and have found out the true way and by walking to and fro have made it worn and easy; must we not lead those whom we love along it and instruct the new-comers?' (p. 99).

Thus, Smith's and Cheke's attempt to recover the classical pronunciation of Greek also recovers a 'civil' speech form – conversation – which enables the questioning of linguistic habits without appearing to do so too radically. Its technique is to expose the process by which customs are created and to provide a yet more 'ancient' style of authority for the beliefs of the different speech community to which Smith and Cheke belong. *De Pronuntiatione Graecae Linguae* is not written as a dialogue, but Smith's Latin treatise on the reform of English orthography is. *De Recta et Emendata Linguae Anglicae Scriptione, Dialogus* (1568) ('On the Correct and Improved Writing of English') is a dialogue between two interlocutors: 'Smith' and a junior

Honest rivalries: Tudor humanism and linguistic and social reform 83

disputant 'Quintus'. It aims to correct English spelling while demonstrating a style of argument – or conversation – which does not appear correctional, and so prevents divisiveness. In this treatise, Smith is putting forward a radical proposal for a more 'rational' or phonetic system of spelling. His choice of the dialogue form, though, is intended to embody an organic process of correction, for he understands – as Gardiner had argued – that 'the meanings of words cannot be temporarily changed at will; but must be fairly and honestly [*bono*] received, and have their source in the common consent of many in nation-wide agreement'.[54]

The dialogue opens with Quintus complaining about a quarrel he has had with a friend 'Stubborn' (Obstinatus) who cannot see the point of worrying about the orthography of English: ' "What difference," said he, "does it make how a word is written, so long as it can be read and is now the received form?" ' Smith responds by arguing that all arts must progress. 'You should have asked Stubborn whether he would be satisfied with nothing but water,' he quips (pp. 17–19). Stubborn is described by Smith as having 'a bitter and obstinate mind' (p. 13), but his views are not dismissed. Quintus is not willing to lose this friendship, despite Stubborn's stubbornness. 'We nearly came to a vulgar quarrel,' says Quintus, observing that Stubborn has always been a faithful friend (pp. 13–15). As a result, Quintus is unwilling to remember past disagreements or to 'allow them to interrupt our daily intercourse and companionship'. Smith responds approvingly: 'That is civilized behaviour, and the only way for your friendship to last' (pp. 14–15). The same consideration is enacted in the dialogue itself which challenges the 'constitution' of an alphabet which already carries common consent. At no point does Smith lecture Quintus. On the contrary, his careful exploration of the classical roots of Anglo-Saxon make his proposal a project of natural restitution, not of wilful imposition. In response, Quintus compares his experience of the conversation to being led out of Plato's cave: 'May I die if I had ever thought how many mistakes were made in writing, or that they were so easy to correct' (p. 91).

Smith's contribution to the debate about linguistic reform is steeped in a classical republican idiom of 'senate' and 'citizenship'. Indeed, his project of linguistic reform aims to recover classical forms of government and association. The writing of *De Pronuntiatione Graecae Linguae* coincides with Smith's appointment as Regius Professor of Civil Law at Cambridge in 1540. (Smith wanted to replace the common law, which seemed to him both antiquated and provincial, with this branch of Roman law.)[55] Meanwhile, between 1562 and 1565 Smith wrote his influential political treatise, *De Republica Anglorum*, which explores ideas of civil speech in relation to national politics. In contrast to Elyot, Smith emphasises the importance of participation in government; he imagines the commonwealth as 'a multitude of free men collected together and united by common accord... for the conversation of themselves as well in peace as in warrre'. Speaking of the conduct deemed appropriate in parliamentary debate, he urges that '[n]o reviling or nipping wordes must be used', especially against the 'Prince or Privie counsell', since such language encourages seditious talk. Of the English parliament, he claims with enthusiastic patriotism, 'such diversitie of mindes, and opinions' are expressed with 'the greatest modestie and temperance of speech that can be used'. This does not make for tame debates. As Smith explains, 'with doulce and gentle termes' speakers can 'make their reasons as violent and as vehement the one against the other as they may ordinarily'.[56] Such views are also expressed by Nicholas Bacon in the opening address to the Elizabethan parliament in January 1559. His address signals the spirit of temperance and negotiation which the new regime hopes will characterise parliamentary debate: 'By councell provision would be made that all contentious, contumelious or opprobrious wordes, as "heretike", "schismatic", "papist", and such like names and nurces of seditious faccions and sectes may be banished out of men's mouthes, as the causers, continuers and increasers of displeasure, hate and malice, and as utter enemyes to all concorde and unitie'.[57]

Whether Smith makes possible a genuine rivalry of views is a different matter. Despite his efforts to discover a form which might represent civil disagreement, his dialogues rely too heavily on an unchallenged, dominant speaker. The effect of this is to suppress criticism and to enforce consensus. Smith may claim in the dialogue on English spelling to respect the linguistic customs of a community, but he evidently does not; this dialogue sets out to expose the irrationality of contemporary linguistic practice (just as elsewhere, Smith expresses impatience with the irrationality of English common law). Smith is also notoriously self-aggrandising. In the treatise on Greek pronunciation he usurps Cheke as the leader of reform; in the dialogue on English spelling the speaker Quintus performs the role of straw man, so highlighting the authority of 'Smith' as an English Cicero to his age (Quintus is Cicero's brother and the addressee of *De oratore*).

Smith's rhetorical strategies did not go unnoticed. Gardiner is distrustful of Smith's apparently gentle and courteous terms. He claims that Smith's personal attack is merely displaced on to other persons so as to avoid defaming him openly. He also singles out Smith's representation of his style of friendship with Cheke as singularly disingenuous. He coolly deconstructs this by pointing to how Smith immodestly models himself on the altruistic Greek hero of *amicitia* narratives, Damon. This hero showed willing to sacrifice his life when his friend Pythias was sentenced to death by the tyrant Dionysius (Damon and Pithias are the two ideal friends praised by Cicero in *De officiis*) (p. 102). Gardiner understands that Smith and Cheke are not really exemplary selfless friends, but that Smith is employing a legendary exemple of classical *amicitia* for a rhetorical end: to disarm the argument that Cheke has behaved autocratically in linguistic matters. In this way, Gardiner's reading of Smith's letter points to a problem with its proposed style of debate, which does not allow genuine rivalry to emerge.

We have been here before with *Toxophilus*. The problem is a frustrating one. The opportunity to question the assumption of social authority, which these texts make possible, is compromised as soon as these writers reclaim that authority for themselves. Some of the dangers of this style of linguistic reform are seen in *Queene Elizabethes Achademy*, written by Humphrey Gilbert and printed in 1588, one year after Gilbert had brutally crushed the Munster rebellion. As Patricia Palmer notes, the academy, a London version of Oxford and Cambridge for the sons of the nobility, is imagined 'as a forcing house of "Civill" and "Martiall policy"' where 'navigation, mapping, artillery' were to be combined 'with a new emphasis on the vernacular'. Gilbert advised that 'oratorical training' should be 'grounded in English, not Latin, and modelled on John Cheke's exercises, so that "ornament will thereby growe to our tongue"'.[58] Even so, it is important to recognise that this vision of reform did not go uncontested. John Hart continued Cheke's and Smith's onslaught against the irrationality of custom in *Orthographie* (1569), arguing that a phonetic system would be cost effective because it allows the unlearned and non-native speakers to acquire reading and writing skills quickly.[59] However, the schoolmaster Richard Mulcaster took a different line in his *Elementarie* (1582), using an explicitly political idiom – that of the mixed constitution – to insist on the rationality of spelling customs. Mulcaster compares the debate about orthography to the overthrow of the tyrant Tarquin and the origins of the Roman republic. He tells how, in the history of writing, 'Sound' became first the monarch and then tyrant. He was eventually restrained out of necessity by the appointment of a council led by 'two grave and great personages', Reason and Custom. '[S]ound like a restrained not banished *Tarquinius*', argues Mulcaster, 'desiring to be restored to his first and sole monarchie, and finding som, but no more then sounding favorers, did seke to make a tumult in the scriveners province, ever after that, *reason* and *custom* were joynd with him in commission'.[60] This represents an important shift away from the 'oligarchic' commonwealth of letters envisaged by Smith. 'By grounding the first stage of language construction in consent and custom', explains Martin Elsky, 'Mulcaster gives language a public, social nature that affects it at every level, for consent can be conferred only where people live and communicate in social circumstances.'[61]

As we will see in chapters 5 and 6 this particular mantle is taken up by one of Mulcaster's pupils, Edmund Spenser, and his Cambridge friend Gabriel Harvey, an admirer of Gardiner's rhetorical versatility.[62] Their collaborative writings will show us how a project of linguistic reform and literary experimentation, inspired by Roman '*honestas*', might be used to imagine a less hierarchical and less coercive manner of social and political interaction. With Spenser, Harvey refines Smith's republican rhetoric to accommodate native English speech and the traditions it embodies, including the common law, often seen as a tool to protect the ancient liberties.[63] In the next chapter, however, I will continue to explore humanist debates about self-interest. I will consider how civil conversation was used by Smith and others to reform an older meaning of 'honesty' as liberality or hospitality. I will also examine the double legacy of this speech form in writings preoccupied with the 'market' as well as its overlap with the Socratic dialogue which is employed in the new husbandry manuals inspired by Xenophon's *Oeconomicus*. As we will see, civil conversation was used both to expose *and* to disguise the self-interest of the honest husbandmen in England and Ireland.

CHAPTER 4

Honest speakers: sociable commerce and civil conversation

Joan Thirsk's *Economic Policy and Projects* has enabled scholars to understand the dramatic development of the English economy in the second half of the sixteenth century. Thirsk detects a shift in the economic mentality of this period: a movement away from the social conscience of the commonwealth thinkers, who were preoccupied with the covetousness of the nobility, to a much more positive recognition of self-interest. This transition, she argues, is embodied in Thomas Smith's *A Discourse of the Commonweal of this Realm of England*. Smith's dialogue was written in 1549, at the height of the ideological contention and tumult provoked by the supposed twin evils of the period's economic change, inflation and enclosure, and printed posthumously in 1581.[1] The subtitle of Thirsk's book, *The Development of a Consumer Culture in Early Modern England*, implies that this transition represents the 'modernising' of the English economy. That is, in this period we begin to see take shape a conception of the market and enterprise that might be considered 'capitalist'. Two key words were to characterise the later decades, Thirsk suggests, 'project' and 'projector'. 'Everyone with a scheme, whether to make money, to employ the poor, or to explore the far corners of the earth had a "project"', that is, 'a practical scheme for exploiting material things'. Smith was himself an enthusiastic, if misguided, projector. Of the several projects in which he invested two in particular – both in the year 1571 – stand out, conspicuous mostly for their ill-foundation and failure. The first was a project to make copper from iron, the second, more ominously, plantation in Ireland.[2]

Smith's *Discourse* is regarded as prescient because it refuses to uphold the traditional complaint against the aristocratic enclosure of common land, or, indeed, to blame any one estate for inflation.[3] Smith's dialogue draws on the complaints tradition employed by the commonwealthsmen Hugh Latimer and Robert Crowley in the 1540s and early 1550s: it opens with the Husbandman's complaint about selfish gentry who have enclosed land for private profit. However, it also includes the Knight's counter-complaint about the Husbandman's high prices. For the *Discourse* is, after all, a dialogue between different estates and different interests. The interlocutors consider various solutions, one of which is the suggestion that the Husbandman should lower his prices. They also debate the consequences of their proposals: in this particular case they recognise the difficulties depreciation would pose for overseas trade.

It is hardly surprising that the text is regarded as prescient. For Neal Wood the insight offered in the *Discourse* is that all of the five estates 'are in some sense victims, if unwitting ones, of the inexorable dynamic of the economy'. Smith is ahead of his time because he seems to understand that the market possesses 'an autonomy from the rest of state and society'.[4] This view is corroborated by Andrew McRae, for whom 'Smith's dialogue structure… emphasises the impersonal and dynamic operations of a market economy' because each personalised complaint is negated by the next.[5] However, I want to suggest that exactly the opposite is being emphasised. Indeed, Smith's choice of a dialogue structure represents his attachment to what Craig Muldrew describes as the 'sociability' of early modern commerce.[6] This commitment is underscored by its opening reiteration of a familiar maxim taken from Plato, and re-used by Cicero in *De officiis*, which it promises to explore in its progress: as the Doctor offers, 'we be not borne onely to our selves, but partely to the use of our Countrey, of our Parentes, of our Kinsfolkes, and partly of our Friendes and Neyghboures' (sig. A3r).[7]

Muldrew is challenging a powerful and familiar narrative, that the early modern period witnessed a 'reorientation of the representation of well-being away from the order and unity of the symbolic body of the community to the accumulating individual'. What occurred, he argues, was rather a 'reordering of notions of community relations' and this included the quite new perception that commerce might create, and not just endanger, social trust.[8] The sense that commerce is sociable was partly a product of circumstance. Widespread debt in early modern England, produced in part by a shortage of ready money, created relations of dependence between individuals and households which often cut across the social hierarchy. Thus, he records that Richard Cholmeley of Brandsby in Yorkshire was often in debt to his servants. 'He once recorded, when paying his servant Alice Crawthorne her wages of 20s, "that I had borrowed on her xxiiis"'.[9] But it is also reinforced semantically. Terms like commerce, communication, and computation share a common root, Latin *committo*, meaning 'to unite or bring together in fellowship'. Conversation was '*the* essential social relation' for Stefano Guazzo in *Civile Conversation*, he remarks, and 'the marketplace, "where there is a bargayning for all things" was described as the most representative forum for such communication, where an exchange of words as well as goods took place'.[10]

Muldrew's emphasis on the sociability of commerce provides economic historians with a new vocabulary for describing the experience of the expanding markets in the sixteenth century, and a means to reconstruct the ethical defence of the use of 'credit' as a way of creating trust. The Reformation, he argues, prompted a shift away from a moral, theological and legal obligation to repay debts, and a corresponding social economy which saw debtors as subordinate to creditors, to a stronger commitment to the 'notion of the justification by faith alone, in which the emphasis was put squarely on man's need to trust unconditionally in the truth of Christ's promises' and which was 'mirrored by an increasing emphasis on trust *within* everyday social relations'. This emphasis on trust was reinforced by humanist interest in *De officiis*. '[T]ruth-telling and honesty', Muldrew notes, were 'one of the main foundations of [Cicero's] social theory.' Indeed, 'honesty' was recognised by Cicero and his sixteenth-century readers as the basic building block of interpersonal relations.[11] The new meaning of honesty as truth-telling in the sixteenth century affects the conception of 'profit'. Cicero's emphasis on the interdependence of moral goodness (*honestas*) and profit (*utilitas*) introduced the idea, in a period anxious about the seditious nature of individual covetousness, that 'the contractual bargaining of trade' could be 'described as mutual benefit' and that the word 'profit' referred to 'the mutual advantage, benefit or profit of two or more parties', rather than to the satisfaction of self-interest.[12]

There remains a need, of course, to distinguish between this idealistic discourse and the often conflict-ridden experience of the economy of obligation. There is an obvious danger that the promise to pursue mutual interest might constitute an empty, if not deliberately misleading, rhetorical strategy. Muldrew's study records the rise in litigation at the end of the century as this economy was put under increasing strain.[13] Even so, we might not want to dismiss this supposed 'honesty' of profit-seeking too quickly. In this period truth-telling was not the only meaning of Cicero's 'honesty', as Ascham's *Toxophilus* demonstrates, nor was it the only way of imagining sociable commerce. In other words, there are other ways of understanding the relationship between *honestas* and *utilitas*. We need to extend Muldrew's argument to acknowledge that 'honest' economic conduct might also include seemingly dishonest gestures (for example, the refusal to admit to superior knowledge), and that this definition might even be sometimes preferable. Such 'honesty' is much closer to Cicero's idea of the decorum – or self-restraint – so important to fair trade dealings; it enables humanists to explore both the dishonesty of apparently disinterested plain-speaking in social and commercial exchange *and* 'conversation' (in its double sense of familiar discourse and commerce) as a negotiation between conflicting interests.

I propose to explore this discourse in relation to two different texts: the anonymous, native conduct book, *Cyvile and Uncyvile Life* (1579) and Smith's *Discourse* (1581). These texts are not related in any obvious way, but they do share an interest in Ciceronian '*honestas*', which they explore with the help of the dialogue form. Moreover, both treatises aim to influence government policy by offering an alternative to the mid-Tudor attack on covetousness. The manuscript *Discourse* of 1549 was probably intended for William Cecil; *Cyvile and Uncyvile Life* is dedicated to Sir Francis Walsingham.

Sixteenth-century conduct books are not usually discussed in relation to the burgeoning markets of early modern England. Only one critic has explored this relationship and for him the books signal 'the new liquidity of mercantile relations' in their assertion of a more private selfhood.[14] The example of *Cyvile and Uncyvile Life*, however, will remind us that such books more commonly contribute to the humanist critique of a self-interested culture of 'hospitality', which they seek to replace with what they see as 'honest' socialising. This treatise is a dialogue between two neighbours, the urbane Vallentine who is visiting his rural residence and a country gentleman, Vincent, who clash over one issue: the relative 'honesty' of the courtier and of the manorial lord. Vincent believes that 'the wealthier man, is the more honest man: and the greater landed Gentleman, the better man of worship' (p. 45). In his idiom 'honesty' is equivalent to hospitable conduct: thus, a wealthy landowner is honest when he keeps an open house. In contrast, Vallentine argues that civil conversation (rather than an open hand) encourages honesty because it exemplifies a restrained manner which allows for a more equal exchange. The dialogue also reflects on how these different types of honesty are implicated in economic behaviour. Vallentine attacks the wasteful chasing after profit of the country gentleman Vincent, which is concealed by his 'frankness': his plain-speaking and liberality. He also exposes Vincent as a gentleman-husband who relies on modern techniques of farming to make a profit from his land at the expense of his tenants, and not the traditional manorial lord who holds together the local community that he claims to be.

Cyvile and Uncyvile Life may not have been an especially influential treatise. It was printed twice, in 1579 and 1586. As we will see, though, it usefully sheds light on a dialogue which is central to the economic history of the period, Smith's *Discourse*, which aimed to establish that commercial activity and social responsibility are intertwined, not antithetical. Attending to this treatise as a civil conversation will help us to see how Smith is attempting to provide a social solution to an economic problem: he is searching for a social and linguistic form to communicate his belief that the market creates 'honest' personal relationships and, with the help of Cicero, he found in conversation a model for the discovery of both self-interest and the negotiation between competing interests.

This chapter intervenes in a debate about the rise of self-interest and an emerging defence of capitalist enterprise in the early modern period by recovering a discourse which made those newly discovered interests subject to negotiation. This discourse, however, was not successful. We know this because we are more likely to agree with early modern anti-court satirists that the courtly 'honesty' of Vallentine is profoundly dishonest. Honesty is a highly unstable term in the sixteenth century. This chapter explores the attempt to make it represent transparent social relations by establishing the importance of self-restraint and accommodation which allow others to express their 'interests', but it also recognises the failure of this discourse, as the definition of 'honesty' as truth-telling and thrifty self-management is established. There are two reasons for this failure. The first reason is a problem of the dialogue's Socratic form. Smith may argue that all interests need to be traded freely in a conversation or the market-place, but the *Discourse* is itself dominated by the figure of the learned 'Doctor' (Smith) who manages – or 'husbands' – consent between the different estates. These are the same problems that we encountered with Ascham's *Toxophilus*. The second reason is contextual. The policy of colonisation supported by Henry Sidney and subsequent lord deputies in Ireland from the 1560s was too good an opportunity for a projector like Smith to miss.[15] Thus, when trying to attract investment in his venture to colonise the Ards in Ireland in the 1570s Smith readily turned to the discourse of the honest – or truth-telling – husband. Three decades later, Lodowick Bryskett contributed to the propaganda by improving the genre of the courtesy book. His attempt to make the Italian courtier 'honest' by translating him into an English husband, I will argue in the final section of this chapter, serves as a metaphor for a policy of agrarian improvement which promises to translate the wild Irishman into a useful husbandman. As *Cyvile and Uncyvile Life* advises, we should not trust such honest men.

TYPES OF HONESTY: COURTIERS *VERSUS* HUSBANDS

Cicero's study of social duties *De officiis* is a difficult text, as its translator Nicholas Grimalde acknowledges in his 1558 bilingual edition. 'This is the fift time, I have redde over this author:' he declares, 'and as oft as I reade him, so oft somewhat I finde, that I marked not before: and that hath neede to be depely pondered: so that I fancied, at the first, he was easie: but now, methinks, he requieres a very heedful, & a musing reader.'[16] Unsurprisingly, it is a text which is vulnerable to misinterpretation. This is owing partly to its hasty composition, which makes it a difficult text even in Latin, but partly, too, because it was not credibly translated into English until the 1550s.

Robert Whytington's translation of *The thre bookes of Tullyes offyces*, which appeared in 1534, reveals just how hard it was to English this treatise. Although Whytington also published a Latin grammar, his skill as a translator is not great.[17] Among other problems is his incomplete account of 'bountyfulness and lyberalyte' discussed by Cicero under the second category of '*honestas*', justice. In book 1 of *De officiis* Cicero argues that beneficence and liberality appeal 'to the best in human nature', but advises the 'exercise of caution' in three respects: first, we should not injure others by any act of generosity; secondly, we should not exceed our means; and thirdly, our gifts should be proportionate to the deserts of the recipient (1. 42). Whytington clumsily translates Cicero's discussion of the first two points, but not of the third. Of Cicero's second rule, he has this to say:

An other place of cautyon and provisyon is this, that our bountyfulnesse shulde not surmounte above our substaunce, bycause they that woll be more liberall than their power may beare, chefely they offende in this poynte, bycause they be injuryous to their neyghbours [*quod iniuriosi sunt in proximos*].[18]

In contrast, Grimalde follows the original more faithfully and he captures Cicero's point immediately because his diction is more appropriate and his word order more natural:

The second point of exception was, that our liberalitie shoulde not be more than our abilitie: because whoso will be lavisher, than their goods will beare: they chiefly offende in this, that they be injurious to their next of akinne. (sig. C4v)

Whytington's translation of Cicero's *proximos* (those who are nearest) as 'neyghbours', while not strictly wrong, does not convey the sense of blood relationship or kinship which Cicero evidently intends.[19] Moreover, his use of 'neyghbours' upholds a more traditional reading of hospitality as the liberality of the head of a feudal household made up of relations, servants *and* neighbours, which later readers of *De officiis* – like the author of *Cyvile and Uncyvile Life* – were keen to reform.

If the grammar-school teacher Whytington expresses a clumsy grasp of *De officiis*, what chance has the ordinary student? The author of the courtesy book *Cyvile and Uncyvile Life* is well aware of the ease with which *De officiis* can be misunderstood. In this dialogue the old-fashioned country gentleman Vincent offers a valiant defence of the 'auncient custome of this Realme of England', when 'all Noble men and Gentlemen... did continually inhabite the countryes, continuing there, from age to age, and from Auncester, to auncester, a continuall house, and hospitallitie, which got them great love amonge their Neighbours, [and] releeved many poore wretches' (p. 12). Meanwhile, the courtier Vallentine launches an attack on his wasteful generosity. As Felicity Heal remarks, Vallentine articulates the two main arguments directed against the culture of hospitality in the sixteenth century: first, that 'it encouraged idleness in the poor and provided for a rabble of beggars', and, secondly, that 'it was a wasteful and uncivilised way of providing reciprocal entertainment for neighbours, friends and men of influence'.[20] However, he also sets out to refine Vincent's understanding of the relationship between the individual and the community by recalling a maxim from Cicero's *De officiis* which he believes Vincent knows, but has not considered.

The allusion to *De officiis* comes early in the dialogue. Vincent has just claimed that the education of the country gentleman is more 'honest' than that of the courtier because it is 'nourished in justice, truth, and plaine dealinge, free from fraude, and dissimulation'. Whereupon Vallentine argues:

I allowe of your zeale to honesty in education, but if you mixe it with some other thinges, I will like it the better. That you study to bring up your children in honesty, which is a vertue, and cheefely justice... I doo not onely allow you, but commend you: Yet if you remember what Tully telleth you (for sure I am you have bin a Scholler), That men are not onely borne to themselves: Then you will ad some other virtues and knowledges to these. (pp. 14–16)

The phrase 'men are not onely borne to themselves', borrowed from *De officiis*, is likely to be familiar to Vincent, but the meaning it is given by Vallentine in the dialogue is supposedly not. Vallentine assumes that Vincent understands the maxim as a justification of his hospitality or generous housekeeping and charity, much as, say, the social complainants of the 1540s and 50s had done. Thus, Hugh Latimer reminds his congregation on Christmas Day 1552 that 'no one person is born into the world for his own sake, but for the commonwealth sake. Let us, therefore, walk charitably; not seeking our commodities'.[21] Here, the maxim is understood to require the suppression of self-interest for the greater good of the community. On this view, the honest social life entails giving up something – that 'something' being defined by one's status – in order to achieve the reciprocity that creates social cohesion. Thus, a local magnate might give up some of his material resources for the entertainment of his neighbours or the support of the poor, but in return he is rewarded with service and loyalty.

Latimer provides an unusual but useful introduction to the fictional Vincent in *Cyvile and Uncyvile Life*, because he argues, from the lowly position of a 'plowman', that manorial hospitality is the prototype of altruistic sociability. In his famous 'Sermon on Plowers', delivered outside St Paul's Church on 18 January 1548, he reminds a wayward aristocracy of the benefits that accrue from hospitality and of the dangers posed by the neglect of social duty. Adopting the voice of the straight-talking plowman of medieval estates satire, he recalls a self-seeking aristocracy to their social duty to the commonwealth – the charitable support of scholars and the poor and the tempering of their desire for personal profit.[22] The 'Sermon on Plowers' is a response to the inflation of the price of grain in the 1540s. The 'villains' are perceived to be land owners who seek to increase their personal profits by enclosing and engrossing land.[23] Latimer attacks, first, 'lordyng' clergymen (clergy who aspire to live like lords), who are given to hunting, hawking and dancing when they should be harvesting souls, and then the lords themselves who are enclosing land for pasture and, in so doing, preventing tillage and other types of agricultural labour. As Latimer proposes, 'there be two kyndes of inclosynge': the one hinders bodily ploughing, the other spiritual. In both cases the commonwealth is deprived of sustenance and comfort (sig. B5r). '[I]nclosynge' here represents both the enclosure of land for grazing and a general selfishness (a separating of the self from the community).

Despite the disparity between these two speakers, one a plowman, the other a country gentleman, they both express a nostalgia for the feudal manorial estate, presided over by the hospitable lord. In *Cyvile and Uncyvile Life* Vincent is honest in the double sense expected by Latimer; he is 'a plaine man, utterly unacquainted with disguising, and superfluous ceremony', and he is frank with his resources (p. 11). He understands that he fulfils his social duty by keeping an open house. Thus, his sociability extends to all his neighbours, regardless of their social status. As he tells Vallentine, this includes 'our honest neighbours, Yeoman of the Countrey, and good honest fellowes, dwellers there about: as Grasiers, Butchers, Farmers, Drovers,

Carpenters, Carriers, Taylors, & such like men, very honest and good companions'. Against such a show of generosity, Vallentine appears to be a penny-pinching snob. On hearing Vincent's roll-call of friends, for example, he remarks tartly, 'your conversinge with them will make you taste of their bluntnes and rusticitie, which will very evill become a man of your calling' (p. 57).

Even so, *Cyvile and Uncyvile Life* sides with Vallentine, not Vincent. The country gentleman has inherited the semantic confusion of the term 'honesty' in the agricultural debates of the sixteenth century, where it could mean either the suppression of self-interest in service to the commonwealth or the thrifty keeping of 'gettings covertlie'.[24] *Cyvile and Uncyvile Life* reveals how the first definition is already implicated in the second: Vincent's 'honesty' – his plain-dealing and hospitality – is a cover for his exploitation of land and tenants. This treatise also introduces a different style of honesty which allows for the recognition of conflicting interests between estates. On this view, Vallentine's insistence on social distance is integral to his attempt to represent the concerns of tenants overlooked by Vincent (and moralists like Latimer). In this way *Cyvile and Uncyvile Life* offers a more penetrating critique of agrarian capitalism than was possible with this once-challenging form of social complaint. A further weakness of the reformers' adoption of the voice of the plain-speaking plowman, however, is that, with this strategy, they can only attack the overt articulation of self-interest. In such mid-Tudor social complaint the villain is easily recognisable. In Crowley's *Philargyrie of greate Britayne* (1551), for instance, the giant Philargyrie ('Love of Silver') openly advises anarchic selfishness:

> Henceforth there shall
> No lawe at all
> Restrayne your Libertie
> But that you maye
> Boeth nyght and daye
> Do your owne wyll freely...
> And where you spye
> Commoditie
> Ther plant your dwelling place
> And then employe
> Your whole study
> To get it up apase.[25]

However, profit-seeking landlords were unlikely to reveal their villainy in this way! Texts like Crowley's and Latimer's competed alongside a new genre of husbandry manual inspired by Xenophon's *Oeconomicus*, books like

John Fitzherbert's *The Boke of Husbandrye* (1523) and Conrad Heresbach's *Foure Bookes of Husbandry* (1570), which employ the persona of the honest labourer to advise aristocratic landlords of their duty to manage thriftily their speech, estate and servants.

A rising population, increased land rents and food prices all made farming a lucrative business in the course of the sixteenth century. When gentlemen took to farming their desmeanes in the first half of the sixteenth century, Joan Thirsk argues, they could turn to these new husbandry manuals to learn about the most efficient methods of farming. There they would also discover 'a new philosophy of estate management and farming, that appealed to them at a time when other religious, social, political and economic pressures were bearing down on them, urging them...to see themselves in the role of responsible patriarchal figures'.[26] These pressures were to shape a different conception of aristocratic social responsibility. In contrast to Latimer, who berates covetous aristocratic landlords, Fitzherbert and Heresbach make the management of the estate and the production of a small surplus essential to the performance of the landowner's social duties, but they do so by using the same language of honest labour as mid-Tudor complaint.

Treatises such as Heresbach's *Foure Bookes of Husbandry* (which appeared in Barnabe Googe's translation in 1577) are firmly on the side of the landowner. Not only would their size have made them too expensive for the lower gentry, as Andrew McRae notes,[27] but the ideal they represent is in any case inspired by Xenophon's attempt in *Oeconomicus* to persuade the Greek aristocracy to return to farming for their private and the public good. *Foure Bookes of Husbandry* is written as a dialogue between a country gentleman, Cono, and an urbane secretary, Rigo. Most of this lengthy treatise is given over to the practical description of various farming technologies. However, the opening pages dramatise a form of anti-court satire popular in the sixteenth century, the debate between the courtier and the countryman, in an attempt to counter the aristocratic disdain for farming.

The city-dweller Rigo has a distaste for the lifestyle of the country gentleman: 'Socrates', he advises, 'affyrmeth wysdome to be learned in Cities, and not among beastes and trees.' However, the knowing Cono, who has read *Oeconomicus*, has a ready response: 'Socrates his judgement, though I wyll not gaynesay, yet it appeareth by his disputations with *Iscomachus* in Xenophon, that he dyd not disalowe the Countrey mans lyfe' (sig. A2r). When Rigo reproves Cono by repeating Cicero's commonwealth maxim – 'You know we are not borne to live to our selves, nor at our owne pleasures:

but for our countrey, our common weale and state whereto we are called' (sig. A1r) – Cono corrects his misappropriation; he patiently explains how the country gentleman contributes to the commonwealth by organising his estate so that he has the time to converse with the gravest philosophers in books. Indeed, his argument discreetly rehearses the thesis of *Oeconomicus*, that 'husbandry' is a public good because it provides a forum for the development of skills required for paternalistic government, namely an ability to order one's resources. The idea that this is a *shared* benefit is indicated in Googe's prefatory dedication of the book to his ex-employer, Sir William Fitzwilliam, a former Lord Deputy of Ireland:

there is, in my fancie, no life so quiet, so acceptable to God, and pleasant to an honest mind, as is the life of the Countrey, where a man, withdrawing him selfe from the miserable miseries, vanities, and vexations of this foolish and nowe totoo much doting world, may geve him selfe to the sweete contemplation of God, and his woorkes, and the profite and reliefe of his poore distressed neighbour. (sig. 2v)

Cono also adopts the persona of an honest labourer familiar to the readers of mid-Tudor complaint. There is 'nothing more honest nor better', nor any other 'trade of life more meete for a Gentleman, nor travayle more acceptable to GOD', argues Cono in defence of his lifestyle, 'then is the tilling of the ground', and he adds that 'people in the olde time... as oft as they would geve a man the name of an honest man, they would call him a good husbande' (sig. A5r).[28] But Cono is not quite what he seems. He is no straight-talking plowman, but rather a husbandman after the fashion of Ischomachus, and therefore a 'woorkemaister', an overseer of the labours of others; his orderly management of the estate is rewarded with the fruits of *otium*:

When my Servantes are all set to woorke, and every man as busie as may be, I get me into my Closet to serve GOD, and to reade the holy Scriptures... that doone, I write or reade such thinges as I thinke most needefull, or dispatche businesse... A litle before dinner I walke abrode, if it be faire, eyther in my Garden, or in the Feeldes, if it be foule, in my Galerie: when I come in, I finde an Egge, a Chicke, a peece of Kid, or a peece of Veale, Fishe, Butter, such like... after dinner I passe the tyme with talking with my wyfe, my servantes, or yf I have any, with my ghestes: I rise and walke about my ground, where I viewe my woorkemen, my pastures, my medowes, my corne, and my cattel'. (sig. A3r)[29]

Cyvile and Uncyvile Life is refreshingly sceptical of the performance of 'honesty' as truth-telling, plain-dealing or an open-handed liberality. Indeed, it offers a sustained critique of the claim of the country gentleman Vincent to be honest in these senses. Its approach to this problem is twofold.

On the one hand, it uses dialogue to demonstrate a kind of honesty which recognises the different interests of tenants and landowners: an ironic and courtly urbanity ('*honestas*'). On the other hand, it discovers that Vincent, the hospitable manorial lord, is really a profit-seeking farmer, and reveals the hidden costs – both financial and personal – of the gentrification of husbandry.

The dialogue opens, I noted above, with Vincent claiming that the education of the country gentleman is more 'honest' than that of the courtier because it is 'nourished in justice, truth, and plaine dealinge, free from fraude, and dissimulation', to which Vallentine responds:

> I allowe of your zeale to honesty in education, but if you mixe it with some other thinges, I will like it the better. That you study to bring up your children in honesty, which is a vertue, and cheefely justice... I doo not onely allow you, but commend you: Yet if you remember what Tully telleth you (for sure I am you have bin a Scholler), That men are not onely borne to themselves.... (pp. 14–16)

Importantly, Vallentine does not try to correct his friend; he understands that he is already sociable, albeit according to a misguided custom. In fact, it turns out that both speakers agree that honesty and justice are interrelated. Even so, Vincent is being discreetly invited to return to book 1 of *De officiis*, to the discussion of the virtue of 'justice' where the maxim 'men are not onely borne to themselves' is first cited and the '*honestas*' of benevolence introduced (1. 42–60). If he were to return to this passage he would discover that benevolence and liberality are recognised as virtues by Cicero when they are governed by decorum or '*honestas*': generosity should not exceed our means; it should reflect the worth of the recipient. Only then can it be described as 'heart-felt' since it aims to satisfy individual need.

However, Vallentine does not offer to explain this passage. Instead, he rather vaguely hints that Vincent might want to 'remember' Cicero's saying. This is because he does not need to be more explicit. The meaning of this maxim is already implicit in his own practice of honest conversation. Thus, Vallentine recycles Vincent's language – 'I will tell you plainely' (p. 13), 'In plain speeche I tell you' (p. 20) – even as he practises gestures which exemplify a dissembling *sprezzatura*. For example, when he tells Vincent 'my meaning... is to remember you, & not to councel you' (p. 18), or when he admits 'I acknowledge you of much more wisdome and judgement then I am' (p. 30).

The author of *Cyvile and Uncyvile Life* is well aware of the economic implications of '*honestas*'. Vincent may have argued at the beginning of the dialogue that the country gentleman is brought up to be honest, just, wise and wealthy, and that these virtues are represented in his hospitality. In its second half, however, he praises the thriftiness of his peers, arguing that the life of the courtier and city dweller is more expensive and wasteful than that of the country gentleman who produces everything he needs – food, fuel, clothing – 'upon his owne demeanes' (p. 48). Vallentine intervenes, reminding his friend of the cost of producing these goods. '[D]are I warrant you', he argues, 'before such time as the same provisions be fit for your use (I meane, your Lande manured, your corne reaped, your woods cut downe, & all things ready, and brought home as they must bee: your trouble and disquiet wilbe much more then ours, that sende twise a day from our house to the Market in the towne where wee dwell...)'. Vincent is forced to agree. 'I had forgotten', he apologises, 'that we have much adoo in seed season', but adds 'all these things yet wee have without money, which you have not'. 'Without money?' comes the prompt response, 'But Syr, by your favour, not without cost' (p. 49).

Vincent's hospitality is shown to be costly. Where there are many strangers in a house, so must there must be many servants, argues Vallentine, all of whom eat up the lord's profits (p. 60). However, it is also costly for the recipients themselves. Vallentine argues that country gentlemen should reside in the city part of the year. On hearing this Vincent anxiously wonders 'How should my house bee kept, and my neighbours love mee?' 'A great deale better', retorts Vallentine, and then explains why there is a need to distinguish between ploughmen and gentlemen (p. 62). Vincent's 'hospitallitie' is revealed to be a 'cloake' which disguises his self-interestedness (p. 63), pursued at the expense of his tenants. He is both self-deceived and deceiving. In 'disposing your selves... to bee Ploughmen', complains Vallentine:

you have learned what every soyle is worth, and so after that rate, set out your land, wherby the poor Husbandman or Farmer payeth so deare for your comming and neighborhood, as hee had rather you lived further off like a Gentleman, though for very flattery or feare, when hee dineth at your Boarde, hee saith, hee is sory your worship should dwell away, when God wotteth, the poore man meaneth nothing lesse: For I have learned that those Tennauntes have best peny worthes of their Farmes, whose Landlordes do least know the Lande, or dwell furthest from it. Wherfore you deceave your selfe, to thinke that your continuall dwelling in the Countrey, doth ease the poore Ploughman. (pp. 62–3)

What Vallentine makes clear is that Vincent is more likely to be a reader of Fitzherbert's *The Boke of Husbandrye* or Heresbach's *Foure Bookes of Husbandry* than Latimer's 'Sermon on Plowers'. Despite his claim to be an old-fashioned, hospitable manorial lord, he is in fact committed to a culture of improvement which encourages a detailed knowledge of one's land and its profitable management. This leads Vallentine to expose the real nature of the exchange between lord and tenant: lords 'give the poore men their Tennants a meales meat twise a weeke worth a groate, and force him to pay a shillinge more than hee was wonte, before his lorde became so skilfull a husband' (pp. 63–4).

Civil conversation provides an idealised model for a fairer exchange. We could say that Vallentine understands from *De officiis* that the irony of the 'genial conversationalist' who pretends ignorance is also the honesty of the man of business who is 'liberal in giving and not inconsiderate in exacting his dues, but in every business relation... [is] fair and reasonable, often yielding much of his own right' (2. 64). Vallentine's courtly simplicity exemplifies an alternative sociability to that offered by the hospitable lord. For Vincent, generosity binds men to him in a relationship of subordination. Vallentine, however, wants him to practise a different kind of exchange. Thus, a gentleman gives up something – say, the right to dominate as the head of the high table – so as to recognise and secure the 'interest' of all interlocutors. He also gives up his right to 'know' his land. In the discussion about husbandry, for instance, Vallentine makes conversational courtesy also the rule of good economic conduct. He advises his friend to assume simplicity in matters of husbandry: 'some Doctors doo thinke it better not to know all thinges, then to knowe them: meaning (as I judge) that every man should not bee to deepe a searcher in an others profession or mistery, least led on with private profit he hindereth the common commodities' (p. 63).

The anonymous *Cyvile and Uncyvile Life* is not an isolated or eccentric contribution to a complex agrarian debate. On the contrary, as I will argue in the next section, it draws our attention to the existence of a quite different response to a nascent capitalism overlooked in a modern critical debate structured around dichotomous categories: the gift and the commodity, feudalism and capitalism.[30] This response exposes the false consciousness of the moral argument that only the denial of self-interest, or its converse, its absolute assertion, are honest. It understands that only negotiation between competing interests can properly be described as both honest and profitable. *Cyvile and Uncyvile Life* also helps us to recognise that the perceived profits of such negotiation inspired the writing of an early English economic text, Thomas Smith's *A Discourse of The Commonweal of this Realm of England*, a response to mid-Tudor complaint which also happens to be written as a civil conversation. By the same token, Smith's *Discourse* will help us to understand why this speech form is not to be trusted, that is, why it was *not* ultimately adequate to the task of negotiating 'honestly' between different interests.

SOCIABLE COMMERCE: THOMAS SMITH

Thomas Smith's contribution to Reformation culture, as we saw in chapter 3, was to defend the role played by civil debate in any decision-making process. That he wants us to attend to his choice of a dialogue form for the economic exposition of the *Discourse* is evident from his preface. '[Y]ee might well say, that there be men of greater wittes then I that have that matter in charge', begins Smith with conventional self-deprecation, 'yet Fooles (as the Proverbe is) sometimes speake to the purpose: and as many heads, so many wittes'. Thus, foolish contributions to a discussion should be tolerated: 'when every man bryngs in his gyfte, a meane witted man may of all these (the best of every mans devise being gathered together) make as it were a pleasaunt and perfect Garlonde to adorne and Decke hys head with all'. All estates must be 'freely suffered, yea, and provoked to tell their Advyses in that matter. For some poynctes in their feates, they may disclose, that the wysest in a Realme cannot unfolde againe' (sigs. AIr–AIv).

Much recent critical work has been dedicated to discovering in literary texts 'an intelligible, formal analogue of the increasingly fugitive and abstract social relations of a burgeoning market society'. In particular, the rhetorical education at the centre of the humanist curriculum has been seen to provide the basis for a disciplining of a 'self' ready to take advantage of the new opportunities in a more intensively mercantile society. Thus, Hutson discovers in Smith's use of the commonplace 'as many heads, so many wittes', 'a kind of dialectical invention; the application of exemplary resources to an existing and baffling situation in order to "discover" it, to render it intelligible and ready for productive exploitation'.[31] However, let us remember that the *Discourse* is a conversation rather than an oration, and that this detail shapes a slightly different sense of Smith's attachment both to the commonplace 'as many heads, so many wittes' and to the complex relationship between literary and social form that the text proposes. Smith is also seeking to enlighten gross English wits enclosed in quarrels about enclosure and out-manoeuvred by 'the finenesse of straungers wits' who treat English customers like children, swapping apples for their jewels (sig. G3v). He wants to bring his audience into civil conversation in its two senses of familiar discourse and trade, and this means showing us something we already know or will come to know: the paradoxical need to cultivate one's interests – both a native capacity for civility and a nation's domestic raw materials – to serve the commonweal. This is a process which is envisaged by Smith as cultivating an inclusive social economy which recognises competing interests: 'as many heads, so many wittes'.

Smith gives voice to competing interests; he also dramatises the negotiation between them. In the second dialogue, after the argument against enclosure has been rehearsed in terms familiar to the complaints tradition, the interlocutors consider the issue from a different perspective. For some, the Knight argues, enclosure has been very profitable. The wealthiest English counties are also those which have suffered most from enclosure: Essex, Kent and North Hamptonshire (sig. E2v). The real issue, suggests the Doctor, is how the benefits of enclosure can be extended from the few to the many. Meanwhile, the real problem lies not with the act of enclosure *per se*, since common land is often badly managed, but with the profitability of sheep farming that is prompting enclosure and adversely affecting tillage. In response the Knight suggests that sheep farmers 'well may be restrained by lawes' to return to tillage. But, answers the Doctor, it 'were hard to make a lawe therein: so many as have profit by that matter resisting it' (sig. E3r).[32] The Knight rehearses his case *for* enclosure by modifying the moral commonplace used against it in the complaints tradition: the need not to interfere with the private commodity of others (sig. E3v). He then offers a solution, cautiously, because he realises the potential unpopularity of his proposal. He proposes that sheep farmers might be encouraged to return to tillage, not by legal restraint, but by the introduction of a custom on raw wool passing overseas and the enhancement of the price of corn. This 'might be brought to passe if yee wil let it have as free passage over Sea at all times, as yee have now for Wooll' (sig. F1r).

The proposal is popular with the Husbandman, but not with the Merchant or the Capper, both of whom anticipate an increase in the price of corn and bread (sigs. F1v-F1r, F2v). In response to their concern the Doctor argues, first, that the Husbandman should have the right to raise prices like everyone else, and then that he has the right to seek a living (sig. F1v). The Husbandman thanks the Doctor 'withall my heart', and then takes the opportunity to explain something of his financial difficulties. 'And to say the very truth', he offers, 'I that have inclosed litle or nothing of my ground, coulde never be able to make up my Lords rent, were it not for a litle herd that I have of Neate, sheepe, swyne, geese, and Hennes, that I doe reare upon my grounde' (sig. F2r). In response the Doctor reminds his fellows of the need to cherish husbandmen; if not, he warns, they will seek to make a living elsewhere, as 'the doings of this honest mans neighbours, which have tourned their erable lands to pasture, because they see more profit by pasture then tillage' so amply demonstrates (sig. F2v). This ambiguous praise of the Husbandman as 'honest', however, signals a cultural shift. Is the Husbandman honest because he has refused to pursue his own interests unlike his neighbours, or because he has admitted to the financial difficulties he labours under? In fact, the Doctor is using the plain-speaking Husbandman's admission to demonstrate the truth of 'an old saying in Latin. *Honos alit artes*' – honour enhances art – which he translates in such a way as to make *honos* equivalent to 'profit': 'that is to say profit or advauncement nourisheth every facultie, whych saying is so true that it is alowed by the common judgement of al men' (sig. F2v).[33] In this case it is the profit-seeking neighbours who are honest.

In contrast to Latimer's plain monologue, this dialogue explores the validity (and reality) of different and conflicting interests, and it *attempts* to offer a model for their negotiation: both social interaction and trade. For example, Smith uses the dialogue form in book 2 to show that the Husbandman's articulation of his interests does not entail a refusal to recognise social duty. Rather, it dramatises the act of negotiation which the Doctor imagines will take place if the Husbandman is given the liberty to trade corn freely. Honesty is produced *in* conversation. When the Knight worries that the newly liberated Husbandman will sell his surplus corn rather than store it against future bad harvests, the doctor underscores the sociability of the commercial relationship he is imagining. If we are envious of our corn, he explains, so will our neighbours be:

God hath ordeyned that no countery shoulde have all commodities, but which that one lackes another brings forth: & that the one countery lacketh this yere, another hath plenty thereof commonly in the same yere, to the intente men may knowe that they have neede one of anothers helpe, & thereby love and societie to growe amonge all men the more. (sig. F4r)

Meanwhile, the Knight is made aware of his position as the privileged interlocutor in this 'conversation' or trade, and he is required to show some restraint. In effect, his profits from enclosure will be restrained by a custom on raw wool passing overseas. This kind of 'restraint' works quite differently to a legal prohibition against enclosure for it promotes the manufacture of domestic raw materials at home. In this respect the Knight is expected to imitate the conduct of the senior interlocutor of, say, *Cyvile and Uncyvile Life*, whose courtesy enables Vincent to join in the 'conversation'.

I say that Smith attempts to offer a model for the negotiation between different interests because, of course, the Socratic dialogue does not actually achieve this. One of the problems with the *Discourse* is that the discussion is tightly managed by the Doctor, the character who stands in for Smith. It becomes apparent that Smith is recommending a well-managed exchange, rather than a genuinely open one, in order to promote his interest. This treatise has a double aim. On the one hand it recommends 'conversation' as a tool to explore and resolve different interests (and this is practised in book 2). On the other hand, it celebrates a new kind of knowledge which can manage such a conversation (the kind of knowledge of which the author of *Cyvile and Uncyvile Life* is suspicious). Smith is revising mid-Tudor social complaint by positioning the university graduate as the intellectual 'husbandman' hero in place of the humble plowman. In this dialogue it is not the plain-speaking husband who provides the solution to 'dearth' in the commonwealth but the 'Doctor' who husbands or manages conversation/commerce between the estates.

The role of the Doctor as intellectual husband is explored in book 1. The Doctor has just heard the complaint of the Husbandman about the Knight's high rents, and of the Knight about the high prices of the Husbandman's produce. He proposes 'that there is none of you but have just cause to complaine' (sig. B2r). At this point the 'honest' Capper intervenes, challenging the Doctor's right to judge in these matters since he has such an easy life.[34] 'I woulde set you to the Plough and Carte', he offers mischievously, 'for the devill a whit of good yee doe with your studies.' At this rebuke the Knight interjects – 'God forbid neighbour that it should be so' – and a defence of the Doctor's university learning begins. Who would counsel princes, or teach the Christian religion, asks the Knight? Who would know the different estates, or have 'conference' with men from other countries (sig. B2r)? The Knight, who represents the highest estate among the interlocutors, is unduly partial to the Doctor. He makes appreciative, ingratiating murmurs at crucial points in the dialogue: such as, 'Of my fayth I am glad it was my chaunce to have you in my company at this time, for of a wise man, a man may alwayes learne' (sig. C2v). The Doctor, however, remains the most powerful spokesman. Not only does he mediate between all the estates (as in the debate about enclosure discussed above), but he also has the opportunity to defend his profession as a service to the commonwealth at considerable length. '[Y]ou good husband', he addresses this companion, 'for the perfection of the knoweledge of husbandry, had neede of some knowledge in Astronomy'. The list grows; a husbandman also needs 'Phisick' or 'Veterimaria' to care for his animals, and geometry 'for true measuring of lande' (sigs. B4v–C1r). Similarly, counsellors and princes need educated men to guide them in the kind of philosophy 'that teacheth of manners': 'doth it not teach first how every man should governe himselfe honestly. Secondly how he should guide his family wisely and profitably. And thirdly, it sheweth how a City or Realme, or any other commonweale should bee well ordered and governed' (sig. C1r). Smith models his Doctor on Xenophon's aristocratic 'husband' Ischomachus, the speaker who answers the question who is 'a good and honest man' thus: someone whose skill in conversation enables him to persuade others to serve his interests voluntarily.

The *Discourse* is a deeply self-interested treatise in the sense that it advertises the professional skills of the Cambridge-educated Smith. As we have seen, Smith has a tendency towards self-aggrandisement, whether he is positioning himself as 'Cicero' in his dialogue on the English alphabet, or supplanting John Cheke as the leader of the reform in Greek pronunciation in the quarrel with Stephen Gardiner. In the *Discourse*, however, such self-aggrandisement is more worrying because Smith is also defending his future economic interests, some of which were partly dependent on the successful colonisation of Ireland. Smith was one of the key supporters of Henry Sidney's policy of colonisation in Ireland 1565–75, the novelty of which lay in the fact that it was to be supported by private individuals or speculators, not the crown.[35] In 1571 Smith petitioned Elizabeth for lands in Ireland, the aim being to make the country 'civil' and to 'people' it 'with natural Englishmen born'. A broadsheet printed to attract investment, Mary Dewar notes, was 'very much a business prospectus more anxious to persuade men of what they have to gain in pounds, shillings and pence'. The venture failed. News of the land granted, notes Dewar, 'had stirred the Irish chieftains' who believed that Elizabeth had given away some of their land. The expedition set out from Liverpool in the winter of 1571 with fewer men than originally anticipated, under the immature leadership of Smith's son. Once in Ireland the expedition ran into trouble; Smith's son was murdered by one of his Irish servants, and the project abandoned.[36] In 1574, however, Smith drew up plans for a second project which was in effect 'a complete blueprint for the organization and government of a colony'. This time Smith proposed the building of a city, to be called 'Elizabetha' or 'Castra colonelli or Smith's Tents', and the establishment of small farming communities.[37] '"Nothing"', writes Smith, '"doth more people the country with men, maketh men more civil, nor bringeth more commodities to the sustenance of men than the plough"'.[38] Smith's praise of the civility of the Husbandman leads to the final stage of my argument: how the 'honesty' of the courtier and the husbandman are merged in the defence of both this kind of personal investment in plantation and the civilising effects of the English language. To explore this development I want to turn to a courtesy book which translates the self-deprecating, dissimulating Italian courtier into the truth-telling English husband, Lodowick Bryskett's *Discourse of Civill Life* (1606). This 'improvement', I will argue, supplements the proposed agrarian reform of Ireland: its successful settlement and government by opportunist individuals.

LODOWICK BRYSKETT'S *A DISCOURSE OF CIVILL LIFE*

The problems with Smith's management of the dialogue provide a backdrop to an ongoing debate about the courtesy books and their homology with the 'English colonial struggle in Ireland'.[39] Greenblatt's suggestion that a homology exists between books advocating civil conduct and books defending acts of violent incivility is prompted by his incomprehension at why 'a man of Spenser's sensitivity and gifts' failed in his notorious Irish tract, *A View of the Present State of Ireland* (c. 1596), to temper 'the extreme policies of ruthless men', or, indeed, even to 'recoil in the slightest from this horror'.[40] Spenser infamously defends famine as a military strategy early in this treatise. For Greenblatt, the 'sensitive' Spenser finds in the courtesy books a discourse which promotes a form of psychic and moral repression. The courtesy books help to justify the act of violence required to establish a civil self and a civil society. The discovery of this justification coincided with a contemporary need to defend a violent act of colonial possession prompted by Henry Sidney's policy of reform which encouraged settlement. The infamous duplicity of courtly conduct – represented by Castiglione's *sprezzatura* – is deemed by Greenblatt an act of repression. It facilitates an 'illusory resolution' of the 'tragic conflict inherent in the fashioning of civility', a studied forgetting of how a moral language legitimates immoral acts.[41] In this way Greenblatt understands and responds to the task which faces all critics of colonial texts, the imperative to tell the truth.

This imperative really matters. It means that when Spenser explains in the second half of the *View* that the military solution proposed in its first half is intended to free the Irish husbandman from the tyranny of the native Irish and Anglo-Irish lords and to bring him into 'conversation' – both familiar discourse and trade – with English settlers, it is possible to see how such 'liberation' also entails the suppression of native culture. The *View*, Greenblatt explains, aims to 'transform the mass of the rural population from cowherds with their dangerous freedom of movement to husbandmen'.[42] Even so, the colonial narrative of cultivation remains extraordinarily powerful, so much so that Debora Shuger has forwarded a defence of the Elizabethan Irish tracts (including the *View*) which gives credence to their georgic idealism.[43] Ironically, Shuger's recovery of this narrative provides a corrective to its earlier deconstruction by Greenblatt and other critics, not *vice versa*, thus creating a new dilemma: who is telling the truth?

The dilemma is created by authors of texts like the *View*. Spenser seems to believe in the 'honesty' of the civilising process he promotes. After all, he voices criticisms of the culture of guesting already articulated in Gaelic sources, as the work of the Irish historian Katherine Simms suggests.[44] This makes it all the more difficult to define the duplicity of such civility, a difficulty which is perhaps registered in the complexity of Greenblatt's argument. One way in which we might respond to the difficult issue of agrarian reform in Ireland in the late sixteenth century is to explore the contribution of a treatise which co-exists hazily somewhere between the genre of the courtesy book and the colonial tract, Lodowick Bryskett's *A Discourse of Civill Life* (1606). Spenser's *View* has received much excellent critical attention. Bryskett's treatise has not, even though it is a likely influence on the *View*.[45] As I want to argue, this translation of an Italian treatise on manners merges the linguistic reforms of Cheke and Smith with new projects of agrarian improvement to legitimate a policy of reform in Ireland based on the settlement or 'planting' of people.

The *Discourse* is a translation and adaptation of Cinthio's *Tre dialoghi della vita civile* first printed in 1565.[46] Book 1 explores the education of a child; book 2 is concerned with early manhood and book 3 with age after 'the heate of youth'.[47] The content of the *Discourse* is not original. It provides a summary of mostly Greek moral philosophy as well as a discussion of the civil conduct available in other courtesy books. This treatise shares much in common with *Cyvile and Uncyvile Life* and *Civile Conversatione* (Pettie's translation of the latter is dedicated to the mother of Captain Thomas Norris, one of Bryskett's correspondents). It is similarly preoccupied with defining 'the foundation of honest and vertuous living' (sig. G1v), and 'honesty' is perhaps one of the words it uses most frequently. Moreover, as we will see, in Bryskett's translation civil conversation is emphasised as an alternative to an oppressive culture of hospitality. Yet, while Bryskett follows his original closely for the most part, he also introduces prefatory material of his own devising. These contributions locate the *Discourse* in a particular context, the Pale in Ireland. They also tend towards a reform of the 'dishonesty' of the Italian courtier. In Bryskett's translation, 'honesty' is redefined as the thrifty government of the truth-telling English husband. This translation of Italian *onesto* is integral to Bryskett's defence of the policy of plantation – both the settlement of English gentlemen and their tenants in Ireland and the cultivation of the land – as part of a civilising process. On the one hand, the *Discourse* reveals a new confidence in the 'civility' of the English vernacular. That is, English is shown to be a fitter language than Italian for planting and growing the seeds of classical moral philosophy. In this way, Bryskett also uses the translation of *Tre dialogi della vita civile* to imagine the agrarian 'translation' or civilisation of Ireland. On the other hand, the existence of this translation is put forward as evidence of a once successful settling of land in Ireland during the 1580s under the government of Lord Grey de Wilton, Lord Deputy of Ireland. The translation of Cinthio's treatise is possible only because Bryskett is himself a good 'husband'.

Many of the sixteenth-century English courtesy books are translations of Italian originals or, like Simon Robson's *The court of civill courtesie* (1577), they pretend to be. Bryskett's treatise, however, is unusual in that its model is translated into a specific context. The three conversations take place in Bryskett's planters cottage on the outskirts of Dublin in the early 1580s. Cinthio's fictional speakers are replaced by Bryskett's actual acquaintance in Ireland, among them Edmund Spenser. For much of the *Discourse* the Irish context does not seem to matter; it merely provides the location for a microcosmic civil society among a group of Bryskett's acquaintance. Thus, the prefatory material which supplements Cinthio's second dialogue, and which explores the ideal of the 'Philosophicall dinner' (sig. N3r), is probably based on the banquet scene in book 4 of *Civile Conversation*. It could as easily have been set in Venice, London or Paris. Bryskett repeats Guazzo's advice on temperate eating. As in *Civile Conversation*, Bryskett's friends pass around a cup of wine and discuss how to savour its 'odour' as well as the importance of temperate eating (sigs. N3v-O1r). This preface complements Cinthio's discussion in the second dialogue of the role played by dining and civil conversation in promoting free exchange between friends and restraining unruly and anti-social passions.

The Irish context to this civil conversation *is* emphasised, however, in the preface to the third book. At the beginning of the third dialogue Bryskett is asked by his anxious friends on their arrival 'whether that company made me not afraide to see them come in such sort upon me being but a poore Farmer: for though they came not armed like souldiers to be cessed upon me, yet their purpose was to coynie upon me, and to eate me out of house and home'. ('Coynie' is the billeting of military followers upon private individuals.) Bryskett's unflustered response is intended to show that the *Discourse* is indicating an alternative to such enforced hospitality, and describing the conditions which have begun to eradicate its practice:

as long as I saw Counsellers in the companie, I neede not feare that any such unlawful exaction as coynie should be required at my hand: for the lawes had sufficiently provided for the abolishing thereof. And though I knew that among the Irishry it was not yet cleane taken away, yet among such as were ameynable to law, and civill, it was not used or exacted. As for souldiers, besides that their peaceable maner of coming freed me from doubt of cesse, thanked be God the state of the realme was such as there was no occasion of burthening the subject with them, such had bin the wisedom, valour and foresight of our late Lord Deputie, not onely in subduing the rebellious subjects, but also in overcoming the forreine enemie: whereby the garrison being reduced to a small number, and they provided for by her Majestie of victual at reasonable rates, the poore husbandman might now eate the labors of his owne hands in peace and quietnes, without being disquieted or harried by the unruly souldier. (sigs. X2r-X2v)

Though Bryskett may have begun the translation as early as 1567, he did not prepare the text for print until 1603, several years after he had been forced to leave Ireland, along with Spenser, following the Tyrone rebellion of 1598. The text was printed in 1606.[48] Its setting during the deputyship of Lord Grey, then, is nostalgic. Bryskett offers a rose-tinted vision of a happy community which supposedly flourished in and around Dublin under the protection of Lord Grey in the 1580s. In this respect, the *Discourse* follows the convention of the *Courtier*, which also depicts a lost idealised world. As the quotation above makes clear, however, this treatise departs from the courtesy tradition. Bryskett's ideal gentleman is fashioned not as a courtier but as a husbandman. Bryskett is a 'poore Farmer' (sig. X2r), albeit one who gives orders rather than works the plough. Meanwhile, Grey is fashioned as the ideal governor or 'husbandman' in the style of Xenophon's Cyrus. As a second interlocutor contributes: 'My Lord *Grey* hath plowed and harrowed the rough ground to his hand' (sig. X2v). It is this act of 'translation' which we need to treat with scepticism.

Bryskett is himself 'in translation'. He was born in London in 1545, to an Italian merchant father from Genoa who had settled in London, Antonio Bruschetto. His *Discourse of Civill Life* is an Englishing project in a double sense; it is both a translation of an Italian treatise into English, and of a London-born Italian bureaucrat into an English gentleman farmer. In the 1560s Bryskett had been a member of the household of Henry Sidney. He first visited Ireland in 1565 when Sidney became Lord Deputy. In 1575, when Sidney was appointed Lord Deputy for the third time, he was given the post of clerk to the Privy Council, a post he resigned on 9 May 1582 because, as he explains in the preface to book 1 of the *Discourse*, his duties were too irksome. Bryskett's reasons are also recorded in two letters he sent to Sir Francis Walsingham in 1581[2], and these letters indicate his discreet involvement in the debate about colonisation forwarded by Sidney and supported by subsequent Lord Deputies, Fitzwilliam (Googe's employer and the dedicatee of Heresbach's *Foure Bookes of Husbandry*) and Grey. In his letters to Walsingham, which may have been intended for a public reading,[49] Bryskett uses the literary and philosophical discourse of the country versus the court, promoted in new husbandry manuals such as Googe's, to explain his desire to become a farmer. He writes to Walsingham on the 15 January 1581[2] that he is 'fully resolved to esteme the course and hard temperate fare of a ploweman voyde of indignities', because he believes it 'farre sweeter then all the dayntie dishes of Princes courts, where . . . I think it easie for a man to fill his belly, and to be puffed up with vanities and never accomplished hopes and expectations, but very hard for an honest man to purchase due rewarde of his service'. Bryskett argues, like Cono in *Foure Bookes of Husbandry*, that one might serve the commonweal as ably in the country as at court. Yet, this is no ordinary retreat. Bryskett is choosing to farm land in the county of Wexford (a county he describes as 'borders'), and his service to the commonweal has a particular aim: 'to see if a just and honest simple lyfe, may not even emong the most Barbarous people of the world breede securitie in him that shall live nere or emong them'. To complete this service, he explains, he needs to be provided by Elizabeth with 'eight horsemen, and a dozen footmen', a number which he promises to match from his own funds. This is not to be a 'perpetual charge', he adds, 'but only for a tyme till I may have planted myselfe and taken roote there'.[50]

The preface to book 3 of the *Discourse* echoes this plan, although there is no sign of the forty soldiers at the Dublin planters cottage. On the contrary, it shows a successful experiment in settlement and agrarian prosperity. Bryskett uses husbandry, first, as an image of happy government, but in such a way as to repress the violent process of conquest this implies (as Greenblatt argues for Spenser's *View*). Thus, Grey is depicted as a good husband, when plowing the land really means vanquishing enemies with the sword.[51] He uses it as an image, secondly, of linguistic translation. Grey's plowing of Ireland has created the right soil in which English men might prosper; such prosperity encourages the harvesting of the fruits of classical moral philosophy in the soil of the English language. This idea of translation as an act of husbandry, moreover, allows Bryskett to insinuate that he has improved Cinthio's Italian treatise. Our translator Bryskett – a 'poore Farmer' – has brought to fruition the classical moral philosophy half-nurtured by Cinthio. He understands what Cinthio does not, that honesty is produced through physical and intellectual husbandry. It is cultivated in the orderly speech and management of land and people.

Bryskett follows Cinthio's definition of 'honesty' or *onesto* in book 1, where it means 'telling the truth' or not lying (elsewhere in the book it is used more broadly to signify 'moral goodness' which includes temperate self-restraint). In book 3, however, Bryskett supplements Cinthio's discussion of the types of virtues with material drawn from other sources on the grounds that the original treatment is occasionally confused and unclear. In fact, Bryskett does not seek to clarify genuine difficulties in Cinthio's text. The maxim 'we are not born for ourselves' is mentioned twice in book 3 to support contrary arguments: on the one hand, the idea that the virtuous man does not seek profit, on the other hand, the idea that Prudence is a virtue which cultivates profit for oneself, friends, family and neighbours.[52] What Bryskett does do, however, is add to Cinthio's list of virtues. One of these new virtues is 'Veritie', and this addition is consonant with his desire to improve the Italian courtier. Thus, Bryskett defines verity as the mean between two vices: boasting and 'dissimulation or jesting, called in Greek *Ironia*'. Of such *Ironia* – the source, of course, for *sprezzatura* – Bryskett complains of its use by unscrupulous and ambitious men 'to purchase reputation and credit, or profit' (sig. Hh4v). The argument of *Cyvile and Uncyvile Life* is reversed: here, it is the dissimulating courtier who is castigated as self-seeking.

This defence of 'husbandry' as civilising is articulated in the theory of translation offered at the opening of the *Discourse*. Bryskett compares the translator to a traveller who visits foreign lands, bringing home grafts of new and varied fruits to plant in his poorer native soil. Like other Elizabethan translators, Bryskett is aware of the assumed poverty and 'incivility' of the vernacular. George Pettie had defended his translation of Guazzo with the argument that it is easier to grasp an idea in one's native language (p. 10). Bryskett develops this modesty topos. He apologises for the poverty of English, describing his translation as a patriotic act, a way of improving a barren vernacular. However, he also suggests more boldly that translation into English is improving. The very limitation of English which promises to make it an unfit soil for the grafts of Greek and Roman moral philosophy, its plainness, in fact make it a superior soil for the clarification *and* cultivation of ideas confusedly discussed by Aristotle, obliquely presented by Plato, and imperfectly translated by the Italians.[53]

This chapter explored two distinct conceptions of 'honesty' embodied, on the one hand, in the self-restraint of the courtier, and, on the other hand, in the thriftiness of the truth-telling husband. Its argument developed the tension between civil and domestical conversation, and between Cicero and Xenophon, which we explored in chapter 1. I argued that this is a genuine tension in *Civile Conversation*. Guazzo may claim that civil conversation grows out of domestical conversation, but his treatise also demonstrates how the social relations of the household undermine the aspirations of male friends. These are also, however, overlapping discourses. Thus, the author of *Cyvile and Uncyvile Life* may construct a conversation between two male friends so as to expose the dishonesty of the gentrification of husbandry, but, by the same token, Bryskett can adapt a civil conversation to 'domesticate' the Italian courtier and the Irish. The same ambivalence attends the two writers we will explore next, Gabriel Harvey and Edmund Spenser. Harvey is infamous for his uncivil castigation of the recently deceased Robert Greene in the early 1590s while Spenser is, of course, Greenblatt's insensitive poet of empire. I have not explored Spenser's *View* in this chapter, although my argument concerning Bryskett's *A Discourse of Civill Life* might extend to it: Spenser's *View* is more circumspect about civil conversation as a tool of reformation, at least without the support of military conquest. In the next two chapters, however, I am interested in Harvey's and Spenser's ground-breaking collaborative writings of the 1570s. These writings bring me to the final stage of my argument. The representation of their friendship attempts a probing reform of the failed conversations of the earlier Cambridge generation, a generation who could not – or would not – ameliorate the dominant male speaker of the Socratic dialogue. Harvey's and Spenser's familiar letters reform and refashion authoritarian schoolmasters; they explore the issue of how an education based on Ciceronian *amicitia* can nurture the talents of young men and create a more inclusive, less 'oligarchic' commonweal.

CHAPTER 5

A commonwealth of letters: Harvey and Spenser in dialogue

The authoritarian character of Tudor educational reform, and the social and political world it imagined, is well known. Thus, Richard Halpern observes that in this period we can take it as 'axiomatic that the primary function of schooling is to reproduce the dominant social order'. He describes 'the tortures of the Tudor schoolroom – sadistic, arbitrary, sometimes explicitly sexual' which 'clearly worked as a political ritual, in which the pedagogue assumed and reinforced the sovereign authority of the monarch or magistrate'.[1] Of course, the whip was not the only tool at the disposal of the schoolmaster. The sixteenth century saw an increase in corporal punishment, but it also saw a debate about more humane ideas of educational method. Roger Ascham's influential *The Schoolmaster*, written between 1563 and 1566 and printed posthumously in 1570, was openly critical of the standard method of learning Latin: rote-learning backed up by the threat of violence. It recommends instead a gentler method which elicits pleasure: imitation or emulation of the kind, encouraging schoolmaster and the classical text. Halpern, familiar with the writings of Michel Foucault and Louis Althusser, knows better than to take these ideas as progressive. The 'mimetic model' of the gentle schoolmaster shapes 'a new class culture within the nascent bonds of "civil society"' and it does so by 'imparting behavioural discipline, encouraging the stylistic assimilation of cultural authority, and distributing individual differences within a regularized system'. Ascham, among others, 'tried to evolve a mode of indoctrination based on hegemony and consent rather than force and coercion', a mode which would produce 'an active embrace of ideology rather than a passive acceptance'.[2]

Ascham's treatise is generally regarded as central to the Tudor debate about educational and social reform. Its conflicted attitude towards the authority of the paternalistic schoolmaster has come to signal a cultural fault-line: a starting point for the unmasking of the dishonest 'humanity' of the reforming pedagogue. My argument in this chapter, however, is that the failure of the attempted reform of Ascham, as well as Smith and Cheke (really, a failure to relinquish authority in social communication) was noted by Harvey and his friend Edmund Spenser a decade later. In their familiar letters they demonstrate an improved model for educational and social exchange which they imagine will liberate the pupil from the tyranny of the schoolmaster. This critique has been lost to us partly because Harvey and Spenser are 'civil' rather than satirical (and therefore their criticisms are not always obvious), but partly too because they engage with a remote linguistic experiment with classical quantification. This metrical system based on the duration of syllables was to be abandoned in the 1590s. Yet, the curious and involved debate about it was central in the 1570s and 1580s to the discussion of a topic which now preoccupies us, male homosociality, and it deserves our attention. In this chapter I will explore how Harvey's and Spenser's contribution to this educational debate is intended to establish the foundations for easy and familiar conversation between teacher and pupil while encouraging literary experiment. In this respect it also aims to offer a less hierarchical model for social communication within the commonwealth.

The detail of this curious debate will be addressed later in this chapter. I want first, though, to explore a different problem. My claim that Harvey, with Spenser, aims to moderate the authority of Smith and Ascham, and to constitute a national, linguistic community which encourages debate, does not chime with his reputation. In the satirical *Have With You to Saffron-Walden, or Gabriel Harvey's Hunt is Up* (1596), Thomas Nashe imaginatively reconstructs a letter from the student Harvey's Cambridge tutor to his father: 'I am uncertaine, but constantly up and downe it is bruted, how he pist incke as soone as ever hee was borne, and that the first cloute he fowlde was a sheete of paper.'[3] In the 1590s Harvey was lampooned as the archetypal ponderous pedant, typified by the bumptious Holofernes of Shakespeare *Love's Labours Lost*. Satirical attacks on Harvey were prompted by his personal attacks on Robert Greene which were seen by Nashe as evidence of his hypocritical pretence to civility. Nashe's criticism is important to consider not only because it has proven to be enduring, but also because it offers a debunking of Harvey's use of the familiar letter as a mode of civil conversation. Nashe offers persuasive criticism of *Three Proper, and wittie, familiar Letters: lately passed betwene two Universitie men. Two Other very commendable Letters, of the same mens writing: both touching the foresaid Artificall Versifying, and certain other Particulars* (1580) in order to expose the incivility of Harvey's attack on Greene in the later printed letter collection, *Foure Letters and Certeine Sonnets* (1592). Evidently, Harvey was vulnerable to the same criticism of paternalism that he levels (more politely) at Ascham

A commonwealth of letters: Harvey and Spenser in dialogue 115

and Smith. It is to this uncivil conversation that I will now turn, partly to place Harvey in context, but partly, too, to try to understand how *not* to read the early letters.

UNCIVIL CONVERSATION

The cause of the infamous quarrel between Nashe and Harvey is not easy to locate. Its origins probably lie in an earlier row between Philip Sidney and the Earl of Oxford which took place on a tennis court in 1579. Harvey's poem *Speculum Tuscanismi*, which appeared in *Three Proper Letters* was taken by John Lyly as a satire against Oxford and an articulation of support for the 'Leicester' camp. Harvey apologised to Oxford, claiming that Lyly had misread the poem. However, the dispute rumbled on. It was transferred to the Martin Marprelate controversy in the late 1580s, and then, in all likelihood, to the Harvey-Nashe quarrel of the 1590s.[4]

Whatever the actual cause the quarrel started in earnest in 1592. The immediate catalyst was Robert Greene's anti-court satire *A Quip for an Upstart Courtier* (1592), which included derogatory remarks about the Harvey brothers, and an attack in the same year on one brother by Nashe in *Pierce Penilesse, His Supplication to the Divell*. Greene's *Quip* – a dialogue between a pair of cloth breeches and a pair of velvet breeches – had originally included the complaint of a Saffron Walden ropemaker (John Harvey) against his three sons: the first, Richard, a divine and 'a vaine glorious asse', the second, John, a physician and a 'foole', and the third, Gabriel, 'the first that invented Englishe Hexamiter' but who was 'orderly clapt in the fleet', supposedly for libel. '[H]onest parents', complains the ropemaker, 'may have bad children'. Meanwhile in *Pierce Penilesse*, under pretence of berating detractors, Nashe rounds on one of his own accusers, Richard Harvey ('some tired Jade...whom I never wronged in my life, hath named me expressely in Print (as I will not do him), and accused me of want of learning...'). '[A]m I subject to the sinne of Wrath I write against, or no, in whetting my penne on this blocke?', he concludes after 'Spurgalling' this 'Asse' (1. 195, 199).

This was all too much for Harvey. Greene died before Harvey could seek legal redress. Instead, he is forced to reclaim the moral high ground in *Foure Letters*. In this text he represents himself as the voice of civility reprimanding scurrilous companions: 'I Wott not what these cutting Huffe-snuffes meane', he writes disingenuously in sonnet VI, 'Of Ale-house daggers I have little skill: / I borrow not my phrase of knave, or queane, / But am a dettour to the Civill quill.'[5] His 'civility' enables him to recognise Nashe's talent and to extend a hand of friendship, even as he ticks him off for falling into the wrong company. But his attack on Robert Greene is unrelenting. For Harvey, Greene is a total degenerate. Poets have a restricted 'Liberty', he declares, which Greene has exceeded by writing invective. This member of a 'riming, and scribbling crew', he explains, 'wil become extremely odious & intollerable to all good Learning, and civill Governement' (sig. A4v).

Harvey seems to think that his claim to wield a 'Civill quill' gives him the right to attack the memory of the recently deceased Greene who is roundly berated for 'his dissolute, and licentious living', 'his fonde disguisinge of a Master of Arte with ruffianly haire', 'his piperly Extemporizing, and Tarletonizing', 'his monstrous swearinge, and horrible forswearing', and 'his continuall shifting of lodginges' or vagrancy (sigs. B2r-B2v). In the same letter, Harvey gives a potted history of Greene's supposed life of debauchery and his horrible death, 'not of the plague, or the pockes, as a Gentleman saide, but of a surfett of pickle herringe and rennish wine' (sig. A4r). Among the concluding sonnets is an address to the 'fine *Castilio* [Castiglione], the Heire of Grace' along with a distasteful composition, the deceased 'John Harveys Welcome to Robert Greene': 'Come, fellow *Greene*, come to thy gaping grave: / ... vermine to Vermine must repair at last'.[6]

It *is* difficult to trust the civility of Harvey in *Foure Letters*. The text opens with an address 'To all courteous mindes' in which Harvey confesses that 'I was first exceeding loath to penne, that is written' and that he only did so 'in mine owne enforced defence, (for I make no difference betwene my deerest frendes, and my selfe)' (sig. A2r). The first letter, written by a Christopher Bird from Saffron Walden (29 August 1592), serves to introduce Harvey to a friend in London, M. Emmanuell Demetrius. In this letter Bird complains that a 'leawd fellow' has 'notoriously deffamed, most spitefully and villainously abuseth an auncient neighbour of mine, one *M. Harvey*, a right honest man of good reckoninge' (sig. A3r). Bird's moral indignation is meant to provide some justification for Harvey's personal attack on Greene in the second letter. In the third letter, which attacks Nashe, Harvey tones down his language in an attempt to close the quarrel. He advises that 'fellow-schollers' and 'fellow-writers, may bee made friendes with a cup of white wine, and some little familiar conference, in calme and civile termes'. 'I offer them my hande', he continues, 'and request their: which I will accept thanckfully: & kisse lovinglye: and ever commende the good Nature, that would; and the better Governemente, that coulde master Affection with Reason and sweeten gall with Humanity' (sig. F3v). The final letter continues the apologies. 'My meaning is not, to teach, but to touch', he claims. He is worried by the 'corruptions in manners, and absurdities in

Arte' that 'have too-lately overflowed the banckes of all good Modesty, and discretion'. He longs only to 'see Learning flourish' and 'Vertue prosper' 'and without empeachment to any, wish[es] all rather to be excellent, with *Socrates*, then to seeme famous, with the Philosopher of the Court' (sigs. H1r-H1v). But Harvey's gesture of goodwill and apologies come too late. They do not take away the bad taste left by his defamation of Greene, nor by his more moderate, schoolmasterly reprimand of the wayward Nashe. No wonder, then, that Nashe was annoyed.

In response Nashe ruthlessly exposes the hypocrisy of Harvey's self-fashioning as a civil gentleman in terms which the latter would recognise. 'Scolding & railing is loud miscalling and reviling one another', he writes in *Strange Newes, Of the Intercepting certaine Letters, and a Convoy of Verses, as they were going Privilie to victual the Low Countries* (1592), 'though it bee never so contrary to all humanitie and good manners', phrases which Harvey clings to in *Foure Letters*. But, Nashe adds, addressing Harvey, 'Such is thy invective against *Greene*' (1. 324). Greene, he records, 'might have writ another *Galatæo* of manners, for his manners everie time I came in his companie: I saw no such base shifting or abhominable villaine by him' (1. 330). By turning the tables on Harvey in this way – that is, by exposing his incivility – Nashe is able to indulge in uncivil name-calling with impunity.[7] To strengthen this impression of Harvey's hypocrisy Nashe deploys a reading strategy first used against him in *Foure Letters*. Much to Nashe's annoyance, Harvey had failed – or pretended to fail – to understand the irony of his persona Pierce Penilesse, thus making him responsible for his creation's parodic supplication to the devil. Nashe *is* Pierce Penilesse, Harvey implies in *Foure Letters*, so ignoring his ironic exposé of the hypocrisy and financial self-seeking of 'moral' authors: 'Penilesse is not his purse but his minde: not his revenue, but his resolution' (p. 47).[8] In response Nashe returns to an earlier printed collection of letters to expose one of Harvey's strategies of self-promotion: the invention of well-wishers.

Three Proper Letters is prefaced by an address 'To the Curteous Buyer, by a Welwiller of the two Authours' which serves as an advertisement for its contents and explains that the letters came to the printer 'by meanes of a faithfull friende, who with much entreaty had procured the copying of them oute, at *Immeritos* [Spenser's] handes'. The printing of these pirated letters is a friendly act, a sharing of the talent of their authors with a broader public: 'shewe me, or *Immerito*', writes the 'Welwiller', 'two Englyshe Letters in Printe, in all pointes equall to the other twoo, both for the matter it selfe, and also for the manner of handling, and saye, wee never sawe good Englyshe Letter in our lives'.[9] 'You must conceit', observes Nashe wryly, assuming the author of the preface is Harvey himself, 'hee was in his chamber-fellowe *wel-willers* cloke when he spake this: the white-liverd slave was modest, and had not the hart to say so much in his owne person, but he must put on the vizard *of an undiscreete friend* (1. 296–7). This strategy makes evident the hollowness of Harvey's gestures of courtesy in *Foure Letters*. If Harvey has a tendency to speak under cover how can we know for certain that he is not also playing a part when he courteously declares at the end of the second letter, 'Let the worlde deale with simple men, as it pleaseath: I loath to be odious to any' (sig. B4v)?

Nashe's demystification of Harvey's *sprezzatura* is entirely believable because, regardless of whether he really is the 'Welwiller' or not, there is plenty of evidence elsewhere to indicate that he did like to praise himself in the third person. His manuscript *Letter-book*, composed in the 1570s, reveals him as a master of 'Renaissance self-forgery'.[10] The letter-book contains draft passages which were to appear in *Three Proper Letters* as well as a number of finished compositions – love poems, letters, prose tales – sometimes in his own name, sometimes under the guise of a persona. The 'book is punctuated by fantasies of publication', notes Katherine Wilson, 'including one epistolary exchange between "E. S. de London", who urges his friend to publish, and the retiring "G. H. de Cambridge" '.[11] Harvey appears as similarly retiring in a tale modelled on Castiglione's courtly debate and the banquet scene in book 4 of Guazzo's *Civile Conversation*, entitled 'A short poeticall discourse to my gentle masters the readers, conteyning a garden communication or dialogue in Cambridge betwene Master G[abriel] H[arvey] and his cumpanye at a Midsumer Comencement, togither with certayne delicate sonnetts and epigrammes in Inglish verse of his makinge'. In this tale, a narrator tells us how the composition of love poetry at this gathering is prompted by one interlocutor quoting a 'common pentameter of Ovid', '*Res est solliciti plena timoris Amor* [it is true that love is full of fear and anxiety]'. The piece includes a poem in adonics ('Hungry vertu') by a supposedly reticent Harvey, but in fact introduced by our author in the third person. The narrator (Harvey) tells how the author (Harvey) pretended that the sonnet was not his, adding that he 'remayne[s] still so persuadid and dare warrant it was of his owne dooinge'. He also tells us that it took much effort on his part to persuade 'Harvey' to copy it for him.[12]

Perhaps the most effective strategy that Nashe uses, however, is to undermine Harvey's confidence in the civilising effects of his style of friendship. This is important because the dispute between Harvey and Nashe is also partly about different styles of male *amicitia*. Greene and Nashe were both contemporaries at St John's College, Cambridge, the erstwhile home of

Cheke, Smith and Ascham. When Nashe mentions the members of this group approvingly in the preface to Greene's *Menaphon* in 1589, Harvey's brother Richard was outraged. As Nashe notes in *Pierce Penilesse*, Richard Harvey 'accused me of want of learning, upbraiding me for reviving, in an epistle of mine [the preface to Greene's *Menaphon* (1589)], the reverent memory of *Thomas Moore*, Sir *John Cheeke*, Doctor *Watson*, Doctor *Haddon*, Doctor *Carre*, Maister *Ascham*, as if they were no meate but for his Maisterships mouth, or none but some such as the son of a ropemaker were worthy to mention them' (1. 195). When Harvey advises in *Foure Letters* that as 'fellow-writers' he and Nashe 'may be made friendes with a cup of white wine, and some little familiar conference, in calme and civile termes', he is calling upon the tradition of male *amicitia* practised at Cambridge. Nashe, though, will have none of this, and he exposes Harvey as deeply self-interested and unfriendly. In *Strange Newes* he observes that Harvey's example of the dangers that beset poets given to invective is his friend Spenser, whose beast fable and anti-court satire *Mother Hubberds Tale* seems to have caused him trouble. 'I must needes say', writes Harvey in *Foure Letters*, addressing the reprobate Greene, 'Mother Hubbard in heat of choller, forgetting the pure sanguine of her sweete Feary Queene, wilfully over-shott her malcontented selfe: as elsewhere I have specified at larg, with the good leave of unspotted friendshipp' (sig. B1r). Who needs friends like this, Nashe responds, refusing to recognise that this is an example of honest rivalry. 'A *pure sanguine* sot art thou, that in vaine-glory to have *Spencer* known for thy friend, and that thou hast some interest in him, censerest him worse than his deadliest enemie would do' (1. 281). Harvey is so full of himself that he has no real friends; indeed, he has no need of friends. To demonstrate this he (mis)quotes Harvey as saying in *Foure Letters* 'I THAT IN MY YOUTH FLATTER'D NOT MY SELFE WITH THE EXCEEDING COMMENDATION OF THE GREATEST SCHOLLER IN THE WORLD etc'. 'Ah neighbourhood, neighbourhood, dead and buried art thou with Robinhood', Nashe laments, 'a poore creature here is faine to commend himselfe, for want of friendes to speake for him' (1. 293–94).[13] A few years later in the mock courtesy book *Have With You* Harvey is portrayed by Nashe as an uncivil conversationalist, a man 'verie seditious and mutinous in conversation, picking quarrels with everie man that will not magnifie and appauld him'. Nashe also suggests that Harvey's attachment to Ciceronian *societas* is opportunistic. He quotes from the fictional letter attributed to a university tutor who complains that Harvey 'useth everie night after supper to walke on the market hill' in Cambridge, carrying his gown high at the waist to show off his fine legs. Should any woman be naive enough to show him 'never so little an amorous regard, he presently boords them with a set speech of the first gathering together of societies, and the distinction of *amor* and *amicitia* out of *Tullies Offices*' (III. 68).

Nashe's critique is persuasive because Harvey is opportunistic. However, the kind of rhetorical games Harvey plays with his personae to 'sell' his talents do not preclude more critical reflection on social and linguistic habits. Nashe's critique is successful partly because it misrepresents the aims of *Three Proper Letters* as being only self-interested promotion, but also, too, because it depends on the opposition (still commonplace today) between self-interest and honesty. The same assumption, of course, informs Greene's estates satire *A Quip for an Upstart Courtier* which exposes the Harvey brothers as upstarts. Nashe makes no distinction between the Harvey of the 1570s and 1590s. On the contrary, he cites *Three Proper Letters* as proof of Harvey's insistent self-aggrandisement, and uses it to unmask the strategies of 'civility' he employs in the later composition, *Foure Letters*. Thus, he deliberately misreads Harvey's practice of friendship in the earlier work as well as his ironic use of personae, and ignores the important difference between the two collections. In *Foure Letters* Harvey is upbraiding two men who have shown themselves unfriendly towards him and his family, whereas *Three Proper Letters* is a civil conversation with a close friend, Spenser. Moreover, *Three Proper Letters* exemplifies the argument that good poetry is produced in conversation between intimate friends. The collection aims to demonstrate that a reformed homosociality – based on the principles of civil conversation – is essential for the growth (or civilising) of the English vernacular and the talents of young men. The work is an optimistic intervention in a cultural debate around the issues of *imitatio*, homosociality and the formation of a national literature; it aims to extend the imperfect demonstration of *amicitia* in Ascham's monologic *The Schoolmaster* and Smith's dialogues with an eye to developing a less rigid practice of classical quantification and social communication.

In *Strange Newes* Nashe mocks the 'authoritarian' Harvey, and then, to avoid the same fault, undermines his own satirical authority: 'am I subject to the sinne of Wrath I write against, or no, in whetting my penne on this blocke?' (I. 199). The quickness of his wit, the cunning with which he questions the wielding of social authority, and the dexterity of his idiomatic prose, do make Harvey look like a self-aggrandising satirist, perhaps after the confident fashion of the paternalistic Horace or Juvenal. As a result it is easy to miss Harvey's attachment to self-parody. What is so interesting about *Three Proper Letters* is the extent to which Harvey repeatedly circumscribes his academic authority. This is evident, for example, in the second letter of the collection which relates 'a prettie conceited discourse' about an eathquake that occurred while Harvey was playing cards with some 'curteous Gentlemen' in the house of a friend in Essex (sig. B1r). The letter gives Harvey the occasion to show off his doctorly learning. He is asked by the company to explain whether the cause of earthquakes is natural or divine. His conclusion, however, is that it is 'almost impossible, for any man, either by Philosophie or Divinitie, evermore to determine flatly the very certaintie either way' (sig. C3r). The same scepticism concerning academic authority occurs in the 'garden communication or dialogue' of the *Letter-book* when Mistress Katherine asks Harvey and other gentlemen to put aside their university learning and speak of love. 'We be all of us nowe scholars', she says, engaging the gentlemen in civil conversation, 'I would God you doctors would enter into sum good substantiall matter of lerninge, or sum witty schoolpoynte, that were not aboove my sonne Antonyes, and my capacity' (p. 96). Mistress Katherine may appear to be the clumsy feminine foil to the self-important scholar Harvey, but she is also a 'teacher' after the fashion of Anniball who invites us to laugh kindly at this pedant trying hard to become a civil conversationalist.

The earthquake letter has much to say about Harvey's attitude to the easy assumption of moral and spiritual authority by doctors of divinity; it is part of his project to find an alternative identity to the 'Doctor' of Smith's dialogues. In this chapter I want to consider how Harvey relinquishes the role of the schoolmaster and university man, as represented by Ascham and Smith, in discussions with Spenser about the art of poetry; he prefers to practise the complex give and take of the relaxed friendship praised by Laelius in *De amicitia* and exemplified by Scipio, a style where 'superior and inferior ... stand on an equality' so as to advance each other's gifts (16. 69). Sometimes he is the older friend and Cambridge scholar to whom Spenser appeals for advice. More often than not, though, he is the friend who refuses to teach because he is struggling with his own practice. Harvey does use the letters to advertise his learning and poetic talents. Indeed, in the 1570s he was seeking employment outside the university, and he represents himself as the natural successor to the men of government, Ascham and Smith. However, he also displays an expectation that he, too, will be overtaken, not least by the talented Spenser and his young brother John. His self-presentation is superbly ironic. In one paragraph he can disguise himself in the first person as the self-deprecating author, and also in the third person, anticipating his prospects as a man of great learning, and then negate both possibilities, while reminding the reader of their responsibility to return something – preferably payment – in exchange for inclusion in this conversation.

CIVIL CONVERSATION

Some aspects of Harvey's and Spenser's correspondence, printed in 1580, are more memorable than others. Spenser's admission that he and Harvey extemporised in quantified English verse in bed together at Westminster is naturally more engaging than his discussion in the same letter of the need to lengthen the middle syllable of the word 'Carpenter'. Unsurprisingly, this correspondence is more interesting to modern readers for the information it gives us about its most exalted contributor rather than for what it reveals about Spenser's peculiarly 'streightlaced' approach to the debate about English versifying.[14] However, as I will argue, the two interests – friendship and quantification – are closely related: Harvey and Spenser understand that the development of English poetry depends on – and enables – a reform of the master-pupil relationship, and indeed, of male friendship.[15]

Male friendship has been carefully scrutinised in recent years. Critics have focused on its careerist, networking aspects; they have also explored how Ciceronian ideas of *amicitia* were employed to disguise the pursuit of self-interest by an educated and mobile elite. Ciceronian *amicitia* did enable the pursuit of self-interest in a culture which valued service to the commonweal, but it also encouraged a re-examination of social relationships; it invited reflection on ways of negotiating between different interests. Spenser and Harvey understand this. *Three Proper Letters* is promotional writing. Its print publication coincides with that of *The Shepheardes Calender* (1579), and it appears at a time when Harvey is seeking employment outside the university.[16] However, it is also an optimistic intervention in a cultural debate around the issues of imitation, homosociality and the formation of a national literature; it aims to extend the imperfect demonstration of *amicitia* by earlier humanists with an eye to developing a less rigid practice of classical quantification and less hierarchical social communication.

The Socratic dialogue was used by mid-Tudor humanists to explore new styles of social communication, and in particular, to inculcate in companions Latin '*honestas*' or self-restraint. This type of honesty – a synonym for decorum – is acquired 'in conversation', that is, from the experience of 'taking turns' in social interaction. The wish to accommodate Latin '*honestas*' to English 'honesty' is apparent in Roger Ascham's dialogue about archery, *Toxophilus* (1545); meanwhile, Thomas Smith's attempts to reform Greek pronunciation and English spelling simultaneously advertise his special friendship with Cheke, which exemplifies the honest rivalry – the give and take – of Ciceronian *amicitia*. Whether these 'friends' ever achieved such honesty is a different matter. Ascham's dialogue *Toxophilus*, like Smith's

A commonwealth of letters: Harvey and Spenser in dialogue 123

treatises on linguistic reform, relies on a dominant 'teacherly' speaker. Honesty or decorum is a difficult concept. Indeed, it is in some sense unteachable. When Cicero tries to explain in *De officiis* how honesty is achieved in conversation he reluctantly offers some 'rules', including, don't be prescriptive, and don't prevent others from participating. Harvey and Spenser understand this pedagogic problem as an opportunity to explore the dynamic of honest rivalry in friendship so as not to lock a junior speaker into a subordinate role. The form of the familiar letter – described by both the courtesy writer Stefano Guazzo and Harvey as a natural extension of 'civil conversation' – is crucial to this intention.[17] For a letter functions as a gift; it demands a return salutation. By virtue of writing a letter, especially with a personal address, an interlocutor is engaging in a trusting, social relationship.

Mercifully, the intricate rules of classical and English quantification will not concern me here.[18] I am rather more interested in Harvey's persistent refusal to divulge its rules. Quantification is an artificial system. Even in classical Latin the quantity of a word was often a matter of a rule which had to be learned and applied rather than a product of its actual pronunciation. That select group of Elizabethan poets (Sidney, Spenser, Harvey, Ascham, Thomas Drant, Thomas Watson, Richard Stanyhurst) who experimented in the imitation of classical metre in the vernacular in the 1570s understood that the success of their project depended to some extent on establishing rules by which English sounds might be measured. For, as Derek Attridge notes, if there 'are no carefully-codified and widely-accepted rules, metre simply does not exist, except as a private game'.[19]

This need is taken up by Spenser in the letters, not the supposedly pedantic Harvey.[20] In one letter Spenser worries Harvey to 'send me the Rules and Precepts of Arte, which you observe in Quantities, or else followe mine, that *M. Philip Sidney* gave me... that we might both accorde and agree in one: leaste we overthrowe one an other, and be overthrown of the rest' (sigs. A3v–A4r). Harvey refuses to comply. He 'dare[s] geue no Preceptes, nor set downe any Certaine General Arte'. He also explains that he is writing down the precepts of his art, yet admits that he is 'not so resolute, but I can be content to reserve the Coppying out and publishing therof, until I have... some farther advize of *Madame Sperienza*' (sig. D4v). He also has little to say about Sidney's rules; he only compares Sidney's and Edward Dyer's 'livelie example, and Practise' to the 'dead Advertizement, and persuasion of *M. Ascham* to the same Effecte: whose *Scholemaister* notwithstanding I reverence in respect of so learned a Motive' (sig. D4r). *The Schoolmaster* does not offer any rules for this art, but it does give an uninspiring example of quantified verse by Thomas Watson, an author identified by Harvey in another letter as a fussy and pedantic classicist. Harvey disparagingly repeats Ascham's praise of Watson who would 'never to this day suffer his famous *Absolon* to come abrode, onely because *Anapæstus in Locis paribus* [anapest in a few places], is twice, or thrice used in steade of *Iambus*' (sig. H4v).[21] He also disagrees with Spenser's claim that his iambic trimeters are 'precisely perfect for the feete (as you can easily judge) and varie not an inch from the Rule' (sig. G4r) and criticises his use of the 'restrictive, & streightlaced terme, Precisely' (sig. H4v).

One reason for Harvey's reluctance to divulge the rules for 'Quantities' is that he is committed to the idea that the length of a syllable in verse should correspond to its actual pronunciation. Thus, he refuses to consent to Spenser's suggestion that the middle syllable of the word 'Carpenter' should be 'an inch longer or bigger than God and his English people have made him'. He also complains that Spenser, who had suggested that 'rough words must be subdued with use' (sig. A3v), 'againste all order of lawe, and in despite of custome' does 'forcibly usurp, and tyrannize uppon a quiet companye of words'. It is wilful for Spenser to prefer to say 'honēstie' rather than 'honĕstie' (sig. F2v). As Richard Helgerson has noted, the discussion of quantification in the letters is politically nuanced: Spenser compares the divining of rules for verse to the making of new laws in parliament, while Harvey invokes the language of custom and common law. For Helgerson, though, Spenser and Harvey 'almost inadvertently' discover 'an oppositional politics' to the absolutist tendencies of the classical culture they seek to imitate and make English – a form of resistance which was to be more fully expressed with the final assertion of the superiority of rhyming verse by patriotic poets in the 1590s. Harvey's accusation of tyranny, Helgerson argues, is 'a local response to a very particular provocation' and its implications are never developed; indeed, Harvey's 'arguments elsewhere contradict them'.[22] Yet, as I want to insist, there is nothing 'inadvertent' or contradictory about this accusation.

Perhaps the first thing to notice about these letters is that it is Spenser, not Harvey, who insists on following rules to write quantitative metre. This is despite the fact that Spenser was already choosing to abandon the project, as the evidence of *The Shepheardes Calender* suggests. Evidently, the dialogue is staged. The second thing to notice is the debate that is being recalled. When Harvey refuses to 'tyrannize uppon a quiet companye of words', he is recalling Richard Mulcaster's criticism of the earlier Cambridge humanists – Cheke, Smith and Ascham – who sought to restore the sovereignty of an old tyrant, 'Sound'. Cheke and Smith tried to introduce the 'correct' or classical pronunciation of Greek at Cambridge, and Smith attempted to introduce a new more 'rational' or phonetic system of English spelling. In his *Elementarie*, Mulcaster compares Smith's spelling reforms to the rule of the tyrant Tarquin, and its overthrow to the beginning of the Roman republic. Harvey is playing the role of Mulcaster's 'Custom' to Spenser's 'Reason'. This is why he refuses the role of law-maker and teacher which Spenser invites him to take up. 'I beeseeche you', Spenser begs, 'without the leaste selfe love of your own purpose, councell me for the beste: and the rather doe it faithfullye, and carefully, for that, in all things I attribute so muche to your judgement, that I am evermore content to adnihilate mine owne determinations, in respecte thereof' (sig. G3v). Harvey's refusal – a gesture of *sprezzatura* - is the means by which he and Spenser will begin to realise the potential of the vernacular to rival Latin and Greek as a literary and political language fit for the aspiring English commonwealth *if* it is allowed to develop organically, by means of relaxed conversation between friends.

Harvey and Spenser do not make it easy for us to discover this insight. This is because the letters are enacting the kind of *amicitia* which they deem integral to the creation of a flourishing national speech community. The letters are full of contradictions, as Helgerson notes. However, these contradictions are carefully placed; failing to recognise this can easily lead us astray. For example, Spenser sometimes sounds uncannily like Thomas Smith. His observation that Philip Sidney and Edward Dyer constitute an areopagus which has pronounced 'a general surceasing and silence of balde Rymers', recalls Smith's representation of the Cambridge community concerned with linguistic reform as a 'senate'. As Spenser boasts, Sidney and Dyer 'have by authoritie of their whole Senate, prescribed certaine Lawes and rules of Quantities of English sillables, for English Verse: having had thereof already greate practise, and drawen mee to their faction' (sig. G3v). To see this allusion as evidence of Spenser simply showing off his aristocratic connections is to miss its irony. The phrase 'authority of their *whole* Senate' (which rests on a membership of two or three) is meant to sound absurd. Indeed, Harvey refuses to accept its authority; he politely praises Sidney's and Dyer's practice or 'conversation', while denying the authority of self-appointed lawgivers.

I will return to Smith later (as we will see, Harvey also impersonates him). First, though, I want to explore how Harvey's careful criticism of the 'dead Advertizement, and persuasion of *M. Ascham*' in the *Schoolmaster* contributes to a critique of prescriptive rule-giving and the refashioning of a more democratic style of friendship. Even as Harvey criticises Ascham, he also claims to 'reverence' his 'learned... Motive'. It is not immediately clear, though, what motive it is that he admires. One contender is his attempt to reform English versifying, although, as I have suggested, Harvey is *not* a 'hard classicist' after the fashion of Ascham: he does not share this schoolmaster's attachment to the rigours of correct quantification. A second contender, however, is Ascham's desire to 'civilise' the educational experience, and it is this desire, I will shortly argue, that Harvey, with Spenser, is explicitly reforming.

The Schoolmaster is preoccupied with the teaching of correct Latin. For an enlightened Ascham, however, this issue cannot be separated from an enquiry into the experience of teaching and learning, and indeed, of male friendship. His treatise is openly critical of one method used for teaching Latin, rote-learning backed up by the threat of beating. It seeks to replace the brutal method of the ignorant master with a more humane technique indebted to Cicero's ideal of friendship in *De amicitia* and the conversational familiarity of *De oratore*. In the preface Ascham explains how *The Schoolmaster* grew out of two conversations prompted by the news that 'divers scholars of Eton be run away from school for fear of beating' (p. 6). The first took place at Windsor Castle in 1563 and it included members of Elizabeth I's council, among them William Cecil. Ascham claims to have been 'courteously provoked' over dinner to defend his thesis that 'young children were sooner allured by love than driven by beating to attain good learning' (p. 7). The second, more private conversation between Ascham and Sir Richard Sackville (father of Thomas Sackville) – the immediate catalyst for the writing of *The Schoolmaster* – took place after dinner. Sackville confesses to Ascham that the beating he received at the hands of his schoolmaster discouraged him from study (pp. 7–8).

The Schoolmaster opens with an attack on 'fond' or foolish schoolmasters whose poor knowledge of Latin is manifested not just in the mistakes they make, but also in their violent and coercive conduct in the schoolroom (which reflects a misunderstanding of the classical texts they teach). But Ascham also aims to change attitudes to learning; in particular, he wishes to communicate the pleasure of disciplined study. Some say, he observes, 'that children of nature love pastime and mislike learning because, in their hand, the one is easy and pleasant, the other hard and wearisome', but 'the matter lieth... in the order and manner of bringing-up by them that be old'. After all, he wisely adds, a child who is beaten by his dance-master, perhaps for missing a step, will learn to hate dancing (pp. 33–4). *The Schoolmaster* also provides practical recommendations on how to 'allure' pupils to learning.

A commonwealth of letters: Harvey and Spenser in dialogue

Much of the advice is obvious: for example, the teacher is advised not to punish a pupil for making mistakes but rather to 'monish him gently' (p. 20). But some advice is not. *The Schoolmaster* also advertises a new(ish) pedagogic method for the 'easy' learning of Latin which will enable the pupil to avoid making mistakes in the first place, 'double translation'.

It will not be immediately obvious how double translation represents an 'allurement' to learning. According to this practice derived from *De oratore*,[23] a tutor should translate 'some other part of Tully' from Latin into 'plain, natural English' and then require his pupil to translate it back to Latin again. 'Here', Ascham explains, the pupil's 'wit shall be new set on work, his judgement for right choice truly tried, his memory for sure retaining better exercised than by learning anything without the book' (p. 78). Double translation is pleasurable in the sense that it is an 'easy' – or rather precise – method to learn Latin. It is also pleasurable, though, because it provides the basis for a friendly bond between master and pupil, both of whom are led by a 'master' text. The pleasure of such translation is dramatised in a story Ascham tells about one of his readings of Cicero's *De amicitia*, shortly after leaving Cambridge, with a younger man, John Whitney, in bed at the house of Sir Anthony Denny in Chesthunt in 1548.[24] As he explains, his bed-fellow Whitney:

> willing by good nature and provoked by mine advice, began to learn the Latin tongue after the order declared in this book. We began after Christmas; I read unto him Tully *De amicitia*, which he did every day twice translate, out of Latin into English and out of English into Latin again. About St Laurence' tide after, to prove how he profited, I did choose out Torquatus' talk *de amicitia* in the latter end of the first book of *De finibus* because that place was the same in matter, like in words and phrases, nigh to the form and fashion of sentences, as he had learned before in *De amicitia*. I did translate it myself into plain English and gave it him to turn into Latin, which he did so choicely, so orderly, so without great miss in the hardest points of grammar, that some in seven year in grammar schools, yea, and some in the universities too, cannot do half so well. (pp. 80–1)

The product of this shared reading belongs to Ascham, not Whitney. Sadly, as Ascham adds, Whitney died a few days after this meeting. However, his death becomes the occasion for Ascham to display his affection and the remarkable rhetorical effects of *their* 'double translation'. Indeed, it becomes clear that double translation is a homosocial as well as a linguistic exercise. It is as if the attempt to embrace an original stylist is comparable to the affectionate relationship between a schoolmaster and his pupil, such as that between Ascham and Whitney. Or, that in double translating *De amicitia* these two friends came to embody the essence of its ideal. As Ascham offers:

though I had never poetical head to make verse in any tongue, yet either love, or sorrow, or both, did wring out of me then certain careful thoughts of my good will toward him which, in my mourning for him, fell forth more by chance than either by skill or use into this kind of misorderly meter:
> Mine own John Whitney, now farewell, now death doth part us twain;
> No death, but parting for a while, whom life shall join again etc. (p. 81)

Double translation, in both senses, enables Ascham to produce spontaneously – or so he claims – an elegy of fourteeners for Whitney in 'natural, plain English'.

Ascham's story of his friendship with Whitney is perhaps the moment where he best captures the notion of 'double translation' as a linguistic exercise and an affectionate and pleasant manner between master and pupil. Key to this relationship between master, pupil and text is the schoolmaster's admission that he is not an authority and is liable to error. Hence the importance attached in *The Schoolmaster* to the repeated return to the original and authoritative master-text, Cicero's *De oratore* (which replaces the schoolmaster as 'corrector'). However, Ascham's levelling of the relationship between master and pupil is undercut by his creation of Cicero – and his mouthpiece Crassus – as absolute authorities. Ascham views *De oratore*, not as a conversation between Crassus and Antonius, but as a text dominated by Crassus, and he thus fails to understand Cicero's 'joke' at the heart of *De oratore*, that Antonius is most artful or most teacherly when he refuses to teach his art, choosing instead to disseminate his oratorical practice by engaging in conversation.[25] This misreading determines the style of *The Schoolmaster*.

Although *The Schoolmaster* grows out of two conversations, the text itself (Ascham's 'poor schoolhouse' (p. 9)) is monologic, and its tone is schoolmasterly. Ascham promises not to 'contemn' but 'gladly teach rules, and teach them more plainly, sensibly, and orderly than they be commonly taught in common schools' (pp. 15–16), choosing to be a plain-speaking counsellor to impressionable young children (and their parents) because he is wary of the vagaries of conversation. On the one hand, he is aware that errors are more likely to creep into spoken rather than written Latin (pp. 16–17). On the other hand, he is fearful of the anarchic tendencies of unregulated speech, illustrated by the example of Catholic Italy. In the infamous Italophobic conclusion to book 1, Ascham complains that Italians inhabit 'some free city, as all cities be there, where a man may freely discourse against what he will, against whom he lust' (p. 74). He does praise one Italian text, the *Courtier*, for joining 'learning with comely exercises' (p. 55). However, he does not recognise its conversational form, and thus fails (or refuses) to recognise Castiglione's argument in the *Courtier* that it is the easy way and the delightful manner – represented in relaxed and light conversation – which encourages honest conduct. He misunderstands the educative effects of the 'honest pleasure' of 'flickeringe provocations' (p. 300).

Ascham's attempt to introduce into England the pedagogic style of Cicero is compromised further by the fact that halfway through the first book he moves from defending the need to allure young children to learning to insisting on the need to discipline young men. 'I wished before to have love of learning bred up in children', he writes midway into book 1, 'I wish as much now to have young men brought up in good order of living and in some more severe discipline than commonly they be'. Among the 'old noble Persions', Ascham notes, 'a young gentleman was never free to go where he would and do what he list himself, but under the keep and by the counsel of some grave governor, until he was either married or called to bear some office in the commonwealth' (p. 38). No son, he continues, should be allowed to marry without his parents' consent. He also discourages parents from sending their boys to the continent, especially to Italy where they might be easily seduced to practise Catholicism. He pours scorn on the English translation of bawdy Italian prose fictions and praise on those 'honest citizens of London' who 'watch at every gate to take misordered persons in apparel' (p. 58). '[L]et the prince', he advises, 'proclaim, make laws, order, punish, command every gate in London daily to be watched' to prevent the entry of those young gentlemen given to wearing effeminate fashions (pp. 57–8).[26]

Ascham may praise Castiglione for joining 'learning with comely exercises'; he may also advise that lessons are to be followed with dancing and other entertainments, but, in contrast to Castiglione, he does not see such exercises as integral to the process of education. On the contrary, *The Schoolmaster* redefines the nature of pleasure and pleasant exchange to include that which is irksome. In book 2 Ascham remembers with affection the 'pleasant talks' he had with Thomas Watson and John Cheke at St John's College. Yet, these enjoyable conversations were about dry, scholarly matters. In one of these recalled conversations the friends are 'comparing the precepts of Aristotle and Horace *De arte poetica* with examples of Euripides, Sophocles, and Seneca' shortly after Watson completed his 'excellent tragedy' *Absalom* (p. 139); in another, they are discussing how Virgil and Horace would have 'brought poetry to perfectness also in the Latin tongue' if they had followed the example of the Greeks properly (p. 145). This revised conception of pleasure informs Ascham's literary values. 'True art' for Ascham, notes

Attridge, 'requires the sustained effort of self-education, and the resultant familiarity with the work of the best practitioners, and with the minutiae of the rules'. Quantification is admired because it is difficult and artificial; meanwhile, Watson's practice of quantification is praised because it shows the strains of educational labour: to 'this day [he] would never suffer yet his *Absalom* to go abroad, and that only because *in locis paribus anapaestus* is twice or thrice used instead of *iambus*' (sig. H4v). In contrast, accentual verse is 'despised because it is the product of some natural instinct, not subject to the ordering and shaping of the higher qualities',[27] in short, because it is too close to everyday, conversational English.

The Schoolmaster is an important source for *Three Proper Letters*. Like Ascham, Harvey and Spenser share with each other (and the reader) information about new experiments in quantification and 'pleasant talks' between budding poets. The intimacy of Ascham's relationship with John Whitney is also captured in the description of Spenser and Harvey reading poems to one another in bed at Westminster. However, their decision to record their quantitative experiments in a series of familiar letters offers a 'livelie example' of a different kind of friendship which is contrasted with Ascham's 'dead Advertizement'. They are friendly conversationalists. They get the joke at the heart of *De oratore* and adapt it for their own purposes, first, to show how English is sufficient of itself to rival Latin and Greek, and secondly, to show how this development depends on a relaxed homosociality. Conversation allows for the exchange of technique and examples in an ordinary and familiar idiom, with the effect that these poets give up trying to apply strictly the rules borrowed from Latin or Greek, and work towards discovering the rules of English versification. This argument is made in the third of *Three Proper Letters*, Harvey's 'A Gallant Familiar Letter', which I will explore below. In this letter, Harvey's refusal to teach Spenser the rules of his art reinforces his argument that the quantities of English words should be based on their customary pronunciation: it is clearly inelegant to extend the middle syllable of 'Carpenter' just to make it fit someone's rules. This relaxed approach is meant to produce natural quantified verse in English. 'I dare geve no Precepts, nor set downe any Certaine General Arte', Harvey explains, adding that he is 'not greatly squaimishe of my *Particular Examples*'. '[H]e that can but reasonably skil of the one, wil give easily a shreude gesse at the other: considering that the one fetcheth his original and offspring from the other'. We should follow the example of Homer in Greek, and Ennius in Latin, whose practice established the quantity of specific words (sigs. D4v–E1r), and thus, the process by which versification developed in Greek and Latin, rather than apply rules natural only to those languages.

Harvey's own examples of metrical verse are as ungainly as those of Watson so it is odd that he should complain of the 'dead Advertizement' of Ascham when he seems to be unable to do little better himself. Ascham's 'dead Advertizement', however, is embodied not just in his citation of Watson's uninspiring experiments, but also in the example of the short-lived Whitney, whose potential is never fulfilled. Harvey exemplifies an alternative method of double translation to that of *The Schoolmaster* which is based on a conversation between master and pupil in English. In the same letter he describes his tutoring of his young brother John in a 'peece of hollydayes exercise'. John is asked to translate a 'Theame out of Ovid' and to 'varie it after his best fashion'. He first offers a paraphrase in four lines of hexameter, then four lines of pentameter, and finally a longer poem in hexameter. After offering an English translation in hexameters of the Italian gloss to Spenser's *October* eclogue in *The Shepheardes Calender*, John is asked to show what he 'can doo in [his] owne Tongue'. Harvey reaches for that 'certaine famous Booke, called the newe *Shephardes Calender*', and invites John to rearrange the two English emblems at the end of the *March* eclogue. John completes this exercise in less than an hour: he refashions each of Spenser's emblems into tetrameter, and then combines them to create two lines of dactylic hexameter.

> Love is a | thing more | fell, than | full of | Gaule, than of | Honny,
> And to be | wize, and | Love, is a | worke for a | God, or a | Goddes peere
> (sigs. E3r–E4r)

In contrast to Whitney, John Harvey transforms English rhyme into metre (his achievements are published in the letter to prove this), and in so doing he experiences the flexibility of his native tongue. In contrast to the nostalgic *Schoolmaster* which dwells mournfully on lost geniuses – Whitney, Lady Jane Grey, Sackville (all three of whom died prematurely) – the *Letters* anticipate the achievements of the next generation: John Harvey and Spenser. Harvey is not seeking to remember the dead, but rather to nurture an ability possessed equally by tutor and pupil alike.

How seriously we should take Harvey's wish to cultivate the potential of a friend 'in conversation' is a different matter. If we give ear to Nashe, who complained that Harvey was boastful and self-regarding, then it is difficult to see how he might be capable of cultivating the potential of anyone. Part of the problem lies with the genre of the familiar letter itself. We can understand why Harvey and Spenser chose this ostensibly intimate form to show how friends in conversation might enhance each other's gifts, but intimacy does not carry over well into print. There is good reason to be sceptical about the use of the printed familiar letter. Lisa Jardine has shown us in *Erasmus: Man of Letters* how the early sixteenth-century scholars Erasmus and Thomas More used the familiar letter and the new technology of print to promote the career of their longstanding friend Juan Luis Vives, who was then teaching at Louvain without any formal qualifications. In one letter More pretends not to know Vives, giving Erasmus the opportunity 'to build a pedigree in print citations as a substitute for diplomas and degrees'.[28] *Three Proper Letters* is working towards the same end; Harvey is eager to be seen as a successor to Ascham (and Smith). However, in contrast to Ascham, Harvey expresses his ambition in a conversation which reveals that he expects to be outperformed.

This shifting role is nowhere more apparent than in the episode in this letter where Harvey tries to advise – and not advise – Spenser of his literary tastes so as to encourage him to rival 'all the most delicate, and fine conceited Grecians & Italians' (sig. F1r). Harvey expresses his preference for Spenser's Apollonian *Nine Muses* (*The Teares of the Muses*) to his 'Hobgoblin' *Faerie Queene*; however, he simultaneously urges him to 'emulate' and 'overgo' Ariosto's great Italian romance *Orlando Furioso* (a source for the *Faerie Queene*) because he recognises that 'nations advaunce themselves' with such works to the 'great admiration, and wonderment of the whole countrey'. The discussion ends with a statement that withdraws Harvey's advice, while also hinting once again at his preference for neoclassical verses: 'I wil not stand greatly with you in your owne matters. If so be the Faerye Queene be fairer in your eie than the Nine Muses, and Hobgoblin runne away with the Garland from Apollo: *Marke what I saye, and yet I will not say that I thought*, but there an End for this once, and fare you well, till God or some good Aungell [Gabriel?] putte you in a better minde' (sig. F1v; my italics).

This style of conversation informs Harvey's rivalrous relationship with one other Cambridge humanist, Thomas Smith, as well as the legal idiom of the letters. In these letters, Helgerson notes, Spenser sounds like a civil lawyer; he compares the divining of rules for verse to the making of new laws in parliament. Harvey, in contrast, appeals to the principles of consensus and custom which characterise the common law. Sometimes, however, the roles are reversed. Harvey also hints at his wish to study civil law. In one letter, he claims to be employed 'in our Emperor Justinians service' (sig. E3r); meanwhile his *Letter-book* includes a letter addressed to Smith in which he asks for advice on a career in civil law (in fact, Harvey took a doctorate in civil law from Oxford in 1585). In his 'Gallant' letter, moreover, it sometimes seems as if Harvey wants to take over Smith's linguistic role as 'law-giver'. Early in the letter, he mentions Smith's Socratic *De Recta et Emendata Linguae Anglicae Scriptione, Dialogus* (1568), with the intention, apparently, of highlighting his greater talents. Uneasy with Spenser's request for rules, Harvey advises that he should 'take this for a general Caveat, and say I have revealed one great mysterie unto you':

I am of Opinion, there is no one more regular and justifiable direction, eyther for the assured, and infalliable Certaintie of our English Artificiall Prosodye particularly, or generally to bring our Language into Arte, and to frame a Grammer or Rhetorike thereof: than first of all universally to agree upon one and the same *Ortographie*, in all pointes conformable and proportionate to our *Common Natural Prosodye*: whether *Sir Thomas Smithes* in that respect be the most perfit, as surely it must needes be very good: or else some other of profounder Learning, & longer Experience, than *Sir Thomas* was, shewing by necessarie demonstration, wherin he is defective, wil undertake shortely to supplie his wantes, and make him more absolute. (sig. D4v)

This advice seems typical of Harvey. We can readily imagine what Nashe might have to say in response! The writer 'of profounder Learning, & longer Experience' than Smith whom Harvey imagines 'shewing by necessarie demonstration' how to 'bring our Language into Arte' is obviously Harvey himself. Harvey cleverly anticipates such identification by denying it: 'My selfe dare not hope to hoppe after him' until 'I see something or other, too, or fro, publickely and autentickly established, as it were by a generall Counsel, or acte of Parliament: and then peradventure, standing uppon firme grounde, for Companie sake, I may adventure to do as other do' (sig. D4v).

Have we finally caught Harvey out? His allusion to an 'acte of Parliament' prescribing correct orthography for English is in fact deeply ironic. He disguises himself under two cloaks: in the third person, as the writer 'of profounder Learning, & longer Experience' than Smith, and in the first person, as the self-deprecating author ('My selfe dare not to hope to hoppe after him') who awaits an 'acte of Parliament'. In fact, Harvey is awaiting no such 'generall Counsel'. '*Interim*, credit me, I dare geve no Preceptes, nor set downe any *Certain General Arte*', Harvey offers, before suggesting that we learn from the example of the Greeks and Romans for whom the art of versification was developed by practise (sigs. D4v–E1r). Thus, no 'acte of Parliament' is required because, as his examples show, he is already engaged in the process of reforming English orthography and prosody with his friend. He is 'not greatly squaimishe of [his] *Particular Examples*' since 'he that can reasonably skil of the one, wil give easily a shreude gesse at the other [the rule]: considering that the one fetcheth his original and offspring from the other' (sig. D4v). Linguistic improvements must carry broad consensus. They cannot be made 'autocratically' after the fashion of, say, Thomas Watson who forces English to fit a borrowed model, failing to understand the social forces which produced classical quantification. Similarly, Harvey hints that doctors of learning (like Smith) must take a back seat. Much as Gardiner argued in 1542, and Mulcaster in the 1570s and 1580s, a senate of self-appointed scholars does not carry the authority to reform English.

This gentle rivalry is apparent also in his private letter to Smith, recorded in the *Letter-book*, in which he asks for advice on a career in civil law. On the one hand, Harvey adopts a tone of deference when addressing Smith, inviting Smith to play the role of 'Crassus' (the senior interlocutor of *De oratore* and a practising lawyer). But the letter also expresses Harvey's understanding of the debate structure of *De oratore* (Crassus's arguments, he notes, are confuted by Antonius) and his concern that any effort expended in the study of civil law may be wasted; as he argues, the common law is our civil law.[29]

The implicit suggestion in *Three Proper Letters*, that Harvey is exceeding his mentor Smith, sounds uncomfortably self-congratulatory. However, there is no reason why Smith should have been bothered by the comments in *Three Proper Letters*. For Harvey adopts Smith's own commitment to the 'progressiveness' of the learning process. In the case of *Three Proper Letters* the point is that it is natural for a pupil to exceed his master, just as Harvey is exceeding the much respected Ascham and Smith, or as John and Spenser are exceeding Harvey. (He accepts Spenser's lighthearted warning, 'beware, leaste in time I overtake you' (sig. G4v).) This idea of progression is developed from Smith who plays Cicero to a young 'Quintus' in order to discover the antiquity of the Anglo-Saxon alphabet while recognising how it can be improved. 'You see all the arts brought to perfection gradually and by intervals of time and ages.'[30] Only in *Three Proper Letters* there is no Socratic 'Smith', no Cicero sound-alike. I have suggested so far that it is Harvey who is playing the role of the 'schoolmaster', even as he declines to offer the rules of his art. But of course the *sprezzatura* is Spenser's ('councell me for the beste for that in all things I attribute so muche to your judgement') and it serves to draw out Harvey who is ambiguously placed in the role of the junior disputant. This is reinforced when Harvey uses Spenser's native pastoral rhymes as a model for his brother's experimentation with classical verse forms.

A commonwealth of letters: Harvey and Spenser in dialogue

It is difficult to reconstruct the social and political significance of a debate about the length of syllables. However, we need to recognise with Harvey that how you set about reforming and improving a language will affect ultimately how a speech community or nation is organised and governed. Several critics, including Helgerson, have established that the linguistic reforms proposed by sixteenth-century humanists serve to produce a top-down model of social interaction in the 'King's' or 'Queen's' English.[31] But it is important to remember that such reforms did not go uncontested. Harvey and Spenser, for example, question the narrow authority of the senate proposed by Smith and others. With Mulcaster they champion the authority of a broader linguistic community. This desire is evident in their choice of print publication; Smith, in contrast, first circulated his work in manuscript.

This commitment, however, does not entail a simple restatement of the commonwealth maxim that 'we are not born for ourselves'. Rather, the letters dramatise a sensitivity to the interplay between self-interest and social duty. It is to the advantage of scholars to engage in civil conversation, Harvey advises. In the manuscript *Letter-book*, where many of the ideas for *Three Proper Letters* are first aired, he takes the scholar to the common fair. However, rather than using his humanistic learning to manage commercial exchange (as Smith attempts to in his *Discourse*), he wonders what price it will fetch.[32] Harvey does worry that the circulation of his poems in the market will discredit him. In one letter he berates Spenser for publishing his experimental verse. 'What greater and more odious infamye for on of my standinge in the Universitye and profession abroade,' he complains, 'then to be reckonid in the Beaderoule of Inglish Rimers, esspecially beinge occupied in so base an objecte and handelinge a theame of so slender and small importance?' (p. 60). But another attitude to the market is hinted at in an earlier section of this letter:

And nowe forsoothe, as a mighty peece of worke not of mine own voluntarile election, which might have chosen a thousand matters both more agreable to my person and more acceptable to others, but muste needs in all haste no remedye be sett to sale in Bartholomewe and Stirbridge fayer, with what lack ye Gentlemen? I pray you will you see any freshe newe bookes? Looke, I beseeche you, for your loove and buie for your moonye. Let me borrowe on crackd groate of your purse for this same span new pamflett. I wisse he is an University man that made it, and yea highly mendid unto me for a greate scholler. I marry, good syr, as you saye, so it shoulde appeare in deede by his greate worke: by my faye he hath taken verye soare paynes, beshrowe my hart else. What? Will iiid fetch it? (pp. 59–60)

Even as Harvey complains about his writings being sold in Stourbridge fair (a fair famous for book-selling), he also reveals his curiosity about their value: 'What? Will iiid fetche it?' he asks, before inviting Spenser to purchase this brand new (or 'new span') pamphlet.[33] Harvey worries about being discredited as an academic by selling his 'goodly wares' in the market, but he also relishes the idea of being credited in other ways. His irony is at work again; it enables him to argue that authors can credibly sell their wares in the market, while acknowledging the discreditable connotations of hack-writing. Harvey is also using the idea of the market to explore the nature of obligation in literary and social exchange. The letter rehearses Harvey's worries about the value of his writings; it also repeatedly asks the reader to consider 'who is obliged to whom'. It depicts these friends as engaging in a dynamic relationship. For instance, the beardless Harvey jokingly advises Spenser to make amends for selling his poetry by sharing some of his facial hair (p. 61). The serious point underlying the joke is that Spenser is obliged to make amends. However, the recipient of the debt keeps changing. Spenser is indebted to Harvey because he needs to make amends for this faux pas but Harvey is also indebted to Spenser for publishing abroad his poems.

These interests are carried over to *Three Proper Letters* where Harvey's friendly exchange with Spenser is described in monetary terms which anticipate a financial return on the publication.[34] These letters carry no aristocratic dedication; indeed, in one letter Spenser reflects on the dangers of the misplaced dedication when he recalls Sidney's displeasure at Stephen Gosson's dedication to him of the anti-theatrical *Schoole of Abuse* (sig. G3v). As I want to suggest, there is an attempt in these letters to create a more dynamic and level relationship with potential patrons (like Sidney), who are invited to regard contributions to the formation of a national literature as being in their interest.

In the letters Harvey claims not to be able to 'recompense' Spenser's 'long, large, Luxurious, Laxative Letters' from his own meagre store (sig. H3r); he promises that he will be better able to 'requite [his] lavishe, and magnificent liberalitie' after a visit to Italy (sig. I1r). Harvey also describes the letters as a shop window, implying that the poems are on display to passing customers ('But seeing I must needes bewray my store, and set open my shoppe wyndowes' (sig. E2r)). Harvey values literary endeavour as a craft rather than a genteel activity for leisured men: poets are akin to the profit-seeking artisans of *Toxophilus*. Quantification is both an art or *techne* and a service to the commonweal, and it requires financial support. To this end

A commonwealth of letters: Harvey and Spenser in dialogue

Harvey reworks Ascham's emphasis on the paradoxical pleasure of labour in *The Schoolmaster*, albeit to the different end of reminding the reader of a necessary, material contribution to this 'conversation'. Like *The Schoolmaster* these letters convey both the ease and difficulty with which English rhymes can be turned into classical verse forms. Thus, Harvey describes how a youth like John can complete these transformations as a 'peece of hollydayes exercise' by following the example of an English poet whom he holds high 'in the Catalogue of our very principall Englishe *Aristarchi*', Spenser (sig. E4r). Elsewhere he suggests the spontaneity of his poetic composition (sigs. E1v–E2r).

However, at other times he admits that versification is a laborious and unrewarding process. After mentioning a composition by his brother which is not yet ready for public viewing, Harvey abruptly proceeds to discourage both John and Spenser from further experimentation: 'I have little joy to animate, & encourage either you, or him to goe forward, unlesse ye mighte make account of some certaine ordinarie wages, at at [sic] the leastwise have your meate, and drinke for your dayes workes.' His advice comes from personal experience. 'As for my selfe', he explains, 'howsoever I have toyed, and trifled heretofore, I am nowe taught ... to employ my travayle, and tyme wholly, or chiefely on those studies and practizes, that carrie as they say meate in their mouth, having evermore their eye upon the Title *De pane lucrando* [earning a living], and their hand upon their halfpenny' (sig. E4v). This complaint reminds us of the emphasis elsewhere in *Three Proper Letters* on the arduous process of revising and rewriting poetry.[35] Harvey concludes this complaint by quoting two stanzas from the *October* eclogue in *The Shepheardes Calender*:

> Piers, I have piped erst so long with payne,
> That all myne Oten reedes been rent, and wore,
> And my poore Muse hath spent hir spared store,
> Yet little good hath got, and much lesse gayne.
> Such pleasaunce makes the Grashopper so poore,
> And ligge so layde, when winter doth her strayne.
>
> The Dapper Ditties, that I woont devize,
> To feede youthes fancie, and the flocking fry,
> Delighten much: what I the bett for thy?
> They han the pleasure, I a sclender prize.
> I beate the bushe, the birdes to them doe flye,
> What good thereof to Cuddy can arise?
>
> (sig. E4v)

Like Smith in the *Discourse of the Commonweal of This Realm of England* Harvey wants to encourage the manufacture of the nation's raw materials; he wants readers to buy English products. This time, however, the product is poetry, and its process of manufacture defends a vision of a national community engaged in various conversations.

Three Proper Letters demonstrate formally how the development of a flourishing English poetry which can rival continental achievements depends on a reconception of social relationships. They dramatise a style of rivalrous and conflictual *amicitia* that nurtures the talents of friends. This style is quite different to the friendship portrayed in the pages of Smith and Ascham, who assume that it is the role of the schoolmaster and university 'Doctor' to maintain social order. In contrast, Harvey and Spenser demonstrate how rivalry with a friend can serve to advance the interests and gifts of each (this perhaps partly explains the mistake Harvey made with Nashe in *Foure Letters*). Thus, even though Harvey claims to prefer Spenser's *Nine Muses* to his 'Hobgoblin' *Fairy Queene*, he does him no disservice in so saying. On the contrary, his criticism is coupled with the recognition that the genre of romance serves the national interest and, also, promotion of *The Fairy Queene* itself. The dispute about the virtues of neoclassical versus native poetic forms is open-ended. Indeed, it is carried over to *The Shepheardes Calender*. This pastoral compendium, which self-consciously appropriates an archaic native idiom and rhyme schemes, is an instance of Spenser playfully refusing to take the advice of his friend. It makes gentle mockery of his seemingly honest admission to Harvey that 'I am, of late, more in love wyth my Englishe Versifying, than with Ryming: whyche I should have done long since, if I would the[n] have followed your councell' (sig. G4r). In so doing, though, Spenser takes the argument of *Three Proper Letters* one step further, countering the objection often raised in mid-Tudor writing that an aspirational *amicitia* threatens social unity. It does so by reforming the gift economy of native English pastoral and estates satire.

CHAPTER 6

A new poet, a new social economy: homosociality in The Shepheardes Calender

Spenser's *The Shepheardes Calender* makes an unusual contribution to the Elizabethan friendship *topos* by privileging the productive potential of male *amicitia* over heterosexual *amor*. This pastoral dramatises a love triangle: Colin loves Rosalind, but she doesn't love him; Hobbinol loves Colin, but Colin doesn't love him anymore. Yet, by the end of its calendric cycle, Hobbinol's love has proven to be enduring and fruitful; he acts as a scribe for Colin's love-stricken outpourings, helping to produce the record of his talent that is the *Calender*. That is to say, the *Calender* tells a double story of triumph and defeat. The text articulates worries about the talents of its 'new Poete'.[1] Will his potential be developed and realised, or will it remain uncultivated? Its final eclogue *December* records the tragic error of Colin's career: his fruitless chasing after the disdainful Rosalind which has left his gift unnurtured ('My boughes with bloosmes that crowned were at firste, / And promised of timely fruite such store, / Are left both bare and barrein now at erst' (lines 103–5)). However, its final two lines also recognise the good faith of Hobbinol: 'Adieu good *Hobbinol*, that was so true, / Tell *Rosalind*, her *Colin* bids her adieu' (lines. 155–6), and the reader is left in possession of the fruits of Colin's gift, the physical book called *The Shepheardes Calender*. It is this second story of discovered talent that I will explore in this chapter. As I will argue, the *Calender* imagines a model of friendship and collaboration which allows desire and aspiration to be expressed and pursued to the advantage of individual poets and the commonwealth.

The *Calender* is not usually recognised as a text about friendship. This is partly because twentieth-century criticism has understood pastoral as abandoning 'the strife of civil and social living and the ordeal of human fellowship for a solitary existence, in communion with nature and with the company of one's own musings and thoughts'.[2] The *Calender* indeed advertises itself as the debut of an independent, fledgling author. However, it is also a self-consciously dependent piece of writing. It is hedged about with alternative voices to those of its supposed author 'Immerito' (Spenser's persona), and it is organised as a series of eclogues or conversations between a variety of characters, not just Colin (Immerito's persona) and Hobbinol, but also Cuddie, Thenot, Thomalin, Piers, Palinode, Willie, Perigot and Diggon Davies. In addition, it is constructed as a dialogue between the poet Immerito and a commentator, the infamous E.K.. Author and commentator treat the text as their own. Immerito dedicates his eclogues to Philip Sidney, 'the president/Of noblesse and of chevalree' (lines 3–4), while E.K. dedicates the text with his commentary to Gabriel Harvey. More confusingly still, E.K. identifies a number of acquaintances who exist outside the text, including Thomas Smith, George Gascoigne and Harvey. There is overlap between fictive and real friendships: Colin and Hobbinol are Spenser and Harvey respectively, while the gloss of E.K. may have been written with Harvey in mind (or, indeed, even with Harvey).[3] Spenser seems to want his readers to recognise the *Calender* as a collaborative venture.

This hint of collaboration in the *Calender* may not have inspired many critics, but it was recognised by contemporaries. As Michelle O'Callaghan notes, the *Calender* provided the Jacobean Spenserians with a 'model for a print community' in which 'meaning is produced collectively'. In the early 1700s the Spenserians created their own print community with the publication of two co-authored pastoral anthologies, *The Shepheards Pipe* (1614) and *The Shepheardes Hunting* (1615). Both pastorals construct an 'oppositional community' of like-minded individuals who are grounded in the social environment of the Inns of Court and the Fleet Street taverns.[4] However, the community hinted at in the *Calender* is rather different. Its location is likely to have been rooms at the Cambridge colleges, various households – for example, Thomas Smith's house Hill Hall, and possibly also Leicester House – as well as London lodgings, not the Inns of Court.[5] Indeed, as I will argue, Spenser's pastoral is contesting an ideal of male friendship developed at the Inns in the 1560s which, despite its apparent neoclassicism, reproduces the values of mid-Tudor reformers such as Crowley and Latimer: in particular, the emphasis on the virtue of altruism for the preservation of the social order. Perhaps the most exemplary instance of this ideal is offered by Richard Edwards in his Inns of Court drama, *Damon and Pythias*. This play, which is inspired by Cicero's *De amicitia*, discovers self-abnegation as the virtue which creates honest friendships. The same virtue is valued in the pastoral anthologies of two other Inns of Court writers with whom Spenser is engaging in the *Calender*, Barnabe Googe and George Turbeville.

The *Calender* is in conversation with earlier pastorals, among them Virgil's eclogues, the *Adolescentia* (1486) of Baptista Spagnuoli or 'Mantuan', and Clémont Marot's eclogues (1531). However, it is also in conversation with the native experiments in pastoral and estates satire of the Reformation poets, Googe and Turbeville. We have already seen, in chapter 4, how Robert Crowley employs estates satire and georgic to attack the selfishness of his contemporaries, who are compromising the project of the Reformation. Pastoral was similarly co-opted. Mantuan, identified as a Reformation prophet, was translated by Alexander Barclay in the 1520s and by Turbeville in 1567. In the early 1560s Turbeville's friend Googe adapted estates satire and the satirical style of Mantuan's *Adolescentia* in his *Eglogs, Epytaphes, and Sonettes* (1563) to attack upstarts who threaten the social order as well as the Marian persecutors of the bishops Ridley, Cranmer and Latimer. Despite his classical education, Googe (like Edwards) reproduces the hierarchical values of medieval estates satire in his *Eglogs*. Its eclogues usually dramatise a dialogue in which a senior speaker advises a junior companion to curb his desires. Meanwhile, the collective contributions to the preface serve to remind the reader of their duty not to disdain his work. There is no ambiguity about where authority lies in this pastoral. The same curtailment of aspiration is performed in Turbeville's translation of Mantuan. In his preface he fashions the poet as an exemplary individual who serves the commonweal; he also introduces the reader to a 'classical' (Horatian) conception of decorum, which insists that style should suit the status of its speaker.[6] Turbeville illustrates another side to this theory, that the low style is also suitable for ungifted – or modest – gentlemen-poets. His translation, he confesses, was completed 'basely and with barren pen' (sig. A3v); he also reminds us that he is not seeking reward, but aiming only to win our good will so as 'to avoyd scotte free from slaunderous snare' (sig. A4v).

The *Calender* is quite different. Immerito confidently flaunts his unworthiness because he knows that therein lie the seeds of future greatness. He also demonstrates a bold new argument: that the expression of disdain and disagreement can strengthen as well as threaten a community. Its characters are outspoken, critical and demanding; indeed, their conversations thrive on debate. They are free to refuse the stifling closeness of a friendship, as well as both good and bad advice. *Februarie*, for example, dramatises a generational conflict between the ancient Thenot and a disrespectful 'younker', Cuddie. When it becomes clear that Cuddie's disregard for his older companion cannot be tempered, Thenot tells a fable about how a cheeky Briar learned to regret the destruction of an ancient Oak which had offered him shelter from the winter cold. In Googe's *Eglogs* disputes are resolved when the sensible advice of a senior speaker is accepted; in *Februarie*, in contrast, the moral of Thenot's fable is briskly rejected by Cuddie. The difficulty the reader finds in locating an authoritative view in this eclogue is compounded by the contribution of E.K. Initially, this commentator seems to side with Thenot. In one gloss he notes that Thenot's fable 'is very excellente for pleasaunt descriptions, being altogether a certaine Icon or Hypotyposis of disdainfull younkers' (like Cuddie presumably) (102, gloss). Like Thenot, E.K. displays his wisdom; like Thenot, too, he takes upon himself the role of corrector (92, gloss). Yet, at the end of the eclogue he unexpectedly sides with Cuddie, concluding (in his commentary on its emblem) that it 'is to playne, to be gainsayd, that olde men are muche more enclined to such fond fooleries, then younger heades'. E.K. is a notoriously unreliable commentator, but not unhelpfully so.[7] His often confusing commentary shapes our approach to the *Calender*. We will discover that meaning is produced collaboratively. We will also discover that no rejection of any speaker – I include here both E.K. and Hobbinol – is ever completed; it is more often a necessary checking of a sometimes misleading, sometimes useful corrector. Spenser is writing a pastoral in English that accommodates Ciceronian *amicitia* in a way that Edwards, Googe and Turbeville do not; that is, he produces a pastoral in which friendly rivalry is productive rather than threatening.

One reason for this difference is the friendship Spenser shares with Harvey. As we saw in chapter 5, Spenser and Harvey develop the kind of rivalry or 'comparison' valued by the 'Athenian tribe' in the 1540s. For example, their friendship accommodates differences of view: Harvey favoured quantification, while Spenser, as the evidence of the *Calender* suggests, came to favour native metres. It also accommodates critical engagement. Harvey may have generously circulated his books, signing many of them '*gabrielis harveij, et amicorum*' (belonging to Gabriel Harvey and friends), but he was also willing to criticise friends in their margins. In his heavily annotated copy of *The Poesies of George Gascoigne Esquire* (1575), for example, Harvey reflects on the strengths and weaknesses of this acquaintance thus:

Want of resolution & constancy, marred his witt & undid himself.
Sum vanity: & more levity: his special faulte, & the continual causes of his misfortunes. Many other have maintained themselves gallantly upon sum one of his qualities: nothing fadgeth with him, for want of Resolution, & Constancy in any one kind. He shall never thrive with any thing, than can brooke no crosses, or hath not learned to make the best of the worst, in his Profession.[8]

This kind of critical engagement is also typical of Harvey's friendship with Spenser, whom he both respects greatly and finds wanting. Alongside a list of archaisms approved by Gascoigne in *Certayne Notes* he notes: 'All theise in Spenser, & manie like: but with discretion: & tolerably, thowgh sumtime not greatly commendably.'[9] More publicly, he takes advantage of 'unspotted friendship' in *Foure Letters and Certeine Sonnets* (1592) to criticise Spenser for writing too satirically in *Mother Hubberds Tale* (sig. B1r). For Harvey, such rivalry is the foundation of a thriving and prosperous commonwealth.

The *Calender* incorporates Harvey's style of encouragement and criticism in the complex give and take of its different dialogues. Many of the tensions between the fictional Immerito and E.K. or Colin and Hobbinol resemble those dramatised as part of Harvey's and Spenser's friendship. We will probably never know for certain if Harvey really did co-script the role of E.K., but we are encouraged to speculate about this possibility. For there is something of the donnish Harvey in this character. Harvey's willingness to adopt fictional personae (as we saw in chapter 5) makes it possible that he was good-humoured enough to be the model for this sometimes helpful, sometimes irritating commentator. However, E.K. does not just sound like a character Harvey might have been willing to play. Occasionally, he sounds *like* Harvey. E.K., for example, shares Harvey's idiomatic usage of the word 'younker' – which could mean either child or fashionable gentleman – in *Three Proper Letters*, where it is applied to Spenser. Moreover, Harvey's dismissal of alliteration in *Three Proper Letters* – 'your gentle Masterships, long, large, lavish, Luxurious, Laxative Letters withal, (now a Gods name, when did I ever in my life, hunt the Letter before?)' (sig. H3r) – reappears in the prefatory epistle: 'I scorne and spue out the rakehellye route of our ragged rymers (for so themselves use to hunt the letter)' (lines. 127–9). Harvey's style of critical commentary is also recalled in a gloss in the elegaic *November*. E.K. glosses the name Philomele thus: 'the Nightingale. whome the Poetes faine once to have bene a Ladye of great beauty' who is raped by her brother-in-law, and then adds some thoughts on one recently deceased author who has 'set forth' Philomele's 'complaintes':

Ma. George Gaskin a wittie gentleman, and the very chefe of our late rymers, who and if some partes of learning wanted not (albee it is well knowen he altogyther wanted not learning) no doubt would have attayned to the excellencye of those famous Poets. For gifts of wit and naturall promptnesse appeare in hym aboundantly. (144)

In this chapter I want to explore how the *Calender* engages in civil conversation with Harvey (disguised as Hobbinol and E.K.) in two eclogues, *Januarye* and *June*; I also want to explore Spenser's conversation in *Januarye* and *October* with two Inns of Court pastoralists, Googe and Turbeville, who were writing about male friendship in the 1560s. There is one other rivalry, though, that I would like to consider briefly here, which exists between

Gascoigne and Spenser. Gascoigne, a Cambridge graduate who joined Gray's Inn in 1555, perhaps came closer than any other contemporary to contributing to an aspirational, literary commonwealth. E.K.'s mention of him in *November* suggests that Immerito will succeed where Gascoigne failed because he does not lack 'partes of learning'. But there may be other reasons too. Gascoigne's later writings articulate the same anxiety about wasted talent and lost opportunity that pervades the *Calender*, but they also demonstrate how *not* to tackle this problem. In an attempt to disarm the criticism that his writings are lascivious Gascoigne made the mistake of appropriating the traditional moral authority of the estates satirist.

On returning from his involvement in Humphrey Gilbert's controversial military campaign in the Netherlands in the early 1570s the impoverished Gascoigne sought to obtain aristocratic patronage through his writing. His first attempt, *A Hundreth Sundrie Flowres* (1573), as G. W. Pigman notes, 'was deemed lasciviously offensive' and was thought to harm the reputation of certain individuals. In the second edition of 1575, *The Poesies of George Gascoigne*, he takes on the identity of a reformed prodigal 'whose early errors "might yet serve as a myrrour for the unbrydled youth, to avoyde those perilles which I had passed"'. Yet the 'sincerity' of his reformation has been questioned.[10] The *Poesies* is prefaced by three letters which lament the author's wasted talents (as befits a reformed prodigal). However, as Robert Maslen notes, they also point to 'the alternative routes his "giftes" might take': 'Read one way, the collection could lead to these gifts being deployed to the benefit of the nation. Read in another, the craftiness they celebrate could lead to the corruption of an entire generation.'[11] Gascoigne publishes *The Poesies* to show that he 'coulde aswell sowe good graine, as graynes or draffe', but he also refuses 'to cast away a whole bushell of goode seede, for two or three graynes of Darnell or Cockle' (p. 361). He describes himself as the victim of 'curious Carpers, ignorant Readers, and grave Philosophers' (p. 365). The only views he claims to value belong to the 'grave Philosophers' (all others are dismissed as malicious); but, giving himself the opportunity to address these 'Philosophers', he merely argues thus:

I must confesse, that as the industrious Bee may gather honie out of the most stinking weede, so the malicious Spider may also gather poyson out of the fayrest floure that growes.

And yet in all this discourse I see not proved, that either that Gardener is too blame which planteth his Garden full of fragrant floures: neyther that planter to be dispraysed, which soweth all his beddes with seedes of wholesome herbes: neyther is that Orchard unfruitfull, which (under shew of sundrie weedes) hath medicinable playsters for all infirmities. (pp. 366–7)

Gascoigne's wasted talents are also considered in the preface to *The Steele Glas* (1576), which includes 'Philomele's complaint', written in 1562. This text appears to offer a more serious attempt at moral reformation because it belongs to the didactic genre of estates satire, the genre which, I am arguing, Spenser leaves behind in the *Calender*. From the perspective of Harvey and Spenser, this old-fashioned, nostalgic satire could be seen to waste Gascoigne's talents. Despite its attachment to the agrarian cycle of labour and reward, it does not provide a 'soil' suitable for the cultivation of its author's talents. The form does not promise to encourage innovation. In fact, *The Steele Glas* is innovative; it is one of few early examples of blank verse (unrhymed iambic pentameter), but the significance of this would have been lost on Harvey and other readers in the 1570s.[12] Rather, its title would have recalled such texts as the forbiddingly titled broadside *A new yeres gift, intitled a Christal Glas For all Estates to look in, wherein they may see the just rewarde, for unsatiate and abhominable Covetousness* (1569).

Gascoigne's dedication of *The Steele Glas* to Lord Grey of Wilton (Spenser's employer in Ireland in the 1580s), contains a moving admission of wrong-doing and unfulfilled potential: 'I have loytred (my lorde) I confesse, I have lien streaking me (like a lubber) when the sunne did shine, and now I strive al in vaine to loade the carte when it raineth. I regarded not my comelynes in the Maymoone of my youth, and yet now I stand prinking me in the glasse, when the crowes foote is growen under mine eye.' Gascoigne asks Grey to allow that he is able to change at this mature stage in life and he advises that he has written *The Steele Glas* to give his detractors a 'rybbe of roste' so that they will 'be no lesse ashamed to have falsely accused me'.[13] The ironic, perhaps satisfying twist in this work (that is, for one who has been so frequently detracted), is that Gascoigne is now able to assume the mantle of social commentator and critic. He usurps the moral authority of the satirist who holds up a 'steele' mirror to each of the different estates, reminding them of their place in the social hierarchy and of their proper duties. 'O Knights, O Squires, O Gentle blouds yborne, / You were not borne, al onely for your selves: / Your country claymes, some part of al your paines', he declares in an attempt to curb the greed of this estate and to remind them of their duty to maintain hospitality (sig. D3v). But the irony backfires. The hero of *The Steele Glas* is trusty, plain-speaking plowman Piers who knows and accepts his place at the bottom of the social ladder. Since estates satire begrudges the desire for social mobility, there was no better form in which the gifted and aspiring Gascoigne might waste his talents. For the 'new Poete' Immerito, displaying his gift in the lowly pastoral mode, the difficult question was how to avoid the same fate.

HONESTY BETWEEN FRIENDS AT THE INNS OF COURT

The Inns of Court were an important location for the forging of friendships in the mid-sixteenth century. Their official function was to certify men to serve as barristers, but they also provided instruction in gentlemanly behaviour, and thus attracted wealthy members who had no intention of studying law. The Inns, Winthrop Hudson notes, were 'a kind of club and common eating place, a center of conversation and fellowship as well as a place of learning, where mutual acquaintance and friendship were nurtured'.[14] In this context political networks formed in Cambridge were sustained and strengthened. Cecil was admitted to Gray's Inn in 1542 after leaving Cambridge (without taking a degree). Many of the men he chose to serve in the new Elizabethan Privy Council had studied with him in Cambridge and were affiliated to one of the Inns. Residence at the Inns also nurtured textual collaboration. Barnabe Googe's *Eglogs, Epytaphes, and Sonettes* (1563) included poems written for friends, and also poems by friends to the author. Conversations carried on across printed texts. Googe's *Eglogs* includes the parodic 'Of Money' which begins 'Give money me, take friendship whoso list'. Four years later George Turbeville printed a friendly response, reminding Googe that the value of friendship cannot be quantified.[15]

Writers at the Inns of Court in the 1560s reworked in vernacular poetry the themes of classical *amicitia* which they were themselves seeking to practise. One of the most important writers on this topic was Richard Edwards (admitted to Lincoln's Inn in 1564), a contributor, along with Gascoigne, to the multi-authored *The Paradise of daynty devises*, printed in 1576, and reprinted with additions a further nine times in the next forty years. This text, as Ros King remarks, is 'evidence for manuscript culture in action'. This is because its 'various manifestations mark a continuing process of exchange: a community of poets, and later of poets and printer, sharing ideas, collecting each other's work, using each other's poems as sources for their own writing'.[16] Many of the poems included in this compilation are concerned with friendship, for example, M. Yloop's (or Pooly's) 'The perfect tryall of a faythfull freend', or F.K.'s 'Nothing is comparable unto a faithfull freend'.[17] Collectively, the poems celebrate the virtues of *amicitia*: true friends are to be valued above material wealth; they are plain-dealing and trustworthy, and they offer immeasurable comfort. As the poet F.K. (F. Kindlemarshe) argues:

Of freendship, groweth love and charitie,
By freendship, men are linked in amitie:
From freendship, springeth all commoditie,
The fruite of freendship, is fidelitie.

(sig. C1r)

Edwards himself is praised as just such a faithful friend in the volume. Responding in the second edition of 1578 to one of Edwards's poems in the original collection ('May'), the poet M.S. praises Edward's benevolence born out of amity: 'He is not for himself, it seemes, but wisheth well to all.'[18] Edwards might well be held up as an example of friendly altruism; it is just such a feature of *amicitia* which his Inns of Court drama *Damon and Pythias* celebrates.

Damon and Pythias is worth pausing over because it engages with a question important to the debate about male *amicitia*: what binds men in true friendship?[19] Its eponymous heroes are the two ideal friends praised briefly by Cicero in *De officiis* (3. 45), and the play is a theatrical reworking of *De amicitia*.[20] Its response to this question is thus conditioned by Edwards's reading of this text. The thesis of *De amicitia* – that true friendship does not follow advantage, but that advantage accrues from true friendship (14. 51)[21] – is dramatised by Damon and Pythias and the new court philosopher Aristippus. The virtue of Damon and Pythias is realised in their shared response to the difficulties they run into during a visit to a city ruled by the tyrant Dionysius. One of Dionysius's parasites, the courtier Carisophus, falsely accuses Damon of spying. When Damon is arrested and sentenced to death by Dionysius, Pythias pawns his life; he offers to take Damon's place in prison so that he can secure his estate before returning to face execution. It is Damon who articulates Cicero's argument that the motive for friendship is love of virtue rather than the desire for profit or 'commodity' (7. 41–8). In contrast, Carisophus illustrates false friendship; his oath of friendship to a fellow courtier, Aristippus, is exposed as meaningless when he advises the audience that 'by my troth, to speak my conscience plainly, / I will use his friendship to mine own commodity' (9.84–5). His pledge of friendship is contrasted with the trust between Damon and Pythias. The audience is guided to an appreciation of a new quality which binds men in mutual friendship and good society. As Damon reminds Dionysius in prison (when commenting on Pythias's self-sacrifice), 'There is no surer nor greater pledge than the faith of a gentleman' (10. 256).

Damon and Pythias is exploring the idea of good faith between gentlemen; it insists that the pledge between friends should not be honoured to the detriment of other social relationships. As Cicero argues in *De amicitia*, we have a right to ask 'of friends only what is honourable', and friends are called upon to give one another 'true advice with all frankness' (13. 44). Friendship must rest not on unquestioning loyalty, but honesty. This point is made in an exchange between Carisophus and Aristippus at the point at which their alliance breaks down. When Carisophus calls upon Aristippus to rescue him from the wrath of Dionysius he receives an education in true friendship. Carisophus complains that the tyrant has begun 'to suspect my truth and honesty' and he asks Aristippus to support him: 'My friend, for my honesty, will you not take an oath'? (14. 15–18). However, Aristippus cannot be persuaded to 'stretch one point to bring [Carisophus] in favour again' (14. 27); instead, he identifies the 'link' that binds true friends:

CARISOPHUS. What link is that? Fain I would know.
ARISTIPPUS. Honesty.
CARISOPHUS. Does honesty knit the perfect knot in true friendship?
ARISTIPPUS. Yea, truly, and that knot so knit will never slip.
CARISOPHUS. Belike then, there is no friendship but between honest men.
ARISTIPPUS. Between the honest only; for '*Amicitia inter bonos*' [friendship exists only between good men], says a learned man.　　　　　　　　(14. 15–38)

There are two problems with Edwards's friends. On the page Damon and Pythias are not easily distinguishable characters; Damon is the elder of the two, and he is responsible for leading Pythias into danger. The two figures, however, share the same philosophy of friendship, and the same willingness to die for the other. It is likely that the differences between them would be emphasised in performance, but it is also possible that the extremity of their shared idealism would lend itself to comic effect.[22] The second problem is the kind of honesty they exemplify. Their evident willingness to die for one another finally persuades the tyrannical Dionysius of the poverty of his rule. (Dionysius has no friends, and he constantly fears for his life.) Yet, Edwards's ideal of shared likeness of mind, willing self-sacrifice *and* truth-telling is implicated in the Reformation culture of 'plain-speaking' which rejects any expression of self-interest. As a result, *Damon and Pythias* offers a partial exposition of '*honestas*' in *De amicitia* and *De officiis*. Edwards does not extend to Inns of Court dramatic dialogue – or to the style of friendship therein enacted – any personal aspiration or independence which Cicero's idea of honesty might yield.

Harvey and Spenser were not members of the Inns of Court.[23] Their relationship was formed in Cambridge and they emulate the friendships of Smith, Cheke and Ascham. The textual exploration of their friendship is best understood as a development of the linguistic and social reforms initiated by the 'Athenian tribe'. In keeping with this project, the *Calender* offers a more careful exploration of honest rivalry than was possible in Edwards's drama and in the Socratic dialogues preferred by Smith and Ascham. The *Calender* does not pause to reflect on the meaning of honesty (in the way, say, that Ascham does in *Toxophilus*), but it does qualify our sense of what it means to speak plainly. It does so by discussing in its prefatory epistle a new conception of decorum as '*honestas*', a self-restraint expressed as self-deprecation which resonates with the promise of its lowly speaker.

One of the perplexing features of this pastoral is its attachment to an archaic and provincial diction which makes it feel old-fashioned. The *Calender* recalls Edwardian Reformation literature, treatises such as Hugh Latimer's 'Sermon on Plowers' which resurrects the voice of the plain plowman of the Chaucerian apocrypha and Langland's *Piers Plowman*. It includes blunt plain-speakers like the shepherds Thomalin (*Julye*), Piers (*Maye*) and Diggon Davie (*September*) who attack the formality of catholic worship and the corruption of the clergy and who display a respect for hard-working agricultural labourers. Spenser also occasionally uses the alliteration, rhyme schemes and stanza forms typical of Reformation complaint.[24] He writes according to the rules of lowly pastoral, described in *October* as the 'base and viler clowne' of the generic hierarchy (line 37); he signs himself Immerito ('unworthy') in the dedication to Sidney, while insisting that his *Calender* was 'base begot with blame' (line 14), and he adopts the namesake of John Skelton's humble plowman, Colin Clout. Meanwhile, Thomalin's claim in *Julye* – 'How be I am but rude and borrell' (line 95), as John N. King observes, 'reduplicates, without the irony of Chaucer's original, the Franklin's protest: "I am a burel man"'.[25] However, Spenser also aims to transcend the role of this limited social critic and to offer a distinctive kind of plainness which is consonant with the *dissimulatio* of Cicero's Antonius and the *sprezzatura* of the modern courtier.

The connection is made for us by E.K. in his epistle to Harvey. Some of Immerito's words are 'hard, and of most men unused', although they are English in origin, deriving from medieval authors such as Chaucer. Commenting on Immerito's interest in Chaucer, E. K. argues:

In whom whenas this our Poet hath bene much traveiled and throughly redd, how could it be, (as that worthy Oratour sayde) but that walking in the sonne although for other cause he walked, yet needes he mought be sunburnt; and having the sound of those aunctient Poetes still ringing in his eares, he mought needes in singing hit out some of theyr tunes. But whether he useth them by such casualtye and custome, or of set purpose and choyse, as thinking them fittest for such rusticall rudenesse of shepheardes, eyther for that theyr rough sounde would make his rymes more ragged and rustical, or els because such olde and obsolete wordes are most used of country folke, sure I think, and think I think not amisse, that they bring great grace and, as one would say, auctoritie to the verse. (lines 32–46)

E.K. offers two possible causes. He first repeats the argument of Turbeville in the preface to his translation of Mantuan, that such diction matches the status of shepherds. However, he then suggests a second cause: that Immerito adopted these words out of habit, as a result of repeated reading of Chaucer. This second explanation is developed through a discreet allusion to Antonius's suntan simile in *De oratore*, an example of the *dissimulatio* or 'pretended ignorance' that informs Castiglione's *sprezzatura*. (E.K.'s ignorance about the cause of the *Calender*'s archaic diction is an example of *dissimulatio*.) This kind of self-deprecation, I have argued in this book, should be viewed as 'honest' because it aims to reveal something of the potential sociability and nobility of another speaker. In this epistle, its use also encourages the reader to think more carefully about the relationship between 'nature' and 'culture', and between speaker and speech, than they would customarily do. The idiom of Spenser's shepherds does not just represent their low estate; it is also aspirational. Just as in the *Courtier*, where *sprezzatura* is employed to explore the idea of natural nobility as a cultural myth, so here, E.K.'s disingenuousness prepares us to think more positively about the nobility of the *Calender*'s unworthy author and his native diction. His *sprezzatura* alerts us to a truism of *Civile Conversation*, that though 'flowers of speache [may] growe up chiefly in the learned, yet you see that nature maketh some of them to florish even amongst the common sort, unknowing unto them' (2. 136). The poet cultivates these 'flowers of speache' in art so that they can flourish naturally in conversation.

The intention to emphasise aspiration rather than stasis is indicated in the discussion which follows. E.K. offers a defence of a vernacular perceived as barbarous or base by its users, and of the virtue or nobility of base poets whose seeds of virtue have come to fruition through intellectual husbandry. Thus, E.K. praises Immerito's use of 'our Mother tonge' (lines 87–8), and reminds us that though the vernacular 'hath long time ben counted most bare and barrein' it 'truely of it self is both ful enough for prose and stately enough for verse' (lines 88–9). In this vein, E.K. suggests that Immerito, our poet who is 'unworthy', will prove to be properly noble since he has cultivated his inheritance: his parent Chaucer, the English 'Tityrus'. Despite his unworthy origins Spenser is not base at all. Rather, he is contrasted with ignoble poets who, ashamed of their native language, have 'patched up the holes with peces and rags of other languages, borrowing here of the french, there of the Italian, every where of the Latine' (lines 91–114). In their 'bastard judgement' (line 111), they fail to understand the innate nobility of English ('theyr rightfull heritage' (line 85)) and its need for careful cultivation or embellishment. This emphasis on potential is also explored in the eclogues.

DISDAINING GIFTS: SPENSER AND GOOGE

At the heart of the *Calender* is a story of unrequited love and rivalry. Immerito's persona, Colin Clout, laments the failure of his beloved Rosalind to return his love. Meanwhile the poet's friend Hobbinol laments Colin's love-lorn state, the concomitant neglect of their friendship and of Colin's poetic talent, all of which he imputes to the cruel Rosalind. The heterosexual and the homosocial cross paths in the first eclogue, *Januarye*. Colin, complaining about Rosalind's coldness, abruptly turns his attention to his relationship with Hobbinol, observing that:

> It is not *Hobbinol*, wherefore I plaine,
> Albee my love he seeke with dayly suit:
> His clownish gifts and curtsies I disdaine,
> His kiddes, his cracknelles, and his early fruit.
> Ah foolish *Hobbinol*, thy gyfts bene vayne:
> *Colin* them gives to *Rosalind* againe.
> (lines 55–60)

In the hierarchy of Colin's affections Rosalind takes precedence over Hobbinol. Confusingly, though, E.K.'s commentary tells a different story. He defends the friendship of Colin and Hobbinol from the insinuation of being 'disorderly' or homosexual love. The gloss to this stanza includes a lengthy paean on proper friendships between men, of which Colin and Hobbinol are considered to be an example. Their affection, E.K. comments, is no 'disorderly love' or 'pæderastice'. On the contrary, he explains, 'who that hath red Plato his dialogue called Alcybiades, Xenophon and Maximus Tyrius of Socrates opinions, may easily perceive, that such love is muche to be alowed and liked of'. As he adds, 'so is pæderastice much to be præferred before gynerastice, that is the love whiche enflameth men with lust toward woman kind' (59, gloss).

How should we understand this apparent rift between Immerito and E.K. so early in the text? Or indeed, E.K.'s unexpected defence of the friendship of Colin and Hobbinol from the 'savour' of 'pæderastice'? One of the problems is that the rejection of Hobbinol is incomplete. After all, Hobbinol will be named as a favoured friend in the closing lines of *December*. Some of the best criticism of this difficult passage is inspired by gay studies and queer readings. Paul Hammond observes of *Januarye* that Colin's 'gesture of denial and containment undoes itself, leaving the sign open to the reader – indeed, inviting him to ponder the possible significance of what E.K. has so usefully drawn to his attenion'.[26] Meanwhile, Jonathan Goldberg patiently discovers in Colin's divided attitude to Hobbinol the articulation of Spenser's erotic desire for a friend (Harvey) in a culture that had no name for homosexuality. He recognises that if E.K. 'rules out' an erotic reading of Colin's and Hobbinol's friendship, he 'rules it into the textual economies of the *Shepheardes Calender*'.[27] For example, E.K. notes that the line 'His clownish gifts and curtsies I disdaine' links *Januarye* directly to Virgil's homoerotic second eclogue about the unrequited love of the shepherd Corydon for his master's favourite, the boy Alexis: 'His clownish gyfts imitateth Virgils verse, Rusticus es Corydon, nec munera curat Alexis' (57, gloss) ['Corydon, you are a clown! Alexis cares nought for gifts'].[28] The association lingers in our minds even though E.K. denies that there is any 'savour of disorderly love' (line 59). Goldberg uses Eve Kosofsky Sedgwick's paradoxical category of 'homosocial desire' to describe the relationship between Colin and Hobbinol, but the question of why Spenser teases us in this way is only partly answered.[29] As I want to argue, the hint of same-sex desire in *Januarye* is a means as well as an end; it also allows Spenser to hint at and to displace the unconventional and unacceptable aspirations which classical male friendship might nurture.

The focus of work by Hammond and Goldberg is on the recovery of the covert expression of same-sex desire, rather than its denigration. We would do well to remember, though, that the double attitude of E.K. in *Januarye* is also inspired by the anxious rejection in early modern writing of the erotic possibilities of Virgilian pastoral and Ciceronian *amor* – a word which encompasses both a benevolent love for one's friends and parents and a 'strong, passionate longing for something, desire and lust'.[30] This anxiety, suggests Alan Stewart, belongs to a Reformation culture that had castigated monastic communities as sodomitical, but which highly valued, and indeed, rested upon, affective male relations.[31] In *Damon and Pythias*, notes Ros King, Richard Edwards 'truncates and adapts' one of Cicero's friendship maxims with the effect of removing any hint of homosexual desire. The maxim '*Nihil autem est amabilius nec copulatius quam morum similitudo bonorum* ("nothing, moreover, is more conducive to love and intimacy than compatibility of character in good men") is shortened in Edwards's drama to *Morum similitudo conciliat amicitias*' because, she explains, the English verb 'copulate' (from the Latin *copulatio*, to 'join together') had developed its sexual connotation by the sixteenth century.[32] However, *amor* can encompass other 'disorderly' desires, including social aspiration. Unease with Virgil's second eclogue is registered by Goldberg in *De Ratione Studii*, where Erasmus advises schoolmasters on how to 'protect the minds' of pupils from this 'ill-formed friendship'. Schoolmasters are to interpret the eclogue thus:

It is a symbolic picture of... an ill-formed friendship.... Corydon is from the countryside, Alexis from the city. Corydon is a shepherd, Alexis is a courtier. Corydon is unsophisticated (for Virgil calls his songs artless), while Alexis is widely read. Corydon is advanced in years, Alexis is in early manhood. Corydon is ugly, Alexis is handsome. In short, they differ in every respect. The prudent man should always choose a friend in tune with his own character, if he wants the affection to be mutual.[33]

Corydon's desire for Alexis is evaded; its impropriety rests on a difference in age and social status, not the sameness of sex, an argument that reflects a very Roman sensibility.[34]

The double impropriety of Virgil's second eclogue, however, is tackled in Barnabe Googe's protestant English pastoral (1563). These *Eglogs* discreetly castigate Corydon's sexual desire and the social aspirations of members of its pastoral community. They restore the culture of hospitality, the cycle of gift-giving and return, which is disturbed in Virgil's second eclogue, and the concomitant harmony of the estates. Gift-giving is a social relationship; as Marcel Mauss so influentially argued, it is always in someone's interest.[35] In Googe's pastoral dialogues, gift-giving serves the interests of an aristocratic social order. The social relationship created by its shepherds recalls the economy of estates satire in which the generosity of a lord (and also here, a noble poet) is rewarded by grateful acceptance and reaffirmation of the perceived status quo. It is this static economy that Colin's rude rejection of Hobbinol's gifts ('His clownish gifts and curtsies I disdaine') is attempting to circumvent. It is to Googe's study of this economy that I will now turn.

Googe (1540–94) is a poet now lost to most modern readers of Elizabethan verse: he rarely finds his way onto student reading lists. However, he was well known in the 1570s. His translation of Palingenius is praised, for instance, by Ascham in *The Schoolmaster*; Harvey praises him three decades later, placing him among those 'vulgar writers' in whom 'many things are commendable, divers things notable, some things excellent'.[36] He is known to us as the translator of Conrad Heresbach's *Foure Bookes of Husbandry* (1577), discussed in chapter 4. Googe matriculated from Christ's College, Cambridge in 1555, and entered Staple's Inn, London in 1559.[37] He was cousin to Alexander and Thomas Neville (the former wrote a prefatory poem to the *Eglogs*, the latter was Harvey's enemy at Pembroke College, Cambridge). Googe would have been known to Spenser for his contributions to Reformation literary culture, including his 'modern' vernacular pastoral.

For all its modernity, however, the *Eglogs* is nostalgic rather than forward looking; the critique offered by its plain-speaking shepherds stifles the expression of desire and aspiration. This is because the text is implicated in a Reformation tradition which relies on a static conception of the social hierarchy represented formally in medieval estates satire. Googe's *Eglogs* dramatises a cycle of exchange – represented in the 'thanks' owed to a senior shepherd by a junior for advice given – which entails an expression of satisfaction with the staus quo. In turn, the *Eglogs* is itself imagined as a gift to English poets who are encouraged to 'thank' the author by offering goodwill and publishing their own experimental poems. However, because Googe denies the reader (and budding poets) the possibility of criticising his *Eglogs* on the grounds that this would be a show of ingratitude, then the possibility of exploring both individual aspiration and the potential of the English language is also denied.

Googe is impatient with the self-indulgent follies produced by all kinds of love. His second eclogue records the lament of the suicidal, love-stricken Dametas; the third eclogue recounts the pains of an unrequited ram, while the fifth records the suicide of the disappointed shepherdess Claudia. Googe's strongest statement against 'love', however, occurs in the first eclogue, a dialogue between the youthful Daphnes and the aged Amintas. Amintas describes 'love' as poisonous before conceding that married love is still better than the 'wicked love' of Jove and Ganymede.

> I shall not need (I think) to bid
>   thee, to detest the crime
> Of wicked love that Jove did use
>   in Ganymede's time.
> For rather would I (though it be much)
>   that thou should'st seek the fire
> Of lawful love that I have told
>   than burn with such desire.[38]

Jove and Ganymede are the most well-known representatives of same-sex desire for the Elizabethans. In this pastoral context, though, we might also recall Virgil's Corydon and Alexis. The allusion to them is displaced; the names appear in the third eclogue, a dialogue between the shepherds Coridon and Menalcas, where a second Coridon, a churlish, upstart shepherd – 'no kin to me', says our speaker Coridon (7. 111) – is held responsible for the persecution of two (Marian) martyrs, Daphnes and Alexis.

Even with Googe, though, it is not the object of desire that really matters. Sexual desire, heterosexual and homosexual, is equated in the *Eglogs* with other types of desire (including social aspiration and the lust for power), all of which entail an assertion of will that is dangerous to the commonwealth. Erasmus worries about the social disparity between Virgil's two shepherds; his argument is that the aged, crippled and rustic Corydon has nothing to offer the sophisticated Alexis. In contrast, Googe castigates the selfishness of lusty lovers. In the *Eglogs*, desiring lovers seeking gratification are no better than upwardly mobile 'carters' eager to leave behind the pastoral life (7. 66). The *Eglogs* laments the destruction of a once harmonious community held together by manorial hospitality where 'giving' requires of the recipient acceptance of the status quo. In the third eclogue Coridon complains to Menalcas that shepherds have become proud, ambitious and individualistic, and he prophesises the decline of hospitality when the ranks of the nobility are infested with men of base descent: 'Nobility begins to fade, / and carters up do spring' (7. 65–6):

> Menalcas, I have known myself,
>   within this thirty year,
> Of lords and ancient gentlemen
>   a hundred dwelling there,
> Of whome we shepherds had relief:
>   such gentleness of mind
> Was placèd in their noble hearts
>   as none is now to find.
>   (7. 69–76)

Meanwhile, the *Eglogs* celebrate the self-sacrifice of Christian love. In the same eclogue Coridon describes approvingly the sacrifice of Daphnes and Alexis who died for something worthwhile: the Protestant faith. In contrast, Dametas and Claudia commit the sinful act of taking their own lives because of disappointed love. In the eighth (and final) eclogue Cornix advises Coridon of the happy state of simple shepherds, of the fall awaiting lusty lovers (like Dametas and Claudia) and ambitious men; he also argues that the only honourable object of love is God:

> CORNIX. Both place and time, my Coridon,
>   exhorteth me to sing,
> Not of the wretched lovers' lives,
>   but of the immortal king,

>   Who gives us pasture for our beasts
>   and blesseth our increase;
>   By whom, while other cark and toil,
>   we live at home with ease;
>   Who keeps us down, from climbing high
>   where honour breeds debate,
>   And here hath granted us to live
>   in simple shepherd's state.   (12. 21–32)

Googe reworks in the pastoral mode the attack on self-interest in Reformation texts such as Latimer's 'Sermon on Plowers'. In Latimer's treatise the possibility of an honest critique of social and economic conditions was not possible. This is because the plain-speech of his acerbic mouthpiece, the plowman, is already implicated in the culture of deference and obedience which reinforces the social and economic authority of the noble lords. In the *Eglogs* obedience is expressed in the offering of 'thanks'. Its ruptured cycle of gift-giving is restored with the ritual of closure – the offer and receipt of thanks and some modest token – enacted at the end of several eclogues. Thus, Daphnes concludes the first eclogue with thanks, the gift of a whistle and acceptance of the didactic tale he has been told (5. 165–73).

This restored cycle also defines a proper response to the *Eglogs*. There are three parts to its preface: a poem by Alexander Neville attacking critics; a letter from Googe to his friend William Lovelace of Gray's Inn explaining that the poems were prepared for print without his knowledge, and an address by Laurence Blundeston to the reader which aims to win goodwill for the work. In his letter Googe notes that his friends will be well aware that he was 'loath' to publish the poems abroad partly because of the 'grossness of [his] style' but partly, too, because he 'feared and mistrusted the disdainful minds of a number both scornful and carping correctors' (2. 1, 6, 8–10). These two arguments persuaded him to 'condemn' his writing to 'continual darkness' (2. 14–15). This is where they would have stayed had it not been for the intervention of a friend who committed them to a printer. Hoping to make the best of a bad situation Googe dedicates his 'fruits' to the 'friendly mind' of 'gentle Master Lovelace' (2. 33–5). He also declares that he seeks no financial reward, but only 'the friendly receiving of my slender gift' by the reader (2. 44–5). The idea that the *Eglogs* constitute a gift – a publication for the profit of others – is developed by Blundeston in his preface, where he also confesses to being the friend who has hazarded their printing. Blundeston 'gives' the *Eglogs* to us and defines the proper remuneration we owe both him and Googe, 'thanks': 'I would be then no more sparing to horde up my treasure from thee than I trust to find thee thankful now in taking this present from me' (3. 15–17). He reminds us that 'the giver, not the gift, is to be regarded' and asks us to 'Accept [his] goodwill and weigh not the value' (3. 27–9). If we do so then we will encourage other poets to share their talents rather than hoard them like the anti-social miser of biblical parable:

so shalt thou encourage others to make thee partaker of the like or far greater jewels, who yet doubting thy unthankful receipt niggardly keep them to their own use and private commodity, whereas being assured of the contrary by thy friendly report of other men's travails, they could perhaps be easily entreated more freely to lend them abroad to thy greater avail and furtherance. (3. 32–8)

Of course, the giving of 'thanks' or goodwill already carries the promise of material reward in a credit-based economy such as that of early modern England. The thanks a poet might receive from an aristocratic patron, as Michael Brennan writes, might include a position in a noble household such as 'chaplain, physician, secretary, tutor and man-servant', but also 'the basic necessities of accommodation and daily sustenance'.[39] Googe did use his literary skills to advance his career and interests. In 1560 he dedicated the second instalment of his translation of Palingenius to Cecil, from whom he was to receive support in the form of offices in subsequent years. However, the language of the *Eglogs* does not honestly acknowledge the credit which Googe is seeking by publishing his work. On the contrary, it claims social duty rather than self-interest as his only motivation.

Googe's economy of 'thanks' also undermines the integrity of social *and* literary critique, both of which are castigated as self-interested. The intention to inhibit criticism is made clear not only in Blundeston's letter but also in Neville's opening poem, which offers a searing attack on 'momish mouths, / reproachful tongues, and vile / Defaming minds' (lines 15–17). According with the circular logic of the *Eglogs*, Neville identifies critics with the upstart carters of the third eclogue; they are men swayed by 'desire of filthy gain' (line 25); they are 'crabfaced, cankered, carlish chuffs' (line 45), 'crabsnouted beasts' and 'raging fiends of hell, / Whose vile, malicious, hateful minds/with boiling rancour swell' (lines 33–6). Googe is urged to aim for the ultimate reward, fame, not money; he is taken out of critical – and commercial – circulation, and in such a way that the potential of future poets is stifled.

Colin's failure in *Januarye* to offer a return on Hobbinol's gifts temporarily lifts him out of this stifling cycle of gift-giving. (In *Aprill* Hobbinoll tells Thenot how he set about 'Forcing with gyfts to winne his wanton heart' (line 24).) In this first eclogue Spenser refuses two 'gifts': the love of Virgil's

Corydon and the advice of Googe's Amintas to restrain desire. On the one hand, *Januarye* understands the constraints implied by Corydon's gifts in Virgil's second eclogue. He explores their rejection from the perspective of the youthful Alexis (Colin). Corydon burns for the love of Alexis; in *Januarye*, a youthful Colin freezes in a wintry landscape with unrequited desire for Rosalind and with coldness towards Hobbinol. Corydon longs to share his rustic home with Alexis; Colin yearns instead to return to the town where his desire for Rosalind was first awakened. Alexis rejects Corydon's love and gifts; Colin recycles Hobbinol's gifts. Virgil's eclogue ends with Corydon's practical return to farming and his dismissal of Alexis ('You will find another Alexis, if this one scorns you' (line 73)), *Januarye* closes with Colin's emblem of hope: 'Anchôra Speme' ('still [there is] hope'). On the other hand, *Januarye* reverses Googe's rejection of Virgil's Corydon. E.K. may echo Amintas's disdain for 'wicked love', but he also asserts the desiring aspect of *amor* when he recalls Virgil's second eclogue, while insisting on the good effects of intimate male *amicitia*. His defence of 'pæderastice' recalls the non-sexual but erotically charged and educative friendship of Socrates and Alcybiades in Plato's *Symposium*. This style of friendship is being both celebrated and modified in the *Calender*.

Januarye introduces the double story of the *Calender*. While Colin complains about his unrequited love for Rosalind, E.K. reconstructs in the gloss to *Januarye* an alternative support system or textual community of male friends. Indeed, his defence of the friendship of Socrates might remind a knowing contemporary of one of Spenser's intimate friends, Harvey, who, in a Latin marginal comment in a copy of his *Rhetor* (1577), expresses his wish to imitate this teacher: 'I would cultivate you as Socrates himself cultivated Alcibiades, and I would compare you and your sermons to Silenus and the Satyrs, as Alcibiades did in the Symposium of that famous Plato'.[40] In fact, Harvey is invoked for all readers to see in a gloss on the word 'couthe'. E.K. explains that it means 'to know or to have skill' and then draws attention to its consideration by Thomas Smith in *De Republica Anglorum*:

As well interpreteth the same the worthy Sir Tho. Smitth [sic] in his booke of goverment: wherof I have a perfect copie in wryting, lent me by his kinsman, and my verye singular good freend, M. Gabriel Harvey: as also of some other his most grave and excellent wrytings. (10, gloss)

The significance of this lateral connection to Smith's brief discussion of the etymology of 'king' in *De Republica Anglorum* is hard to fathom. (Smith 'can not tell' whether the origins of 'king' 'commeth of *cen* or *ken* which betokeneth to know & understand, or *can*, which betokenth to be able or to have power' (sig. C1r).) However, it does make sense when the emphasis on friendship in *Januarye* is considered; it draws attention to an alternative circle of friends outwith the *Calender* who share their writings prior to print publication and who practise Ciceronian *amicitia*. More importantly still, the allusion reminds us of how this shared interest in linguistic reform is implicated in rethinking conventional ideas about power and authority. Smith's rumination on the etymology of 'king', for instance, invites readers to reflect on the source of authority: is it knowledge and virtue (as many humanists argue) or simply 'power'? In the context of *Januarye*, though, this model is only partly accepted. *Januarye* and other eclogues break away from the Socratic style which informs so much Elizabethan dialogue, including Googe's eclogues *and* Smith's defence of the linguistic authority of a law-giving 'senate' of Cambridge humanists. Colin is no Alcibiades; he is not searching for a Socratic teacher in Hobbinol (even if Hobbinol would like to play that role). But he also cannot manage without his friends. *Januarye* allows Colin to reject the gifts of his friend (the idea of disdaining the advice of a senior speaker is picked up in *Februarie*). However, *June*, the only eclogue in which Colin and Hobbinol engage directly in a conversation, will help us to understand how the odd rejection and embrace of a close friend in *Januarye* can be productive. *June* develops the *amicitia* theme of *Januarye* to explore a number of rivalrous relationships: between Colin and Hobbinol, Immerito and E.K., Spenser and Harvey and, ultimately, between the native and classical literary traditions.

Initially, *June* seems to rehearse the same stasis as *Januarye*. It opens with Hobbinol inviting Colin to share his *locus amoenas*. Colin refuses. He is an 'unhappy man' (line 14) who is forced to wander in the wilderness, searching for a new home. Hobbinol tries again:

> Then if by me thou list advised be,
> Forsake the soyle, that so doth thee bewitch:
> Leave me those hilles, where harbrough nis to see,
> Nor holybush, nor brere, nor winding witche:
> And to the dales resort, where shepheards ritch,
> And fruitfull flocks bene every where to see.
>
> (lines 17–22)

This pastoral landscape sounds ideal for the cultivation of Colin's talents. It is populated with 'frendly Faeries' and the 'systers nyne, which dwell on *Parnasse* hight' (lines 25, 28). Again, though, Colin refuses the invitation. He is growing too old to enjoy such a place, and besides, he suffers from unrequited love. It is Colin's turn to play the hapless Corydon. His admission 'Tho would I seeke for Queene apples unrype, / To give my *Rosalind*' (lines 43–4) is noted by E.K. as an imitation of the complaint of Corydon in Virgil: '*Ipse ego cana legam tenera lanugine mala*' ['My own hands will gather quinces, pale with tender down'].[41] The emblem at the end of *June*, '*Gia speme spenta*' indicates that the hope of *Januarye* has been extinguished. Yet, even as Colin repeats the complaint of *Januarye* – that Rosalind does not return his gifts – so a different 'gift' is being nurtured by Hobbinol and E.K., the poetic talent upon which the status of Colin rests. '*Colin*, to heare thy rymes and roundelayes', declares Hobbinol, '… I more delight, then larke in Sommer dayes' (lines 49–51). He suggests that Colin outperforms the muses to their shame: 'when they came, where thou thy skill didst showe, / They drewe abacke, as halfe with shame confound, / Shepheard to see, them in theyr art outgoe' (lines 62–64). Such strong praise prompts Colin's *sprezzatura*, a gesture in keeping with his shepherdly persona:

> Of Muses *Hobbinol*, I conne no skill:
> For they bene daughters of the hyghest *Jove*,
> And holden scorne of homely shepheards quill.
> For sith I heard, that *Pan* with *Phœbus* strove
> Which him to much rebuke and Daunger drove:
> I never lyst presume to *Parnasse* hyll,
> But pyping lowe in shade of lowly grove,
> I play to please my selfe, all be it ill.   (lines 65–72)

Colin modestly acknowledges that his 'homely shepheards quill' is scorned by the nine muses; he also refuses to aspire to rival them, as Hobbinol invites him to do. Pan, with whom Colin is associated, is described in *Januarye* as the god of shepherds (line 17). The story of Pan and the god of poetry, Phoebus (or Apollo) 'striving for excellencye', E.K. explains in *June*, is 'well knowne' (68, gloss). Colin's *sprezzatura* is repeated in the following stanzas. 'I wote my rymes bene rough, and rudely drest', he confesses (line 77); he also compares himself unfavourably with his teacher, Tityrus, 'the God of shepheardes' (line 81).

Mike Pincombe helpfully links *June* to Harvey's comparison of Spenser's native *Fairy Queene* with the *Teares of the Muses* in *Three Proper Letters*. In preferring the former to the latter, Harvey argues, Spenser has allowed 'Hobgoblin' to run away with 'the Garland from Apollo' (sig. F1v). Pincombe detects in this eclogue a 'muted conflict' between Spenser and Harvey over the issue of quantification.[42] Colin's *sprezzatura* is also Spenser's polite rejection of Harvey's neoclassical project. However, I suggest that this rejection is part of the same performance of rivalry we discovered in *Three Proper Letters* and *Januarye*. Spenser shares Harvey's ambition to accommodate native and classical traditions in such a way that the former is not subordinated to the latter; like Harvey, he rejects Smith's totalising refashioning of the English language and the nation's social and political organisation on classical models. Harvey is present in the eclogue in the guise of faithful Hobbinol and, also, in the figure of E.K. This commentator is not exactly a parody of a pedantic Harvey; after all, Harvey mocks the strict classicism of 'academic' writers like Thomas Watson in *Three Proper Letters*. Rather, Harvey is woven into the fabric of *June* in complicated ways which repeat the ambiguous embrace and rejection of Hobbinol in *Januarye* and his own style of friendship with Spenser outside the text. In a gloss on Hobbinol's claim to share the dales with 'frendly Faeries' the rationalist E.K. tartly responds: 'But to roote that rancke opinion of Elfes oute of mens hearts, the truth is, that there be no such thinges, nor yet the shadowes of the things, but onely by a sort of bald Friers and knavish shavelings so feigned' (25, gloss). Hobbinol (or Harvey) is shown to be a superstitious country fellow by E.K. Ironically, though, E.K. also sounds most like Harvey here: both the rational author of the earthquake letter in *Three Proper Letters*, who offers a critique of superstition, and the Harvey of the *Letter-book*, who is happy to mock himself in the third person.

E.K.'s gloss brings the two traditions favoured by Colin and Hobbinol into conversation. Colin's *sprezzatura* is answered by E.K., who enables the rhetorical flowers of this homely poet to flourish in our sight. The gloss re-enacts a rivalry in the eclogue between the classical and native traditions, a rivalry which is represented in the name of Colin's 'teacher', Tityrus: both Virgil and Chaucer. *June* does not accommodate Greek and Latin metre. It offers instead a daring experiment in native rhyme: each stanza offers two rhymes across eight lines (*ababbaba*). However, native and classical traditions are interwoven naively in the gloss in such a way as to create an impression of conversation between them. Colin's description of Chaucer ('Tityrus') as the 'God of Shepheards', E.K. explains, is also Cicero's description of Lentulus.[43] E.K. reveals that Colin is 'Virgilian' even when he sounds Chaucerian (for example in the sixth stanza). He uses Greek rhetorical terms to describe Colin's native turn of phrase (in the exclamation 'O why' he discovers 'A pretye Epanorthosis or correction' (90, gloss)). But E.K. also glosses plain English words with Latin terms. The verb 'To make' (82, gloss) is glossed as 'to versifie', just as in *Januarye* 'Neighbour towne' is explained unnecessarily (and inexplicably) as 'the next towne: expressing the Latine Vicina' (50). E.K.'s classicism is mocked here;

at the same time, homely English words are raised in status as the clarifying function of the gloss is reversed.

RETURNING GIFTS: SPENSER AND TURBEVILLE

The emphasis on refusing gifts seems to lift the *Calender*'s author out of commercial circulation. Colin refuses to reward Hobbinol's gifts in *Januarye*; does this then mean that the reader can refuse to reward Colin's 'gifts'? This might seem to be the conclusion of the one eclogue which complains about poor patronage, *October*. E.K. tells us in the Argument of *October* that this eclogue reveals how poetry is 'no arte, but a divine gift and heavenly instinct not to bee gotten by laboure and learning, but adorned with both: and poured into the witte by a certain ενθουσιασμος. and celestiall inspiration'. In this eclogue, we are asked to consider how poets should be rewarded for this 'gift' which comes to them so freely: the shepherd-poet Cuddie complains about the lack of material reward for his literary labour, to which his correspondent Piers replies that poets are both inspired and rewarded by taking up the role of moral reformer and teacher of virtue (lines 21–3). When Cuddie rejects this argument, Piers advises him to aspire to 'flye backe to heaven apace' (line 84). Cuddie indicates some kind of acceptance of the role of divinely inspired poet. 'The vaunted verse a vacant head demaundes', he argues (line 100). However, he then reiterates his request in a modified form. 'Let powre in lavish cups and thriftie bitts of meat', he asks potential patrons, 'For *Bacchus* fruite is frend to *Phoebus* wise' (lines 105–6). As the editor of the Yale edition, Thomas H. Cain, advises, Cuddie asks that his cups be filled 'lavishly' and that he be given 'only a little food' since 'wine stimulates the ability to compose poems'.[44] As Jane Tylus notes, the Spenserian poet yearns to be lifted out of a stifling and unrewarding cycle of exchange, 'a system of patronage almost feudal in nature', and aspires to the independence of the divinely inspired *vates*.[45] In *October*, the poet appears to be placed outside patronage relations, and poetic composition is seen to be dependent only on spiritual or divine, not material, support.[46]

In this final section I want to consider the kind of 'economy' of return which Spenser is recommending in this eclogue. That is, I want to consider what Cuddie's request for 'lavish cups and thriftie bitts of meat' might mean in the context of pastoral fashioned as a civil conversation. So far, it looks as if *October* is asserting the model of altruistic giving proposed by earlier English poets in this mode, Googe and also Turbeville, both of whom claim not to be writing for gain. In the preface to his translation of Mantuan's

Eglogs (1567), Turbeville emphatically values his 'gift' of poetry over and above any material reward. In his dedication to the printer Hugh Bamfield, Turbeville explains that he attempted the translation of Mantuan 'without hope of recompense'. His aim was to 'gratifie hys well deserving friendes'. The translation is described as a 'slender gift' (the same phrase is used by Googe to describe his *Eglogs*) and is committed to Bamfield's 'Patronage and Defence'. What is curious about this emphasis on goodwill, however, is that it explicitly disregards the sympathies of Mantuan's fifth eclogue, that poets should be materially rewarded. I want to argue that it is this failed argument of Mantuan which Spenser is repeating in *October*, albeit in a new 'civil' form. Or rather, Spenser is seeking both to recover and ameliorate the strident request for reward which is the trademark of Mantuanesque pastoral in order to satisfy his own social and cultural aspirations.

The Italian Carmelite monk Mantuan has already been noted as an important influence on English pastoral. He was regarded as a 'second Virgil' by contemporary readers, and his *Bucolica* was a school textbook. This admiration is difficult for modern readers to understand, as Nancy Jo Hoffman notes, since Mantuan is a rather unsubtle satirist. Mantuan, she complains, has 'no sense of Virgil's multilayered syntactic structures'; he also 'misses the Virgilian implication that poetry, in building an integral world, can make that world echo or resound with song'. In Virgil, 'Poetry transcends the poverty of daily life', whereas Mantuan 'merely complains about a medieval, astrologically determined *fortuna*'. Poetic creativity 'is ruled by a fate outside the self'.[47] Mantuan combines 'pagan Virgilian convention with the trappings of Renaissance Catholicism'; he brought to Virgil's pastoral a 'moralizing piety' and a 'literal use of ancient convention'. It is for his didacticism, not Virgilian emotional range, that he is celebrated by Tudor poets.[48]

Mantuan is valued mostly for his satirical attack on the abuses of the Catholic clergy, but he may also have been appreciated as a social critic. The argument of Mantuan's fifth eclogue, for instance, would have been familiar to Tudor readers versed in Reformation attacks on aristocratic covetousness and the decline of hospitality. What is surprising about the articulation of this argument (in Turbeville's translation), though, is the vehemence with which the poet Candidus defends his right to payment, and the stupidity of his miserly patron Silvanus, who remains convinced throughout only of his antagonist's greed. The eclogue offers a subtle reflection on the misplaced attribution of greed to needy labouring poets by greedy (and wealthy) patrons, but it is also interested in the failure of a moral defence which calls upon a tradition of hospitality. It opens with Silvanus's complaint that Candidus has given up piping, and the poet's explanation that he cannot afford to continue.

> Vaine praise and painted woordes
> in recompence you give:
> Meanwhile the shepherd hunger stervde,
> in thirst and colde doth live.
>
> (sig. G2r)

Silvanus is convinced that a shepherd can find a 'vacant time' to 'make Verses' even while attending to his sheep (sig. G2r). In response Candidus paints a more realistic picture of his agricultural duties, and reminds Silvanus that 'A Verse it is a stately thing/and craves a cruell paines' (sig. G2v). However, his argument only convinces the miser that he is ambitious and 'desiring' of better fortune. Everyone is allotted their fortune by the gods, Silvanus argues. Some are given 'the Golde and kingly seat', others, like Candidus, are given the gifts of Mercury, 'wit, / tong, harpe and Verses feate'. 'That is thy lotted hap', he concludes, 'why doest thou gape for pelfe?' The poet is strongly advised to rest content with his divinely ordained lot in life and to 'resigne the rest / to us that wealthie are' (sigs. G3v-G4r).

The dialogue carefully exposes through the figure of Candidus the double standards of the rich man who refuses to match gift with gift. It also represents the distrust which exists between a wealthy patron and a poor petitioner. Candidus describes his vocation as a trade in an attempt to show why he is deserving, and, when Silvanus berates him for being selfish, he exposes the miser's eagerness to improve his own lot by invading the 'bowndes' of another (sig. G4r). If Silvanus wants to feast on Candidus's songs (the 'iuncket of the eare') then he must requite him with proper hospitality: 'set my chaps a worke with cates, / for so thou standest bound / By love, and law of God'. Silvanus is reminded of the interdependence of individuals in a commonwealth. God gives men different gifts so that no individual is self-sufficient but rather 'standes in want of helpe / and of some forraine ayde' (sig. G4v). Later Candidus explains that the 'gift' of poetry is not given freely to its audience. However, all of these arguments fail. Finally Candidus tries to explain how modest his needs are:

> I neyther long to have
> The fluent wealth of *Cosmus*, 'tis
> no silken cloake I crave.
> No roabe of Purple staine

> or Die that came from Tyre
> Nor costly cates of mighty Kings
>   nor Bankets I desire...
> I crave attire and vittailes in
>   a thacched Coate ywis...
> Give me *Pythagors* homely fare,
>   and *Codrus* garments thinne.
>   (sigs. G6v-G7r)

Candidus is asking for very little indeed. However, this argument also proves unsuccessful. The eclogue ends abruptly and surprisingly with the poet's angry rejection of Silvanus's promise of a gift. Attempting to close the quarrel Silvanus offers to 'be thy helpe at last'. However, this promise is understood by Candidus as a delaying tactic; Silvanus is merely putting off having to requite him (sig. H3v).

Spenser follows Mantuan's eclogue in *October* in the first half of the poem. In the second half, suggests Cain, he 'turns away from Mantuan to let Piers and Cuddy focus on the rising career of Colin'.[49] Thus, Cuddie echoes Candidus's complaint that poets are not requited satisfactorily (who 'feedes him once the fuller by a graine?'), while Piers, who appears to be a more sympathetic version of Silvanus, recommends the rewards of praise and the pleasure that comes from teaching others. Piers also advises Cuddie to leave behind lowly pastoral and to write of wars, chivalric tournaments and 'doubted Knights' (line 41), just as Silvanus advises Candidus to seek his fortune in Rome. However, Spenser departs from Mantuan with this recommendation. Piers recognises that the prince's palace is not yet a proper home for poetry, and he advises his companion to 'make thee winges of thine aspyring wit, / And, whence thou camst, flye backe to heaven apace' (lines 83–4). While Silvanus would no doubt continue to argue his case and insist on the need for material support, Cuddie hesitates: Colin might harbour such aspirations were he not 'with love so ill bedight' (line 89). Piers rejects mundane affairs on the poet's behalf: love should 'teach him climbe so hie' and rescue him from 'the loathsome myre' of his body (lines 91–2), 'For lofty love doth loath a lowly eye' (line 96). At this point Cuddie swaps Pier's adjective 'lofty' for his own, 'lordly'. He offers a critique of 'lordly love' (the ongoing theme of the *Calender*) and repeats his request for a return on his poetic gift.

> All otherwise the state of Poet stands,
> For lordly love is such a Tyranne fell:
> That where he rules, all power he doth expell.

> The vaunted head a vacant head demaundes,
> Ne wont with crabbed care the Muses dwell.
> Unwisely weaves, that takes two webbes in hand.
>
> Who ever casts to compasse weightye prise,
> And thinks to throwe out thondring words of threate:
> Let powre in lavish cups and thriftie bitts of meate,
> For *Bacchus* fruit is frend to *Phœbus* wise.
> And when with Wine the braine begins to sweate,
> The nombers flowe as fast as spring doth ryse.
>
> (lines 96–108)

Cuddie's request is more modestly stated than Candidus's, but it is a request for a return nonetheless. (The modesty of Cuddie's expression is commented on by E.K. in a gloss on the phrase 'peeced pineons' which, he remarks, is 'Spoken wyth humble modestie' (87, gloss).) I suggest that we accept Harvey's reading of *October* in *Three Proper Letters* as a request for a style of patronage which does not fix the poet into a relationship of obligation to his lord. A system of patronage modelled on the cycle of hospitality is replaced by one informed by the values of civil conversation. Cuddie's adjective 'thriftie' can mean not 'only a little', as Cain advises, but also 'proper' or 'decent' in accordance with its use by Chaucer (*OED*). *October* is introducing a different social economy to that present in both Googe's and Turbeville's eclogues. These lines should be read against the idea of the civil symposium, the 'smal and easie banquet' described in courtesy books like *Civile Conversation* (4. 134). In contrast to Candidus, Cuddie relinquishes the role of pastoral satirist, but he does retain a critical voice. The moral role of the poet is to 'restraine' (line 21) by his own example noble readers; this entails inculcating in them a proper sense of their social duty to 'return' on intellectual labour.

Does Spenser avoid wasting his talent in the *Calender*? George Gasgoigne's adoption of the moralising voice of Piers Plowman in *The Steele Glas* (1576) perhaps failed to convince patrons to invest in his talent partly because of its transparency. Mantuan's fifth eclogue recognised this problem: poets who call upon a tradition of hospitality are as vulnerable to the accusation of self-interestedness which they level so freely at rich patrons. One way in which Spenser attempts to escape this is by practising a form of exemplary self-restraint. Spenser does not just articulate his request for patronage in a more restrained or more civil form than Mantuan's Candidus, he also teases the reader with the promise of what might be. In so doing, he both whets our appetite for more (by hinting repeatedly that he is holding back his best work), and implicates the reader in the virtual life or death of this poet's talent. The *Calender*, I have suggested, tells a double story of triumph and defeat. Will Immerito's potential be developed and realised, or will it remain uncultivated? The dilemma is articulated in the three wintry eclogues. The concluding stanzas to *October* hint at what Cuddie and Colin might achieve. 'Thou kenst not *Percie* howe the ryme should rage,' declares Cuddie, 'O if my temples were distaind with wine' (lines 109–10). In the gloss E.K. notes that 'He seemeth here to be ravished with a Poetical furie'. But as soon as Cuddie is transported, he is brought down to earth again: 'ah my corage cooles ere it be warme' (line 115). In *November*, the eclogue in which E.K. remembers the wasted talent of Gascoigne, we see Immerito surpassing the conventional form of elegy: his lament for Dido is turned around when the poet imagines her apotheosis. Colin's companion Thenot, who anticipates the 'greater gyfts for guerdon' which the inspired Colin 'shalt gayne' (line 45), does not know 'Whether [to] rejoice or weepe for great constrainte' (line 205). Meanwhile *December* offers a double portrait of failure and success. It records the fruitlessness of Colin's career, but also ends with Colin's salute to Hobbinol, the friend who has published the fruits of his talent: 'Adieu good *Hobbinol*, that was so true,/Tell *Rosalind*, her *Colin* bids adieu' (lines 155–6). The question is left unanswered: whether Immerito will develop his potential or not depends very much on how readers – potential patrons – contribute to this conversation.

Conclusion

This study has been concerned with the negotiations which took place among a group of Cambridge humanists across two generations over the form and use of civil conversation as a means to explore social, economic and political exchange. This exploration took place in a culture which was self-consciously in transformation and where there was a close link between linguistic and social and political reform. The 'Reformation' involved debates about and changes to social interchange as well as theological doctrine and the practice of worship. It also involved attempts to reform the English language; in this period, speech was understood as the essential bond of human societies. The speech form of civil conversation – recovered from Cicero and, to a lesser extent, Plato – enabled the humanists to explore and debate the interplay between self-interest and social duty in personal relationships as well as within local and national government. It also provided a framework for discussion of the opportunities (and costs) offered by expanding markets and colonisation.

Making this argument has involved a wholesale re-reading of the courtesy books. These treatises have long been regarded as a source for a 'courtly rhetoric', that is, a style of language and conduct appropriate to the male elite. It is believed that they represent a departure and a decline from a classical, republican rhetorical culture. I have argued that the opposite is true. Many of these books offer a sophisticated interpretation of Cicero's rhetorical values and political philosophy and had a much wider appeal than is usually supposed. They may well have been read eagerly by aspirational courtiers but they were also translated and discussed by humanists who were committed to linguistic and social reform, and they contributed to the debate about the language and style of opposition in the service of Reformed religion. In particular, they encouraged debate about the use of power in social relationships. For example, the exploration of the meaning of Ciceronian 'honesty' that we find in these books supported the attempt of humanists to imagine an alternative style of communication to that implied in the influential ideology of the 'estates'. The latter model is articulated in medieval 'estates satire', a genre revived and adapted by Reformers in the 1550s. This form resolved the tension between self-interest and social duty by organising society into a hierarchy of ranks, and by urging each one to recognise its duty to the commonwealth. Inevitably, this implied the virtue of resting content with one's ordained place and the inhibition of all personal aspiration regardless of rank. Such a mode of writing also failed to offer an adequate response to the complex social structures and processes of the sixteenth century. It became apparent in the second half of the century that the ideal of the plain-speaking social critic who exposes the abuse of privilege was insufficient. Worse, this figure might be deployed in debate by knowing landowners (among others) to conceal exploitation. Humanists like Cheke, Smith, Ascham, Harvey and Spenser, explore an alternative style of 'honesty' which requires the practice of self-restraint in social and commercial exchange and which aims to recognise the existence of different interests.

This style of honesty was not always successful; it too could be used pragmatically to conceal interests. One reason for the failure of civil conversation as a critical discourse, I argued, is that the humanists inherited a distinct but overlapping conception of 'honesty' from the husbandry tradition, which relied on the less open Socratic dialogue. This tradition made the cultivation of 'honesty' – chastity, silence and obedience – in wives and servants the recipe for, and a secret of, masculine civility. Though both Castiglione and Guazzo depict women as central to the civilising process in their dialogues, in the English writing we have considered women are noticeably absent. Thus, Spenser's excludes Rosalind from the exemplary friendship he represents in the *Calender*, while Harvey's attempts to represent women in civil conversation in his letters seem clumsy and paternalistic. This exclusion also affects the representation of male interaction for it conceals the concomitant need for subordination, silence and obedience in relationships between men of different status.

Nevertheless, civil conversation should still be seen as contributing to critical thought in the sixteenth century. This is because it understands that meaning and values can only be arrived at through collective discussion. 'Truth' does not belong to the lone moral satirist or plain speaker. Indeed, courtesy books written as conversations are aware of the complexity of the concept of honesty in social practice. The authors of these books also understand that there is an important relationship between social or political and literary structure. The critical possibilities of this discourse continued to shape political debate, to structure responses to cultural encounters and to define radical ideas in the seventeenth century. John Milton, for example, uses this speech form to explore the possibilities and problems of civil exchange in the heavenly 'republic' of *Paradise Lost*. Recognising this ongoing interest in civil conversation will contribute to our knowledge of how defences of the commonwealth against Royalist private interest in the seventeenth century were also engaging in an intricate debate about the relationship between self-interest and social duty which had been initiated by the Tudor humanists.

Notes

INTRODUCTION

1. For an account of this change see Anna Bryson, *From Courtesy to Civility: Changing Codes of Conduct in Early Modern England* (Oxford: Clarendon Press, 1998), p. 19. See also Peter Burke, Brian Harrison and Paul Slack, eds., *Civil Histories: Essays Presented to Sir Keith Thomas* (Oxford University Press, 2000).
2. See Paul Langford, *A Polite and Commercial People* (Oxford University Press, 1989), pp. 4–5, and Lawrence E. Klein, *Shaftesbury and the Culture of Politeness* (Cambridge University Press, 1994); J. G. A. Pocock, 'Virtues, Rights, and Manners', in *Virtue, Commerce and History: Essays in Political Thought and History, Chiefly in the Eighteenth Century* (Cambridge University Press, 1985), pp. 35–50, pp. 48–9; Lawrence E. Klein, 'Liberty, Manners and Politeness in Early Eighteenth-Century England', *The Historical Journal* 32 (1989): 583–605 and Albert O. Hirschman, *The Passions and the Interests: Political Arguments for Capitalism before its Triumph* (Princeton University Press, 1977). On nineteenth-century etiquette see Marjorie Morgan, *Manners, Morals and Class in England, 1774–1858* (Basingstoke: Macmillan, 1994).
3. Bryson, *From Courtesy to Civility*, pp. 20–1.
4. See Frank Whigham, *Ambition and Privilege: the Social Tropes of Elizabethan Courtesy Theory* (Berkeley: University of California Press, 1984). See also Jean-Christophe Agnew, *Worlds Apart: the Market and the Theater in Anglo-American Thought, 1550–1750* (Cambridge University Press, 1986), chap. 2.
5. See Daniel Javitch, *Poetry and Courtliness in Renaissance England* (Princeton University Press, 1978), chap. 1, esp. pp. 43–8.
6. Bryson's excellent *From Courtesy to Civility* remains indebted to the work of the eighteenth-century historian of ideas, Pocock (esp. *Virtue, Commerce and History*), see esp. chap. 2. Bryson takes no account of the impact of the Reformation on the discourse of civility; she also understands the courtesy books as essentially 'aristocratic'.
7. See Markku Peltonen's *Classical Humanism and Republicanism in English Political Thought, 1570–1640* (Cambridge University Press, 1995), which establishes the presence of a vocabulary of classical republicanism in political debate in the period prior to the 1650s. A 'republic' may not have been a 'constitutional goal', he observes, but 'a theory of citizenship, public virtue and true nobility based

essentially on the classical humanist and republican traditions, was taken up, studied and fully endorsed throughout the period', p. 12. The courtesy books are one source for the exploration of these traditions.
8. Howard Jones identifies a huge increase in the popularity of Cicero's works in the late sixteenth century. '[O]f the sixty-seven editions published between 1500 and 1600', he remarks, 'all but seven were products of the second half of the century, one from the reign of Edward VI, one from the reign of Mary Tudor, and fifty-eight from the reign of Elizabeth I'. *De officiis* is the most frequently reprinted of Cicero's writings. See Jones, *Master Tully Cicero in Tudor England* (Nieuwkoop: De Graaf Publishers, 1998), p. 131.
9. See esp. Alan Stewart, *Close Readers: Humanism and Sodomy in Early Modern England* (Princeton University Press, 1997) and Lorna Hutson, *The Usurer's Daughter: Male Friendship and Fictions of Women in Sixteenth-Century England* (London: Routledge, 1994).
10. The phrase is John N. King's in *English Reformation Literature: the Tudor Origins of the Protestant Tradition* (Princeton University Press, 1982), p. 16.
11. On the continuing importance of ideas of community in the period see esp. Alexander Shepard and Phil Withington, eds., *Communities in Early Modern England: Networks, Place, Rhetoric* (Manchester University Press, 2000).
12. See, for example, chap. 2 of Onora O'Neill's *A Question of Trust: the BBC Reith Lectures 2002* (Cambridge University Press, 2002).
13. See, for example, the argument of Stewart in *Close Readers* that 'whatever Ascham's text [the *Schoolmaster*] achieves in the way of pedagogical reform is secondary to its function in fulfilling the continuity of Ascham's hard won social status through his children', p. 115.
14. Spenser's account of the benefits that 'daily conversation' between the native Irish and settler English will bring takes place in the second half of this treatise; the first half justifies the need for military conquest. See Edmund Spenser, *A View of the Present State of Ireland*, ed. W. L. Renwick (Oxford: Clarendon Press, 1970), esp. pp. 153–66.
15. John Leon Lievsay, *Stefano Guazzo and the English Renaissance 1575–1675* (Chapel Hill: University of North Carolina Press, 1961), p. 34.
16. Catherine Gallagher and Stephen Greenblatt, *Practicing New Historicism* (University Chicago of a Press, 2000), p. 5.
17. Sigmund Freud, *The Standard Edition of the Complete Psychological Works of Sigmund Freud vol. XXI (1927–1931): The Future of an Illusion, Civilization and its Discontents and Other Works*, trans. James Strachey in collaboration with Anna Freud (London: Vintage, 2001), p. 111. All citations are to this edition.
18. Stephen Mennell, *Norbert Elias: Civilization and the Human Self-Image* (Oxford: Basil Blackwell, 1989), esp. p. 100. See Norbert Elias, *The History of Manners: the Civilizing Process*, vol. 1, trans. Edmund Jephcott (New York: Pantheon Books, 1978).
19. Freud, *Psychological Works*, p. 97. See Stephen Greenblatt, *Renaissance Self-Fashioning: from More to Shakespeare* (University of Chicago Press, 1980, rpt. 1984), pp. 173, 179, 184–8.
20. Gallagher and Greenblatt, *Practicing New Historicism*, p. 9.

Notes to pages 9–14

21. Philibert de Vienne, *The Philosopher of the Court*, trans. George North (London, 1575), sigs. H6v, H7r-v.
22. Greenblatt, *Renaissance Self-Fashioning*, p. 164.
23. Daniel Javitch, '*The Philosopher of the Court*: a French Satire Misunderstood', *Comparative Literature* 23 (1971): 97–124.
24. The speaker is Crassus in Cicero's *De oratore*, 2 vols, trans. E. W. Sutton and H. Rackham (London: William Heinemann; Cambridge, MA: Harvard University Press, 1988), 1.47. All citations are to this edition.
25. Antonio de Guevara, *A Dispraise of the life of the Courtier, and a Commendacion of the life of the labouryng man*, trans. Sir Francis Bryant (London, 1548), sigs. D8v-E1r; E5v; F2r-v; M8v.
26. See Hannah Arendt, 'Truth and Politics' in *Between Past and Future: Eight Exercises in Political Thought* (Harmondsworth: Penguin, 1968 rpt, 1954), pp. 227–64, p. 241.
27. Terry Eagleton, *The Idea of Culture* (Oxford: Blackwell, 2000), p. 109.
28. See the comments on dialogue in Freud's *Future of an Illusion*: 'An inquiry which proceeds like a monologue, without interruption, is not altogether free from danger. One is too easily tempted into pushing aside thoughts which threaten to break into it, and in exchange one is left with a feeling of uncertainty which in the end one tries to keep down by over-decisiveness', *Psychological Works*, p. 21.
29. Elias views the courtesy books as the catalyst for the 'civilising process', prompted by the centralisation of court culture in late medieval/early Renaissance Europe; on social mobility and the decline of noble families see Lawrence Stone's *The Crisis of the Aristocracy, 1558–1641* (Oxford: Clarendon Press, 1966); the shift from a lineage to a civil society is discussed in Mervyn James's *Family, Lineage and Civil Society: a Study of Society, Politics and Mentality in the Durham Region 1500–1640* (Oxford: Clarendon Press, 1974), esp. pp. 177–98.
30. Whigham, *Ambition and Privilege*, p. 6, citing Stone, 'Social Mobility in England, 1500–1700', *Past and Present* 33 (1966): 48, 16.
31. Whigham, *Ambition and Privilege*, pp. 18–19.
32. *Ibid.*, p. 28. Whigham is commenting on the contradictory attitude to noble birth in these books.
33. Giovanni della Casa, *Galateo of Master John Della Casa*, trans. Robert Peterson (London, 1576), sig. B4v.
34. Simon Robson, *A new yeeres gift. The courte of civill courtesie: assembled in the behalfe of all younge gentlemen, to frame their behaviour in all companies* (London, 1577), sig. A2r.
35. *Cyvile and Uncyvile Life* in *Inedited Tracts: Illustrating the Manners, Opinions, and Occupations of Englishmen during the Sixteenth and Seventeenth Centuries*, ed. W. C. Hazlitt 1868 (New York: Burt Franklin, 1964), p. 30.
36. Harvey's copy (now held at the Newberry Library) contains copious marginalia. For discussion of these see Caroline Ruutz-Rees, 'Some Notes of Gabriel Harvey's in Hoby's Translation of Castiglione's *Il cortegiano* (1561)', *Publications of the Modern Language Association of America* 25 (1910): 608–39.

37. Gerald M. Sider, 'The Ties that Bind: Culture and Agriculture, Property and Propriety in the Newfoundland Village Fishery', *Social History* 5 (1980): 1–39, pp. 21, 2.
38. Whigham, *Ambition and Privilege*, p. 18. The phrase 'untowardly asseheades' is Count Baldassare Castiglione's in *The Book of the Courtier*, trans. Thomas Hoby, ed., Virginia Cox (London: Everyman, 1994), p. 35. See also Eduardo Saccone, '*Grazia, Sprezzatura, Affettazione* in the *Courtier*', in Robert W. Hanning and David Rosand, eds., *Castiglione: the Ideal and the Real in Renaissance Culture* (Cambridge, MA: Harvard University Press, 1983): 45–67, p. 60.
39. I mean by 'negotiation' the kind of personal exchange – the give and take of social interaction – advised by Theodore B. Leinwand in 'Negotiation and New Historicism', *Publications of the Modern Language Association of America* 105 (1990): 477–90, not the model of exchange between the individual and the state or its institutions which encourages 'docile self-regulation' that is described by Greenblatt in *Shakespearean Negotiations: the Circulation of Social Energy in Renaissance England* (Oxford: Clarendon Press, 1988), chap. 1, p. 16.
40. Alexandra Shepard and Phil Withington, intro. to *Communities*. See also Craig Muldrew, *The Economy of Obligation: the Culture of Credit and Social Relations in Early Modern England* (Basingstoke: Macmillan, 1998) and Keith Wrightson, *Earthly Necessities: Economic Lives in Early Modern Britain* (New Haven: Yale University Press, 2000).
41. Shepard and Withington, *Communities*, pp. 4, 6. Quoted from David Sabean, *Power in the Blood: Popular Culture and Village Discourse in Early Modern Germany* (Cambridge University Press, 1984), p. 27.
42. Shepard and Withington, *Communities*, p. 6.
43. *De amicitia* argues that friends should 'vie' with each other 'in a rivalry of virtue [honesta certatio]', Cicero, *De senectute, De amicitia, De divinatione*, trans. William Armistead Falconer (London: William Heinemann; New York: G. P. Putnam's Sons, 1923), 9. 32.
44. Jonathan Barry, 'Civility and Civic Culture in Early Modern England: the Meanings of Urban Freedom', in Burke *et al.*, eds. *Civil Histories*, 181–96, p. 181.
45. *Ibid.*, pp. 192–93.
46. See Peter Mack, 'The Dialogue in English Education in the Sixteenth Century' in M. T. Jones-Davies, ed., *Le Dialogue au temps de la Renaissance* (Paris: J. Touzot, 1984), pp. 189–212, and Peter Burke, 'The Renaissance Dialogue', *Renaissance Studies* 3 (1989): 1–12.
47. Roger Ascham, *The Schoolmaster (1570)*, ed., Lawrence V. Ryan (Charlottesville: University Press of Virginia, 1967), p. 56.
48. See Winthrop S. Hudson, *The Cambridge Connection and the Elizabethan Settlement of 1559* (Durham, NC: Duke University Press, 1980), p. 3. They gained the title 'Athenians', he notes, 'because of their enthusiasm for classical studies', p. 43.
49. *Ibid.*, p. 49.
50. Castiglione, *Courtier*, p. 7. All citations are to Virginia Cox's edition.

51. I am grateful to Phil Withington for sharing with me the manuscript of his forthcoming book on citizenship and incorporation, 'The Politics of Commonwealth' (Cambridge University Press).
52. See Peltonen, *Classical Humanism*, p. 57, and for his detailed discussion of Barston, see pp. 59–73. Guazzo, *Civile Conversation of M. Steeven Guazzo*, 2 vols., books 1–3 translated by George Pettie (1581), book 4 by Bartholomew Young (1586), (London: Constable and Co. Ltd; New York, Alfred A. Knopf, 1925), I. 42. All citations are to this edition. (Citations refer to book and page number.)
53. Harvey's copy of Hoby's translation, is signed and dated on the title page and sig. Yy3v '1572'; sig. Aaa1v is signed and dated '1580'. He also owned a copy of Bartholomew Clerke's Latin translation (1571), a copy of Guazzo's *La civil conversatione* (Venice, 1581), which he dated 1582, and a copy of Pettie's 1581 translation, also dated 1582. See Virginia Stern, *Gabriel Harvey: his Life, Marginalia and Library* (Oxford: Clarendon Press, 1979), pp. 205–6, 217. See also Harvey's *Commonplace Book* (Add MS. 32, 494 Br. Mus.) in G. C. Moore Smith, ed., *Gabriel Harvey's Marginalia* (Stratford upon Avon: Shakespeare's Head Press, 1913), pp. 97–9.
54. Gabriel Harvey, *Letter-Book of Gabriel Harvey AD 1573–1580*, ed., Edward John Long Scott (London: Nichols and Sons, 1884), see esp. pp. 78–9. All citations are to this edition.
55. Spenser became a member of the household of Leicester House not later than 1578; he was appointed secretary to Lord Grey, Lord Deputy of Ireland, in July 1580 (*Dictionary of National Biography*); Gabriel Harvey's *Letter-Book* includes a 'garden communication' between Harvey and some friends, pp. 95–100.
56. See James McConica, 'Scholars and Commoners in Renaissance Oxford' in *The University in Society*, vol. I, ed., Lawrence Stone (London: Oxford University Press, 1975), pp. 51–81, 59–63 and Hugh Kearney, *Scholars and Gentlemen: Universities and Society in Pre-Industrial Britain 1500–1700* (London: Faber and Faber, 1970), chap. 1.
57. Harvey, *Letter-Book*, p. 4. Harvey also reports Neville's complaint that he spent the Christmas holiday studying while the other fellows played cards, p. 14.
58. Patrick Collinson, *De Republica Anglorum. Or, History with the Politics Put Back*, Inaugural Lecture 9 November 1989 (Cambridge University Press, 1990), pp. 15, 20–1.
59. See Sir Thomas Smith, *Literary and Linguistic Works. Part 2. A Critical Edition of De Recta et Emendata Linguae Graecae Pronuntiatione (Lutetiae 1568)*, ed., Bror Danielsson (Stockholm: Almquist and Wiksell International, 1978), pp. 109–11.

1. TYPES OF HONESTY: CIVIL AND DOMESTICAL CONVERSATION

1. Bryson, *From Courtesy to Civility*, pp. 26–7.
2. *Urbanitatis*, p. 13, lines 19–20 in *Manners and Meals in Olden Times*, ed., Frederick J. Furnivall (London: N. Trübner and Co., 1868).

3. Bryson, *From Courtesy to Civility*, p. 28.
4. Furnivall, *Manners and Meals*, p. lxxxiv.
5. *Boke of Nurture* in Furnivall, *Manners and Meals*, pp. 77–8, lines 241, 243, 229.
6. Bryson, *From Courtesy to Civility*, p. 28.
7. *Stans puer ad mensam* in Furnivall, *Manners and Meals*, p. 28, line 30.
8. *Boke of Nurture* in Furnivall, *Manners and Meals*, p. 75, lines 165–8; p.86, lines 137–40.
9. On the shift from communal to private dining see Felicity Heal, *Hospitality in Early Modern England*, (Oxford: Clarendon Press, 1990), chap. 3.
10. *Ibid.*, p. 43.
11. Alice T. Friedman, *House and Household in Elizabethan England: Wollaton Hall and the Willoughby Family* (University of Chicago Press, 1989), pp. 8–9.
12. Stewart, *Close Readers*, pp. 171, 180, 170.
13. Cicero, *De officiis*, I. 12.
14. John R. Searle *et al.*, *(On) Searle on Conversation*, intro. Herman Parret and Jef Verschueren (Amsterdam, Philadelphia: John Benjamins Publishing Co., 1992) recognises the limits of models of the speech act for understanding 'speech acts' in 'real life' and 'collective behavior', pp. 7, 21. See also Sandy Pelney, *Speech Acts and Literary Theory* (London: Routledge, 1990).
15. Peter Burke, *The Art of Conversation* (Cambridge: Polity Press, 1993), p. 93; see also the warning of Jon R. Snyder, *Writing the Scene of Speaking: Theories of Dialogue in the Late Italian Renaissance* (Stanford University Press, 1989), pp. 16–17.
16. Burke, *Art of Conversation*, pp. 91–2.
17. Lynne Magnusson, *Shakespeare and Social Dialogue: Dramatic Language and Elizabethan Letters* (Cambridge University Press, 1999). See also Penelope Brown and Stephen C. Levinson, *Politeness: Some Universals in Language Usage* (Cambridge University Press, 1978, rpt 1987).
18. Burke's 'A Civil Tongue: Language and Politeness in Early Modern Europe' offers a critique of Brown and Levinson.
19. Magnusson, *Shakespeare and Social Dialogue*, pp. 92, 37.
20. Burke, 'A Civil Tongue', p. 33; see also his discussion of the 'humiliative mode', pp. 44–5.
21. Magnusson, *Shakespeare and Social Dialogue*, pp. 24–6, 93.
22. Virginia Cox, *The Renaissance Dialogue: Literary Dialogue in its Social and Political Contexts, Castiglione to Galileo* (Cambridge University Press, 1992), pp. 12–13. See also Roger Deakins, 'The Tudor Prose Dialogue: Genre and Anti-Genre', *Studies in English Literature* 20 (1980): 5–23 on the English dialogue. For other excellent discussions of the Italian dialogue see David Marsh, *The Quattrocento Dialogue: Classical Tradition and Humanist Innovation* (Cambridge, MA: Harvard University Press, 1980) and Snyder, *Writing the Scene of Speaking*.
23. Mary Margaret McCabe, *Plato and his Predecessors: the Dramatisation of Reason* (Cambridge University Press, 2000), p. 25.

24. Snyder, *Writing the Scene of Speaking*, p. 35. See also C. J. R. Armstrong, 'The Dialectical Road to Truth: the Dialogue' in *French Renaissance Studies 1540–1570: Humanism and the Encyclopedia*, ed., Peter Sharatt (Edinburgh University Press, 1976), pp. 36–51.
25. McCabe, *Plato and his Predecessors*, p. 6.
26. This fourth category of *honestas* is usually translated as 'temperance' only, which misses the connection with 'decorum'.
27. 'quod decet, honestum est et, quod honestum est, decet'.
28. Thomas Wilson, *Arte of Rhetorique*, ed., Thomas J. Derrick (New York: Garland Publishing Inc., 1982), p. 325.
29. *OED* 3c.
30. Steven Shapin, *A Social History of Truth: Civility and Science in Seventeenth-Century England* (University of Chicago Press, 1994), p. 36.
31. William Empson, *The Structure of English Words* (Harmondsworth: Penguin, 1995), pp. 185, 189, 187. *OED* 3c records an obsolete meaning of honesty: 'generosity, liberality, hospitality'.
32. *The Dictionary of syr Thomas Eliot knight* (London, 1538), sig. Kiv; see Thomas Cooper, *Thesaurus linguae Romanae & Britannicae* (London 1565), sig. Lll3v.
33. Cicero, *De senectute, De amicitia, De divinatione*, trans. William Armistead Falconer (London: William Heinemann; New York: G. P. Putnam's Sons, 1923).
34. In contrast see Daniel Tuvill's Tacitean account of civil conversation, 'Of Civil Carriage and Conversation', pp. 88–94, in *Essays Politic and Moral and Essays Moral and Theological*, ed., John L. Lievsay (Charlottesville: University Press of Virginia, 1971).
35. Thomas Pritchard, *The schoole of honest and vertuous lyfe* (London, 1579), sigs. C2r, F2v.
36. James Cleland, *The Institution of a Young Noble Man* [facsimile of the 1612 edition], ed., Max Molyneaux (New York: Scholar's Facsimiles and Reprints, 1948), pp. 168–69, 176.
37. See the discussion of nobility at *ibid.*, 2. 174–98.
38. For a recent analysis of the *Courtier* and other courtesy books which aims to expose the ideological tensions inherent in the treatment of nobility see David M. Posner, *The Performance of Nobility in Early Modern European Literature* (Cambridge University Press, 1999), esp. pp. 15–16. For a study which takes seriously the contribution of *Civile Conversation* to an English classical humanism and the debate about 'true nobility' see Peltonen, *Classical Humanism*, esp. pp. 35–6.
39. Cleland, *Institution*, pp. 169, 192, 186.
40. Cox, *Renaissance Dialogue*, pp. 66–8.
41. See Richard Halpern, *The Poetics of Primitive Accumulation: English Renaissance Culture and the Genealogy of Capital* (Ithaca, NY: Cornell University Press, 1991), chap 1.
42. See Guazzo, *Civile Conversation*, 1. 56; 2. 123; 2. 161–2; 2. 174.

43. See Helen Hackett, 'Courtly writing by women', in *Women and Literature in Britain, 1500–1700*, ed., Helen Wilcox (Cambridge University Press, 1996), pp. 169–89, p. 169.
44. Xenophon, *Xenophons treatise of house holde*, trans. Gentian Hervet (London, 1532). The question is asked by Socrates of Ischomachus: what 'maketh you to be called a good and an honest man?' (sig. C5r).
45. Kathleen M. Davies, 'The Sacred Condition of Equality – How Original were Puritan Doctrines of Marriage?', *Social History* 5 (1977): 563–80, p. 563.
46. Hutson, *Usurer's Daughter*, chap. 1.
47. *Ibid.*, esp. pp. 29, 31.
48. *Ibid.*, p. 30.
49. See introduction to Xenophon, *Oeconomicus: a Social and Historical Commentary*, trans. Sarah B. Pomeroy (Oxford: Clarendon Press, 1994).
50. See Hutson, *Usurer's Daughter*, pp. 30–41.
51. Lena Cowen Orlin, *Private Matters and Public Culture in Post-Reformation England* (Ithaca, NY: Cornell University Press, 1994), p. 138.
52. As Pritchard soberly explains in *The schoole of honest and vertuous lyfe*: 'Dame Nature provident of the vertue of scilence, and of the consequent commodities thereof, incarcerated our tunges in a turret, invironed with sharpe teethe' (sig. C1v).
53. Conrad Heresbach, *Foure Bookes of Husbandry*, trans. Barnabe Googe (London, 1577) (Amsterdam: De Capo Press, 1971), sig. A5r.
54. See Pomeroy in Xenophon, *Oeconomicus*, p. 259; Helen North, *Sophrosyne: Self-Knowledge and Self-Restraint in Greek Literature* (Ithaca, NY: Cornell University Press, 1966), p. 221.
55. Quintilian, *Institutio Oratoria*, 4 vols, trans. H. E. Butler (London: William Heinemann; New York: G. P. Putnam's Sons, 1921), 9. 2.15.
56. In Pomeroy's translation of Xenophon: '"What should I be able to do to help you? What ability have I got? Everything depends on you. My mother told me that my duty is to practise self-control"', *Oeconomicus*, p. 141.
57. See Pomeroy's discussion of the dialogue form of *Oeconomicus* pp. 19–20, and the indoctrination of the wife, pp. 272–3, n. 10. As she notes, there is no articulation of opposing views in this dialogue. She also notes that the wife is being tamed like an animal.
58. See, for example, Gerald P. Mohrmann, '*The Civile Conversation*: Communication in the Renaissance', in *Speech Monographs* 39 (1972): 193–204, esp. p. 201.
59. Guazzo's use of *Oeconomicus* can be found at 3. 18 and 3. 21–3 where Anniball advises William to marry a 'young gyrle' who may be more easily turned into a thrifty and obedient wife.
60. Castiglione, *Courtier*, pp. 214–17.
61. Jean Bethke Elshstain, *Public Man, Private Woman: Women in Social and Political Thought* (Princeton University Press; Oxford: Martin Robertson, 1981), p. 119.

2. FROM RHETORIC TO CONVERSATION: READING FOR CICERO IN *THE BOOK OF THE COURTIER*

1. Eugenio Garin, *Italian Humanism: Philosophy and Civic Life in the Renaissance*, trans. Peter Munz (Oxford: Basil Blackwell, 1965), p. 78.
2. From Garin, *L'educazione in Europe 1400–1600* (Bari, 1966), pp. 140–1, trans. Daniel Javitch in *Poetry and Courtliness*, pp. 10–11, n. 6.
3. Thomas M. Greene, '*Il Cortegiano* and the Choice of a Game' in eds., Hanning and Rosand, *Castiglione: the Ideal and the Real*, pp. 5, 6.
4. Lauro Martines, *Power and Imagination: City-States in Renaissance Italy* (New York: Vintage Books, 1979, rpt. 1980), p. 228.
5. See Fritz Caspari, *Humanism and the Social Order in Tudor England* (University of Chicago Press, 1954), p. 85; also John Major, *Sir Thomas Elyot and Renaissance Humanism* (Lincoln: University of Nebraska Press, 1964).
6. *Il cortegiano* appeared in Spanish in 1534 and in French in 1537. A German translation appeared in 1566.
7. See G. K. Hunter, *John Lyly: from Courtier to Humanist* (London: Routledge and Kegan Paul, 1962), p. 32 and Javitch, *Poetry and Courtliness*, pp. 43–8.
8. All references will be to Castiglione, *The Book of the Courtier*, trans. Thomas Hoby, ed., Virginia Cox (London: Everyman, 1994, rpt. 1974); references to the Italian version, when they appear in my text, will be to *Il libro del cortegiano*, ed., Vittorio Cian (Firenze, 1947) and follow the references to the English version.
9. See esp. Whigham, *Ambition and Privilege*, esp. pp. 18–21.
10. John Strype's *The Life of the Learned Sir Thomas Smith, Kt. D.C.L. Principal Secretary of State to Edward the Sixth and Queen Elizabeth* (Oxford: Clarendon Press, 1820), includes a treatise listed as *Il Cortegliano* [sic] in Smith's library collection, Appendix VI, 'Sir Thomas Smith's Library, 1 August 1566, in his gallery at Hill Hall', pp. 274–81. This text is listed under 'Philosophica'.
11. David Norbrook, *Poetry and Politics in the English Renaissance* (London, Boston: Routledge and Kegan Paul, 1984), p. 77.
12. The original was sent to Cheke by Bucer. See John Strype, *The Life of the Learned Sir John Cheke, Kt. First Instructor, Afterwards Secretary of State to King Edward VI* (Oxford: Clarendon Press, 1821), p. 56.
13. Euan Cameron, '"Civilized Religion" from Renaissance to Reformation and Counter-Reformation' in Burke et al., eds., *Civil Histories*, pp. 49–66, 49.
14. See Jerrold E. Seigel, '"Civic Humanism" or Ciceronian Rhetoric? The Culture of Petrarch and Bruni', *Past and Present* 34 (1966): 3–48, and also Hanna Gray, 'Renaissance Humanism: the Pursuit of Eloquence', *Journal of the History of Ideas* 24 (1963): 497–514, and Paul Oskar Kristeller, *The Classic and Renaissance Thought* (Cambridge, MA: Harvard University Press, 1955). For humanism as a *vita activa politica* see Hans Baron, *The Crisis of the Early Italian Renaissance: Civic Humanism and Republican Liberty in the Age of Classicism and Tyranny*

(Princeton University Press, 1955, rpt. 1967). On republican speech acts see David Norbrook, *Writing the English Republic: Poetry, Rhetoric and Politics, 1627–1660* (Cambridge University Press, 1999), pp. 11–14.

15. For example, Javitch in *Poetry and Courtliness*, and Victoria Kahn, *Rhetoric, Prudence and Skepticism in the Renaissance* (Ithaca, NY: Cornell University Press, 1985), pp. 184–5.
16. Harvey, *Letter-Book*, pp. 167–8.
17. Guazzo, *La civil conversatione* (Venice, 1581), sig. **6. Copy held at the British Library.
18. See chap. 2, 'The Humanists: the Primacy of Speech', in Martin Elsky, *Authorizing Words: Speech, Writing, and Print in the English Renaissance* (Ithaca, NY: Cornell University Press, 1989), p. 38.
19. Or at least, while Castiglione's debt to specific passages in Cicero's *De oratore*, for example, to the discussion of jokes in book 2, has been widely recognised, his imitation of the pedagogic method and aim of *De oratore* has not. See esp. Javitch, *Poetry and Courtliness*, chap. 1 and Kahn, *Rhetoric, Prudence and Skepticism*, p. 184.
20. On Antonius's recantation as a compromise see George Kennedy, *The Art of Rhetoric in the Roman World, 300 BC–AD 300* (Princeton University Press, 1972), p. 207. M. L. Clarke characterises it as a 'lame device' in *Rhetoric at Rome: a Historical Survey* (London: Cohen and West Ltd, 1953), p. 52. See also Brian Vickers's criticism of the inefficiency of the dialogue form of *De oratore* in *In Defence of Rhetoric* (Oxford University Press, 1988), p. 34.
21. P. O. Kristeller, 'Humanism and Scholasticism', in *Studies in Renaissance Thought and Letters* (Rome, Edizioni di storia e letteratura, 1956–96), vol. III: 553–83, p. 560.
22. Kennedy, *Art of Rhetoric*, p. 226.
23. *De oratore* 2. 6.
24. Andrew R. Dyck, *A Commentary on Cicero, De officiis* (Ann Arbor: University of Michigan Press, 1996), pp. 275, 309.
25. 'Socrates far passed all others for accomplished wit in this strain of irony or assumed simplicity [dissimulantia]' (2. 270).
26. *Tusculan Disputations*, trans. J. E. King (London: William Heineman; New York, G. P. Putnam's Sons, 1927), 3. 2.
27. See Cox's discussion of Castiglione's 'rhetoricization of ethics', *Renaissance Dialogue*, p. 57.
28. On temperance as the restraining of hubristic manliness see North, *Sophrosyne*, chap. 1, and also Helen F. North, *From Myth to Icon: Reflections of Greek Ethical Doctrine in Literature and Art* (Ithaca, NY: Cornell University Press, 1979), chap. 1.
29. Aristotle, *The Nicomachean Ethics*, trans. H. Rackman (London: William Heinemann; New York: G. P. Putnam's Sons, 1926), 7. 9. 6.
30. Michel Foucault, *The Use of Pleasure. The History of Sexuality*, vol. II, trans. Robert Hurley (Harmondsworth: Penguin, 1985, rpt. 1987), pp. 64, 68, 69; Greenblatt, *Self-Fashioning*, chap. 4; Lorna Hutson, 'Chivalry for Merchants;

or, Knights of Temperance in the Realms of Gold', *Journal of Medieval and Early Modern Studies* 26 (1996): 29–59.
31. North, *Sophrosyne*, pp. 38–45. (Foucault, *Use of Pleasure*, and Hutson, *Usurer's Daughter*, are similarly indebted to North's studies.)
32. Quentin Skinner, *The Foundations of Modern Political Thought. Vol I: The Renaissance* (Cambridge University Press, 1978, rpt. 1996), p. 125, quoting Francesco Patrizi, *De regno et regis institutione* (Prato, 1531), pp. 371, 392.
33. Skinner, *Foundations*, p. 117.
34. Michael C. Schoenfeldt, *Bodies and Selves in Early Modern England: Physiology and Inwardness in Spenser, Shakespeare, Herbert and Milton* (Cambridge University Press, 1999), p. 11.
35. Joan Kelly, 'Did women have a Renaissance?' in *Women, History and Theory: the Essays of Joan Kelly* (University of Chicago Press, 1984), pp. 19–50, esp. pp. 36–47.
36. North, *Sophrosyne*, p. 233.
37. Peter Burke, *The Fortunes of the* Courtier: *the European Reception of Castiglione's* Cortegiano (Cambridge: Polity Press, 1995), chaps. 3 and 4.
38. For example, 'Mr Martin being asked of Mrs Hubert, how Doctour... her Physician looked in his sicknes; answerd, Mr Doctor lookes like the further end of a fiddler', *The Book of the Courtier*, trans. Thomas Hoby (London, 1561), sig. aa4v.

3. HONEST RIVALRIES: TUDOR HUMANISM AND LINGUISTIC AND SOCIAL REFORM

1. Hirschman, *Passions and the Interests*, p. 32.
2. On the aspirational elitism of the humanist movement see Caspari, *Humanism and the Social Order*, chap. 1; on the careerism of the humanists see Lisa Jardine, *Erasmus, Man of Letters: the Construction of Charisma in Print* (Princeton University Press, 1993) and Stewart, *Close Readers*.
3. Hunter, *John Lyly*, p. 31. Abraham Fleming, trans. Virgil's *Georgics* (1589), sig. A2v, and Cooper, *Thesaurus* (1569), sig. Lll6v, cited in Mike Pincombe, *Elizabethan Humanism: Literature and Learning in the Later Sixteenth Century* (Harlow: Longman, 2001), pp. 5–6.
4. Pincombe, *Elizabethan Humanism*, pp. 8–9.
5. Caspari, *Humanism and the Social Order*, pp. 81, 83. See also John M. Major, *Sir Thomas Elyot and Renaissance Humanism* (Lincoln: University of Nebraska Press, 1964), p. 61.
6. Steven W. May, *The Elizabethan Courtier Poets: the Poems and their Contexts* (Asheville, NC: Pegasus Press, 1991 rpt. 1999), pp. 1–2; see also pp. 11–20, 29–30.
7. King, *English Reformation Literature*, p. 55.
8. Robert Crowley, *The Way to Wealth, wherein is plainly taught a most present remedy for sedition* (London, 1550), sig. A3r.
9. See Anthony Fletcher, *Tudor Rebellions* (Harlow: Longman, 1968, rpt. 1983), chap. 6. Kett's manifesto, argues Fletcher, 'leaves a strong impression of social

conservatism, of the desire to recapture a past where everyone knew his place and function', p. 61.
10. Ruth Mohl, *The Three Estates in Medieval and Renaissance Literature* (New York: Columbia University Press, 1933), p. 277.
11. Keith Wrightson, 'Estates, Degrees, and Sorts: Changing Perceptions of Society in Tudor and Stuart England' in Penelope J. Corfield, ed., *Language, History and Class* (Oxford: Basil Blackwell, 1991), pp. 30–52, p. 32; Mohl, *Three Estates*, pp. 189–90.
12. John D. Cox, *Shakespeare and the Dramaturgy of Power* (Princeton University Press, 1989), p. 51.
13. *Ibid.*, chap. 2.
14. See Vernon Hall, *Renaissance Literary Criticism: a Study of its Social Contexts* (New York: Columbia University Press, 1945), esp. pp. 208–14. The most recent restatement of this theory is to be found in Adam Fox's *Oral and Literate Culture in England, 1500–1700* (Oxford: Clarendon Press, 2000), esp. pp. 100–11.
15. Wrightson, 'Estates, Degrees and Sorts', p. 30.
16. Joseph M. Williams, '"O! When Degree is Shak'd": Sixteenth-Century Anticipations of some Modern Attitudes towards Usage' in Tim William Machan and Charles T. Scott, eds., *English in its Social Contexts: Essays in Historical Sociolinguistics* (Oxford University Press, 1992), pp. 69–101, p. 75.
17. Wrightson, 'Estates, Degrees and Sorts', pp. 40, 36.
18. Thomas Elyot, *The Boke Named the Governour* (London, 1531), ed., Foster Watson (London: J. M. Dent; New York: E. P. Dutton and Co., 1907), p. 4; cited in Wrightson, 'Estates, Degrees and Sorts', p. 36.
19. Wrightson, 'Estates, Degrees and Sorts', pp. 47, 52.
20. Elyot claims that simplicity is 'properly justice', *Governour* p. 208, just as Cicero describes justice as one part of *honestas* in book 1 of *De officiis*.
21. Cox, *Shakespeare*, p. 52.
22. John Cheke, trans. *The Gospel according to Saint Matthew and Part of the First Chapter of the Gospel according to Saint Mark*, intro. and ed., James Goodwin (London: William Pickering; Cambridge: J. J. and J. Deighton, 1843), p. 12.
23. *Ibid.*, p. 15.
24. On the variety of plain styles see esp. Kenneth J. E. Graham, *The Performance of Conviction: Plainness and Rhetoric in the Early English Renaissance* (Ithaca, NY: Cornell University Press, 1994). On the Ciceronian plain style see Alvin Vos, 'The Formation of Roger Ascham's Prose Style', *Studies in Philology* 71 (1974): 344–70, pp. 345–6. Janel M. Mueller has made a case for regarding the euphuistic style of John Lyly as plain, *The Native Tongue and the Word: Developments in English Prose Style 1380–1580* (University of Chicago Press, 1984), chap. 6.
25. See esp. Williams, '"O, when Degree is Shak'd"', pp. 79–80. See also Wrightson, 'Estates, Degrees and sorts'.
26. Fletcher, *Tudor Rebellion*, p. 54.
27. Reverend A. H. Johnson, *The History of the Worshipful Company of the Drapers of London* (Oxford: Clarendon Press, 1914), vol. II, p. 88.

28. For a discussion of the farming manuals see my chap. 4. *A Knack to Know a Knave* [1594] ed., G. R. Proudfoot (Oxford University Press, 1964), sig. A3r. Mopsa's 'honesty' is commented on ironically at p. 94; Dorus professes his honesty to Miso, p. 166, and the shepherds are said to possess 'honest liberty', p. 213, in Philip Sidney, *The Countess of Pembroke's Arcadia (The Old Arcadia)*, ed., Katherine Duncan-Jones (Oxford University Press, 1999).
29. Christopher Brooks, 'Apprenticeship, Social Mobility and the Middling Sort, 1550–1800' in Jonathan Barry and Christopher Brooks, eds., *The Middling Sort of People: Culture, Society and Politics in England, 1550–1800* (Basingstoke: Macmillan, 1994), pp. 52–83, p. 77, quoting from Johnson, *History of Drapers*, vol. 1, p. 265.
30. Christopher Brooks, 'Professions, Ideology and the Middling Sort in the Late Sixteenth and Early Seventeenth Centuries' in Barry and Brooks, eds., *The Middling Sort of People: Culture, Society and Politics in England, 1500–1800* (Basingstoke: Macmillan, 1994), pp. 113–40, p. 124; Brook's source is John Stow, *A Survey of London*, 2 vols., ed., C. L. Kingsford (Oxford: Clarendon Press, 1971), vol. 1, p. 272.
31. Barnaby Rich, *The Honestie of this Age* (London, 1614), sig. A3r.
32. Shepard and Withington, *Communities*, p. 1.
33. For an illuminating discussion of Elyot's use of the word 'simplicity' to which I am indebted see R. W. Maslen, *Elizabethan Fictions: Espionage, Counter-Espionage, and the Duplicity of Fiction in Early Elizabethan Prose Narratives* (Oxford: Clarendon Press, 1997), chap. 1, 'The Fiction of Simplicity in the Sixteenth-Century Treatise'. See also Mueller, *Native Tongue*, chap. 5 and Richard Foster Jones, 'The Moral Sense of Simplicity', *Studies in Honor of Frederick W. Shipley* (St Louis: Washington University Studies, 1942), pp. 265–87.
34. As Mueller notes in the *Native Tongue*, Elyot 'reworks the colloquialism [of the Bible] into formality', p. 258. His movement away from conversation gives rise to an 'imperious presence in his narratives', p. 257.
35. See esp. Caspari, *Humanism and the Social Order*, who writes eloquently of the conservatism of humanist intellectuals like Elyot, pp. 1–2.
36. Cox, *Shakespeare*, pp. 43–4.
37. For commentary on this tale see Maslen *Elizabethan Fictions*, pp. 26–8 and Hutson, *Usurer's Daughter*, pp. 57–64.
38. See *Pasquil the Playne* in Roger Ascham, *The English Works of Roger Ascham*, ed., James Bennett (London: White, Cochrane, and Co., 1815).
39. Mueller suggests in *Native Tongue* that *Toxophilus* 'may be a deliberate outgrowth of the last chapter of book 1 of the *Governour*', pp. 324–25.
40. Roger Ascham, *Toxophilus: the schole of Shootinge* (London, 1545) (Menston: Scolar Press, 1969), sig. A4v.
41. See Ascham, *Schoolmaster*, pp. 80–81, discussed in my chap. 5.
42. Ascham, *English Works*, p. 369.
43. See Smith, *Literary and Linguistic Works*, pp. 199–201.
44. Hudson, *Cambridge Connection*, pp. 18–19, 41–2, 26–31.

45. *Ibid.*, p. 35.
46. For discussion of the strong resistance to the settlement see Christopher Haigh, ed., *The English Reformation Revised* (Cambridge University Press, 1987), pp. 7–8. For an account of the progress of the Act of Supremacy see Norman L. Jones, *Faith by Statute: Parliament and the Settlement of Religion 1559* (London: Swift Printers Ltd; Atlantic Highlands: Humanities Press Inc., 1982), chap. 5.
47. Jones, *Faith by Statute*, p. 147, quoting from B. L., Cotton Vespasian D. 18, fols. 90v-91.
48. Sometimes the connection is made explicitly in Smith's treatise, for example, when he argues thus: 'shall we, who are at this moment asserting that miracles are unnecessary to prove the most serious of doctrines of our faith, seek for miracles to decide these contests of vowels and consonants?', p. 99. On the association of custom with catholic doctrine see part 2, chap. 1 'The Double Game of Custom' in Lawrence Manley, *Convention, 1500–1700* (Cambridge, MA: Harvard University Press, 1980).
49. King, *English Reformation Literature*, p. 23.
50. Stephen Gardiner, *The Letters of Stephen Gardiner*, ed., James Arthur Miller (Cambridge University Press, 1933), pp. xxviii, xxxiv.
51. John Foxe, *Acts and Monuments*, ed., Reverend George Townsend, 8 vols. (New York: AMS Press Inc., 1965), vol. VII, p. 587.
52. See Gardiner: 'You maintain that this is done incorrectly. It is precisely there that the point at issue lies. My contention, indeed, is not that it is done because it is correct but that because it is done it is the correct thing to do', *Letters*, p. 104.
53. The complaint is quoted by Smith, *De Recta et Emendata Linguae Graecae Pronuntiatione*, p. 167.
54. Smith, *Literary and Linguistic Works*. Part 3. Danielsson (Uppsala: Almquist and Wiksell, 1983), pp. 40–1.
55. See Brian P. Levack, *The Civil Lawyers in England 1603–1641: a Political Study* (Oxford: Clarendon Press, 1973), chap. 4, esp. p. 132.
56. Thomas Smith, *De Republica Anglorum* (1583) (Menston: Scolar Press, 1970), sig. F4v.
57. *Proceedings in the Parliaments of Elizabeth I, 1558–1581*, ed., T. E. Hartley (Leicester University Press, 1981), vol. 1, p. 35. I am grateful to Dermot Cavanagh for this reference.
58. Patricia Palmer, *Language and Conquest in Early Modern Ireland: English Renaissance Literature and Elizabethan Imperial Expansion* (Cambridge University Press, 2001), pp. 110–11. See Gilbert Humphrey, *Queene Elizabethes Achademy*, ed., F. J. Furnivall (London: N. Trübner & Co., 1869), pp. 2–3.
59. John Hart, *An Orthographie*, 1569, ed., R. C. Alston (Menston: Scolar Press, 1969), sigs. 4r-4v. For a discussion of Hart see Paula Blank, '"niu ureiting": the Prose of Language Reform in the English Renaissance' in Elizabeth Fowler and Roland Greene, eds., *The Project of Prose in Early Modern Europe and the New World* (Cambridge University Press, 1997), 31–47. See also Cathy Shrank's

forthcoming monograph, 'Writing the Nation: Humanism, Literature and English Identities, 1530–1580'.
60. Richard Mulcaster, *The First Part of the Elementarie which Entreateth Chefelie of the Right Writing of our English Tung* (London, 1582) (Menston: Scolar Press, 1970), pp. 68, 64.
61. Elsky, *Authorizing Words*, p. 46.
62. In his copy of Quintilian's *Institutio Oratoria* Gardiner is identified by Harvey as a great man and orator; see Moore Smith, *Harvey's Marginalia*, p. 122.
63. Levack has revised the exaggerated view of some legal historians of the opposition between a radical, puritan tradition of common law and the Royalist and autocratic tradition of civil law. Both traditions could be used to support or limit the power of the monarch. Nonetheless, he notes, 'Almost invariably the civil lawyers supported the monarchy and the English Church in the political divisions of the early seventeenth century', whereas the common lawyers were divided in their allegiance. See *Civil Lawyers*, intro., esp. pp. 2–3.

4. HONEST SPEAKERS: SOCIABLE COMMERCE AND CIVIL CONVERSATION

1. It was printed under the copious title of *A Compendious or brief examination of certayne ordinary complaints of divers of our country men in these our dayes: which although they are in some parte unjuste & frivolous, yet are they all by way of dialogues throughly debated and discussed*. All citations are to this edition. This treatise is attributed to William Stafford (STC 23133). However, Mary Dewar argues that Smith is the more likely author. See Smith, *A Discourse of the Commonweal of This Realm of England*, attributed to Sir Thomas Smith, ed., Mary Dewar (Charlottesville: University Press of Virginia, 1969), pp. xviii–xxvi. See also Dewar, 'The Authorship of the "Discourse of the Commonweal"', *Economic History Review*, 2nd ser., 19 (1966): 388–400.
2. Joan Thirsk, *Economic Policy and Projects: the Development of a Consumer Culture in Early Modern England* (Oxford: Clarendon Press, 1978), pp. 1, 9.
3. See Joan Thirsk, *The Agrarian History of England and Wales, vol. IV, 1500–1640* (Cambridge University Press, 1967), intro. to chap. 4 'Enclosing and Engrossing' for a discussion of the inflationary pressures prompted by the enclosure of land and for an account of the clash between the individualistic and the communal systems of farming in the mid-sixteenth century, pp. 200–55.
4. Neal Wood, 'Foundations of political economy: the new moral philosophy of Sir Thomas Smith', eds., Paul A. Fideler and T. F. Mayer, *Political Thought and the Tudor Commonwealth: Deep Structure, Discourse and Disguise* (London: Routledge, 1992), pp. 140–68, pp. 143, 151.
5. Andrew McRae, *God Speed the Plough: the Representation of Agrarian England, 1500–1600* (Cambridge University Press, 1996), p. 55.
6. Craig Muldrew, *The Economy of Obligation: the Culture of Credit and Social Relations in Early Modern England* (Basingstoke: Macmillan, 1998), pp. 123–5. For a discussion of the impact that modern theories of economics have had

on our understanding of the early modern experience of emerging market relations see also Craig Muldrew, 'Interpreting the market: the ethics of credit and community relations in early modern England', *Social History* 18 (1993): 163–83.
7. See *De officiis* 1. 22: 'we are not born for ourselves alone, but our country claims a share of our being, and our friends a share'.
8. Muldrew, *Economy of Obligation*, pp. 2, 5. See also Wrightson, *Earthly Necessities*, esp. intro. For an important literary study tackling this issue see Ceri Sullivan, *The Rhetoric of Credit: Merchants in the Early Modern World* (London: Associated University Presses, 2002).
9. Muldrew, *Economy of Obligation*, p. 97.
10. *Ibid.*, pp. 138, 139, citing Guazzo, *Civile Conversation*.
11. Muldrew, *Economy of Obligation*, pp. 131–2; p. 140.
12. *Ibid.*, p. 140. See *De officiis* 2. 10: 'whatever is morally right is also expedient [*quicquid honestum sit, idem sit utile*].'
13. Muldrew, *Economy of Obligation*, chap. 8.
14. Agnew, *Worlds Apart*, p. 59. See also the comments of Halpern, *Poetics of Primitive Accumulation*, chap. 1.
15. On Sidney's policy see Nicholas P. Canny, *The Elizabethan Conquest of Ireland: a Pattern Established, 1565–1576* (Hassocks: Harvester Press, 1976), chap. 3. Sidney planned to plant English colonies in land seized from the defeated rebel Shane O'Neill. This policy was distinctive because it was to be funded by private individuals, p. 65.
16. Cicero, *Marcus Tullius Ciceroes thre bokes of duties, turned oute of latine into english, by Nicholas Grimalde* (London, 1558), sigs. ¶2v–¶3r.
17. He tends to follow Cicero's word order, and he has an incomplete command of the Latin subjunctive, so that, as Howard Jones advises, 'for those who could read Latin even moderately well, the original may have been in many places a good deal easier to comprehend', *Master Tully*, p. 135.
18. *The thre bookes of Tullyes offyces, bothe in latyn tonge & in englysshe, lately translated by Robert Whytington* (London, 1534), sig. C5r. '*Alter locus erat cautionis, ne benignitas maior esset quam facultates, quod, qui benigniores volunt esse, quam res patitur, primum in eo peccant, quod iniuriosi sunt in proximos*', *De officiis*, 1. 44.
19. See 1. 54–5 where Cicero argues that the closest bond in society exists between 'husband and wife', then 'parents and children', then 'brothers and sisters'.
20. Felicity Heal, 'The Idea of Hospitality in Early Modern England', *Past and Present* 102 (1984): 66–93, pp. 86–7.
21. Hugh Latimer, *Sermons and Remains (Sermons 1552–1555, and Letters)*, ed., G. E. Corrie (Cambridge University Press, 1845), p. 88.
22. Hugh Latimer, *A notable Sermon of the reverende father Maister Hughe Latemer, whiche he preached in the Shrouds at paules churche in London on the xviii. daye of Januarye* (London, 1548). For discussion of Crowley's adaptation of medieval complaint see King, *English Reformation Literature*, chap. 7. Latimer's contribution to Protestant plainness is discussed by King at pp. 142–3. See

also chap. 1 of John N. King's *Spenser's Poetry and the Reformation Tradition* (Princeton University Press, 1990).
23. Volume III of *Tudor Economic Documents*, eds., R. H. Tawney and Eileen Power (London: Longmans, 1924) contains excerpts from documents concerned with enclosure. See esp. Lever's Sermon at St Paul's Cross (1550): pp. 47–50.
24. Thomas Tusser's *Five hundreth pointes* (1573) (first printed as *A hundredth good pointes of husbandrie* in 1557), 'The Ladder to Thrift': 'To folow profit earnestlie/but medle not with pilferie./To get by honest practisie,/and keepe thy gettings covertlie.' Cited in McRae, *God Speed the Plough*, p. 147, and quoted from *Five Hundred Points of Good Husbandry*, ed., Geoffrey Grigson (Oxford, 1984), p. 13.
25. Crowley, *Philargyrie of greate Britayne*, sigs. A4v–A5r.
26. Joan Thirsk, 'Making a Fresh Start: Sixteenth-Century Agriculture and the Classical Inspiration' in Michael Leslie and Timothy Raylor, eds., *Culture and Cultivation in Early Modern England: Writing and the Land* (Leicester University Press, 1992), pp. 15–34, p. 19.
27. Andrew McRae, 'Husbandry Manuals and the Language of Agrarian Improvement', in Michael Leslie and Timothy Raylor, eds., *Culture and Cultivation in Early Modern England*, 35–62, p. 39.
28. Conrad Heresbach, *Foure bookes of Husbandry*, trans. Barnabe Googe (London, 1577), sig. A5r. For discussion of this text as gentlemen's reading see Thirsk, 'Making a Fresh Start'.
29. For a similar argument see Francis Bryant's translation of Guevara's *A Dispraise of a life of a Courtier*, sigs. E5v, M8v. Heresbach's intervention in this debate influenced the subsequent representation of the 'courtier' as a spendthrift. See esp. Nicholas Bretan's popular anti-court satire *The Court and Country, or A Briefe Discourse betweene the Courtier and the Country-Man* (1618), also in Hazlitt, *Inedited Tracts*, esp. pp. 183–4.
30. For criticism of this dichotomy see John Frow, *Time and Commodity Culture: Essays in Cultural Theory and Postmodernity* (Oxford: Clarendon Press, 1997).
31. Agnew, *Worlds Apart*, p. 10; Lorna Hutson, *Thomas Nashe in Context* (Oxford: Clarendon Press, 1989), p. 48.
32. See Thirsk, *Agrarian History*, pp. 213–38, for discussion of the agricultural acts and statutes passed to encourage tillage: 1489, 1515, 1536, 1550, 1552 and 1563.
33. The maxim comes from Cicero's *Tusculan Disputations* I. 4: '*Honos alit artes*' [Public esteem is the nurse of the arts].
34. The Capper is described as 'honest' on sig. A3r.
35. On Smith's involvement see Canny, *Elizabethan Conquest of Ireland*, pp. 85–8. Canny argues that Smith wanted 'to drive out the ruling elite and retain the majority of the population as docile cultivators', p. 130. See also David Beers Quinn, 'Sir Thomas Smith (1513–1577) and the Beginnings of English Colonial Theory', *Proceedings of the American Philosophical Society* 89 (1945): 543–60.
36. See Mary Dewar, chap. 4 of *Sir Thomas Smith: a Tudor Intellectual in Office* (London: Athlone Press, 1964), esp. pp. 159–70. For Smith's broadsheet see *A letter sent by J.B. Gentleman unto his very friend and master R.C. Esquire*,

wherein is contained a large discourse of the peopling and inhabiting the country called the Ardes and other adjacent in the North of Ireland and taken in hand by Sir Thomas Smith, one of the Queen Majesty's Privy Council and Thomas Smith Esquire his son.

37. Dewar, *Sir Thomas Smith*, p. 164. The proposal was discovered among the Smith family papers at the Essex Record Office in 1955 (E.R.O. D/D Sh. 01/1–7), Dewar, *Sir Thomas Smith*, p. 165, n. 2.
38. Quoted in Dewar, *Sir Thomas Smith*, p. 166.
39. Greenblatt, *Renaissance Self-Fashioning*, p. 179. The same question is asked by Ciaran Brady in 'Spenser's Irish Crisis: Humanism and Experience in the 1590s', *Past and Present* 111 (1986): 17–49.
40. Greenblatt, *Renaissance Self-fashioning*, p. 186.
41. Greenblatt, *Renaissance Self-Fashioning*, p. 178.
42. *Ibid.*, p. 187.
43. Debora Shuger, 'Irishmen, Aristocrats, and Other White Barbarians', *Renaissance Quarterly* 50 (1997): 494–525.
44. Katherine Simms, 'Guesting and Feasting in Gaelic Ireland', *Journal of the Royal Society of Antiquaries of Ireland* 108 (1978): 67–100.
45. See Andrew Hadfield, *Edmund Spenser's Irish Experience: Wilde Fruit and Salvage Soyl* (Oxford: Clarendon Press, 1997), Willy Maley, *Salvaging Spenser: Colonialism, Culture and Identity* (Basingstoke: Macmillan, 1997), Andrew Murphy, *But the Irish Sea Betwixt Us: Ireland, Colonialism, and Renaissance Literature* (Lexington: University of Kentucky Press, 1999), and more recently, Palmer, *Language and Conquest*. On Bryskett see the appendix to Janet Spens, *Spenser's Faerie Queene: an Interpretation* (London: Edward Arnold and Co., 1934) and Henry R. Plomer and Tom Peete Cross, *The Life and Correspondence of Lodowick Bryskett* (University of Chicago Press, 1927).
46. *De gli Hecatommithi di M. Giovanni Battista Giraldi Cinthio, nobile Ferrese. Nella quale si contengono tre Dialoghi della vita Civile* (Vinegia, 1566).
47. Lodowick Bryskett, *A Discourse of Civill Life* in *Literary Works*, ed., J. H. P. Pafford (Gregg International Publishers Ltd, 1972), sig. X3r.
48. Plomer and Cross, *Life*, pp. 77–8. They suggest that it is likely that the preliminary material to each division was added later, but probably before 1586.
49. On the public reading of diplomatic letters and the use of courtly dialogue in correspondence see Rivkah Zim, 'Dialogue and Discretion: Thomas Sackville, Catherine de Medici and the Anjou Marriage Proposal, 1571', *Historical Journal* 40 (1997): 287–310.
50. Cited in Plomer and Cross, *Life*, pp. 33–4.
51. On Spenser's similarly 'plastic' use of metaphors of cultivation see Eamon Grennan, 'Language and Politics: a Note on some Metaphors in Spenser's *A View of the Present State of Ireland*', *Spenser Studies* 3 (1982): 99–110.
52. The virtuous man 'knoweth that he is not borne to himselfe alone, but to civill societie and conversation', sig. Dd3v. Prudence 'works' in a man the understanding 'that as he travels to attain for himself profit & goodnes; so acknowledging himselfe to be borne for the good also of others, endevoreth to

direct the affaires also of his parents, friends and Common-weale to the same end of profit & goodnes', sig. Kk2v.
53. On the qualities of English see sigs. B2r–B2v; on the obscurity of Aristotle and Plato see sig. D4v.

5. A COMMONWEALTH OF LETTERS: HARVEY AND SPENSER IN DIALOGUE

1. Halpern, *Primitive Accumulation*, pp. 22, 26. On the reform of schools see chap. 4 'Social change and educational expansion 1530–1640' in John Lawson and Harold Silver, *A Social History of Education in England* (London: Methuen and Co. Ltd, 1973). The most comprehensive study of Cambridge and Oxford universities in the period remains Mark H. Curtis, *Oxford and Cambridge in Transition, 1558–1642: an Essay on Changing Relations between the English Universities and English Society* (Oxford: Clarendon Press, 1959).
2. Halpern, *Primitive Accumulation*, pp. 45, 28. Not all critics, however, are comfortable with this narrative. See Rebecca W. Bushnell, *A Culture of Teaching: Early Modern Humanism in Theory and Practice* (Ithaca: Cornell University Press, 1996), esp. pp. 73–4.
3. *Have With You to Saffron-Walden*, III. 62, in Thomas Nashe, *The Works of Thomas Nashe*, 5 vols., ed., Ronald B. McKerrow (Oxford: Basil Blackwell, 1958). All citations to Nashe are to this edition. Citations refer to volume and page number.
4. For accounts of this quarrel see Stern, *Gabriel Harvey*, pp. 85–124, and Nashe, *Works*, v. 65–110.
5. Gabriel Harvey, *Foure Letters and certaine Sonnets, especially touching Robert Greene, and other parties, by him abused* (London, 1592), sig. H4v. All citations are to this edition.
6. Sonnet XII, 'His Court of Honour', sig. I2v; sonnet XVIII, sig. I3v.
7. Harvey is, among other things, a 'common coosener of curteous readers', a 'grosse shifter for shitten tapesterly jests', 'a selfe-love surfetted sot', 'a scholer in nothing but the scum of schollership' and 'a stale soker at Tullies *Offices*', *Strange Newes* in *Works*, I. 304, 302.
8. See Hutson's excellent discussion of Nashe's irony in *Nashe*, esp. chap 9.
9. *Three Proper, and wittie, familiar letters: lately passed betwene two Universitie men. Two Other very commendable Letters, of the same mens writing: both touching the foresaid Artificiall Versifying, and certain other Particulars* (London, 1580), sig. A2r. All citations are to this edition.
10. James Nielson, 'Reading between the Lines: Manuscript Personality and Gabriel Harvey's Drafts', *Studies in English Literature, 1500–1900* 33 (1993): 43–82, p. 44.
11. Katherine Wilson, 'Revenge of the Angel Gabriel: Harvey's "A Nobleman's Suit to a Country Maid"', in Mike Pincombe, ed., *The Anatomy of Tudor Literature: Proceedings of the First International Conference of the Tudor Symposium (1998)* (Aldershot: Ashgate, 2001), pp. 79–89, p. 83.

12. Harvey, *Letter-book*, pp. 95, 96, 98–9.
13. In fact, Harvey had merely said in *Foure Letters* that he was commended by some of the greatest scholars in the world', pp. 27–8.
14. The adjective is Harvey's, *Three Proper Letters*, sig. H4v.
15. In the sixteenth century, Alan Bray notes, the word 'friend' signifies a 'network of subtle bonds amongst influential patrons and their clients, suitors, and friends at court', but it also carried the modern connotation of intimacy and companionship. See Alan Bray, 'Homosexuality and the Signs of Male Friendship in Elizabethan England', in Jonathan Goldberg, ed., *Queering the Renaissance* (Durham, NC: Duke University Press, 1994), pp. 40–61, p. 42, and also Stewart, *Close Readers*, pp. xxiii, xlii, xliv, xlv; see Bray also for a discussion of the friend as a 'bedfellow'.
16. On Harvey's employment as a reader or 'facilitator' in the household of the earl of Leicester see Lisa Jardine and Anthony Grafton, '"Studied for action": How Gabriel Harvey Read His Livy', *Past and Present* 129 (1990): 30–78. See also the intro. to Stern, *Gabriel Harvey*.
17. See Guazzo, *Civile Conversation*, 4. 216: William tells Anniball at the close of the dialogue, 'I will not altogether leave you solitarie, because there shall come (during our absence) letters from mee, to holde you still in talke', and he hopes he will 'talke and converse with mee after this guise and manner'. See also Harvey in the *Letter-book*, p. 76: 'What ar letters amongst frendes byt familiar discourses and pleasant conferences?'
18. For these rules see Derek Attridge, *Well-Weighed Syllables: Elizabethan Verse in Classical Metres* (Cambridge University Press, 1974), pp. 7–13.
19. *Ibid.*, p. 138. On quantification see also O. B. Hardison, Jr., *Prosody and Purpose in the English Renaissance* (Baltimore, MD: Johns Hopkins University Press, 1989).
20. The fact that Harvey is usually read as the more rigid classicist says much about the success of satirical portraits of him. Hardison, *Prosody and Purpose*, describes Harvey as a 'hard classicist' like Ascham and Gascoigne as a 'moderate classicist', pp. 113–14; p. 105. Spenser is also the more boastful of the two in the *Letters*; see sig, A4v.
21. Roger Ascham, *The Schoolmaster (1570)*, ed., Lawrence V. Ryan (Charlottesville: University Press of Virginia), pp. 139–40.
22. Richard Helgerson, *Forms of Nationhood: the Elizabethan Writing of England* (University of Chicago Press, 1992), chap. 1, esp. p. 28.
23. *De oratore* 1. 154–5, Ascham, *Schoolmaster* pp. 83–4.
24. For a fascinating reading of the possible politics of this friendship see chap. 4 of Stewart's *Close Readers*.
25. 'Tully in the person of Lucius Crassus, whom he maketh his example of eloquence and true judgment in learning, doth not only praise specially and choose this way of translation for a young man, but does also discommend and refuse his own former wont in exercising *paraphrasin* and *metaphrasin*', *Schoolmaster*, pp. 83–4.

26. See especially Maslen, *Elizabethan Fictions*, who argues that *The Schoolmaster* is 'among other things, an impassioned plea for state control over language', p. 45.
27. Attridge, *Well-Weighed Syllables*, p. 94.
28. Lisa Jardine, *Erasmus, Man of Letters*, p. 18.
29. Harvey, *Letter-book*, p. 165.
30. Smith, *De Recta et Emendata Linguae Anglicae Scriptione*, p. 19.
31. See esp. Helgerson, *Forms of Nationhood*, chap. 1, Paula Blank, *Broken English: Dialects and the Politics of Language in Renaissance Writings* (London: Routledge, 1996) and Cathy Shrank, 'Rhetorical constructions of a national community: the role of the King's English in mid-Tudor writing' in eds., Shepard and Withington *Communities*: 180–98.
32. Such an argument will surprise some critics. See Alexandra Halasz, *The Marketplace of Print: Pamphlets and the Public Sphere in Early Modern England* (Cambridge University Press, 1997), who contrasts Harvey the 'failed capitalist' with the entrepreneurial Nashe, chap. 3.
33. On book-selling at Stourbridge fair see Alison J. Roberts-Roddham, *Fairs in England 1580–1680* (Bristol: Stuart Press, 1999), p. 6.
34. Harvey's financial difficulties in the 1570s are noted by Stern, *Gabriel Harvey*, p. 50.
35. Referring to Spenser's *Stemmata Dudleiana* and some 'nine Englishe Commoedies', for example, Harvey writes, 'whiche two shal go for my money, when all is done: especiallye if you woulde but bestow one sevennights pollishing and trimming upon eyther', sig. D1v. For similar complaints see sigs. A3v and D2r. Harvey repeatedly revised his work; his surviving copy of *Three Proper Letters*, held at Peterborough Cathedral, includes many marginal corrections. See David McKitterick's list of marginal corrections in his review of Virginia Stern's *Gabriel Harvey*, *The Library* 6 (1981): 348–53.

6. A NEW POET, A NEW SOCIAL ECONOMY: HOMOSOCIALITY IN *THE SHEPHEARDES CALENDER*

1. Edmund Spenser, *The Yale Edition of the Shorter Poems of Edmund Spenser*, eds., William A. Oram, Einar Bjorvand, Ronald Bond, Thomas H. Cain, Alexander Dunlop and Richard Schell (New Haven, CT: Yale University Press, 1989), p. 13. All citations are to this edition.
2. Renato Poggioli, *The Oaten Flute: Essays on Pastoral Poetry and the Pastoral Ideal* (Cambridge, MA: Harvard University Press, 1975), p. 2.
3. See Renwick who argues that Thenot, Cuddie, Piers, Thomalin and Willie are 'evidently members of the Cambridge group of friends; but they say and do nothing to make their identification vitally important', in Edmund Spenser, *The Shepherd's Calender*, ed., W. L. Renwick (London: Scolartis Press, 1930), p. 166. The most detailed analysis of the authorship of E.K. is offered by Louise Schleiner in 'Spenser's "E.K." as Edmund Kent (Kenned/of Kent):

Kyth (Couth), Kissed, and Kunning-Conning', *English Literary Renaissance* 20 (1990): 374–407. Her view is that Spenser 'primarily wrote the apparatus, with the initial help and general inspiration of Harvey', p. 380.
4. Michelle O'Callaghan, *The 'shepheards nation': Jacobean Spenserians and Early Stuart Political Culture, 1612–1625* (Oxford: Clarendon Press, 2000), pp. 2, 11.
5. Lisa Jardine's study of Harvey's copy of Livy's *Decades* has located one such reading community. His marginalia are a record of a debate which took place at Smith's home, Hill Hall, Theydon Mount 'in which Livy's historical commentary stimulated a lively topical discussion of Elizabethan military strategy' between Thomas Smith, his son, Sir Humphrey Gilbert and Walter Haddon, probably in 1570 or early 1571. See 'Mastering the Uncouth: Gabriel Harvey, Edmund Spenser and the English Experience in Ireland', in John Henry and Sarah Hutton, eds., *New Perspectives on Renaissance Thought: Essays in the History of Science, Education and Philosophy in Memory of Charles B. Schmitt* (London: Duckworth, 1990), pp. 68–82, pp. 73–74.
6. Mantuan, *The Eglogs of the Poet B. Mantuan Carmelitan, Turned into English Verse, and set forth with the Argument to everye Egloge by George Turbevile Gent.* (London, 1567), sig. A4r. All citations are to this edition.
7. For discussion of E.K.'s unreliability see Richard Rambuss, *Spenser's Secret Career* (Cambridge University Press, 1993), pp. 50–53.
8. Harvey, *Marginalia*, pp. 166–7. Gascoigne died on 7 October 1577. Harvey's reading is dated September 1577. See Harvey, *Marginalia*, p. 165.
9. *Ibid.*, p. 170.
10. George Gascoigne, *A Hundreth Sundrie Flowres*, ed., G. W. Pigman III, (Oxford: Clarendon Press, 2000), p. xxxviii, p. 361.
11. Maslen, *Elizabethan Fictions*, p. 118.
12. See Attridge, *Well-Weighed Syllables*, pp. 108–11 for a discussion of the reasons for this delayed appreciation of blank verse.
13. George Gascoigne, *The Steele Glas* (London, 1576), sigs. A2v, A3r.
14. Hudson, *Cambridge Connection*, pp. 38–9. See Bryson, *From Courtesy to Civility*, pp. 148–9 and also Wilfrid R. Prest, *The Inns of Court under Elizabeth I and the Early Stuarts 1590–1640* (Harlow: Longman, 1972).
15. See Turbeville, *Epitaphes, Epigrams, Songs and Sonets* (London, 1567), sigs. Q2r–Q2v.
16. Ros King, ed., *The Works of Richard Edwards: Politics, Poetry and Performance in Sixteenth-Century England* (Manchester University Press, 2001), p. 42.
17. Richard Edwards, *The Paradyse of daynty devises, aptly furnished, with sundry pithie learned inventions* (London, 1576), sigs. A3r, B4v.
18. Edwards, *Paradyse of daynty devises* (London, 1578), sig. D3r.
19. *Richard Edwards*, ed., Ros King, includes a recent edition of *Damon and Pythias*; she also discusses John Bereblock's eyewitness account of *Palamon and Arcyte*, pp. 66–70. All citations are to this edition. (Citations refer to scene and line number.)

20. Edwards entered Corpus Christi College, Oxford as an undergraduate in 1539 and become a probationer fellow in 1544. See King, ed., *Richard Edwards*, pp. 2–3.
21. '*Non igitur utilitatem amicitia, sed utilitas amicitiam secuta est.*'
22. King, ed., *Richard Edwards*, describes the 'gales of laughter' at a Globe performance in 1996 which met the scene in which Damon and Pythias each attempt to 'gain the moral advantage in self-sacrifice', pp. 59–60.
23. It is unlikely that they could have afforded to join. Prest notes that the Inns of Court were more expensive than the universities because members had to pay to stay (approximately £40 a year between 1590 and 1640), *Inns of Court*, pp. 27–8.
24. King, *Spenser's Poetry and the Reformation Tradition*, chap. 1
25. *Ibid.*, p. 26. *Franklin's Prologue*, line 8.
26. Paul Hammond, *Love between Men in English Literature* (Basingstoke: Macmillan, 1996), p. 33. See also Jonathan Goldberg, chap. 3 'Spenser's Familiar Letters' in *Sodometries: Renaissance Texts, Modern Sexualities* (Stanford University Press, 1992), 63–101.
27. Goldberg, *Sodometries*, p. 66. Goldberg is developing the argument of Alan Bray, who advises on the varied meanings of 'sodomy' and 'buggery' in early modern English, which included bestiality and anal sex with women, in *Homosexuality in Renaissance England* (New York: Columbia University Press, 1982, rpt 1995), see esp. chap. 1.
28. Virgil, *Eclogues, Georgics, Aenied* I–VI, trans. H. Rushton Fairclough (Cambridge, MA: Harvard University Press, 1999), 2nd eclogue, line 56.
29. Eve Kosofsky Sedgwick, *Between Men: English Literature and Male Homosocial Desire* (New York: Columbia University Press, 1995). Sedgwick is exploring the 'radically discontinuous relation of male homosocial and male homosexual bonds', p. 5.
30. See Charlton T. Lewis and Charles Short, eds., *Latin-English Dictonary (Oxford: Clarendon Press, 1966)*. *De amicitia* advises that 'it is love [*amor*], from which the word 'friendship' [*amicitia*] is derived', 8. 26.
31. Stewart, *Close Readers*, p. xxviii–xxix; see also his chap. 2 on John Bale, 'Remapping the Bounds of Sodomy'.
32. King, ed., *Richard Edwards*, pp. 47–8, quoting *Damon and Pithias*, I. 102. See *De amicitia* 17. 56 for the maxim.
33. *De Ratione Studii* ('On the Method of Study'), trans. Brian McGregor in Desiderius Erasmus, *Collected Works of Erasmus. De Copia and De Ratione Studii*, vol. XXIV, ed., Craig R. Thompson (Toronto University Press, 1978), p. 686.
34. Paul Veyne, 'Homosexuality in Ancient Rome', in *Western Sexuality*, eds., Philippe Ariès and André Béjin (Oxford: Blackwell, 1985), 26–35.
35. Marcel Mauss, *The Gift: the Form and Reason for Exchange in Archaic Societies* (London: Routledge, 1989).
36. Harvey, *Pierces Supererogation, or A New Prayse of The Old Asse* (1593), in *The*

Works of Gabriel Harvey, 3 vols., ed., Alexander B. Grosart (London, 1884), vol. II, p. 290.
37. For Googe's biography see Mark Eccles, 'Barnabe Googe in England, Spain and Ireland, *English Literary Renaissance* 15 (1985): 353–70.
38. Barnabe Googe, *Eclogues, Epitaphs, and Sonnets*, ed., Judith M. Kennedy (Toronto University Press, 1989), 5. 149–56. All citations are to this edition. (Citation follows Kennedy's numbering of prefatory material and eclogues and includes line numbers.)
39. See Michael Brennan, *Literary Patronage in the English Renaissance: the Pembroke Family* (London: Routledge, 1988), p. 11.
40. '[C]oloremque ut Socratem ipsum Alibiades; teque ac sermones tuos Silenis, atque Satyris, ut ille illius in Symposio Platonis, compararem', trans. Schleiner, 'Spenser's "E.K."', pp. 392–3, quoted from Harvey, *Marginalia*, pp. 65–6.
41. Virgil, *Eclogues*, 2nd eclogue, line 51.
42. Pincombe, *Elizabethan Humanism*, p. 135. Schleiner argues that we can see Spenser outgrowing Harvey in the gloss, 'Spenser's "E.K."', p. 396.
43. In *Post Reditum in Senatu* (4.8). See Cain's note in Spenser, *Shepheardes Calender*, p. 117.
44. See Cain's note in Spenser, *Shepheardes Calender*, p. 175.
45. See Jane Tylus's excellent essay, 'Spenser's Virgil, and the Politics of Poetic Labor', *English Literary History* 55 (1988): 53–77, esp. p. 54.
46. See Louise Schleiner, 'Spenser and Sidney on the *Vaticinium*', *Spenser Studies* 6 (1988): 129–45.
47. Nancy Jo Hoffman, *Spenser's Pastorals: The Shepheardes Calender and 'Colin Clout'* (Baltimore, MD: Johns Hopkins University Press, 1977), pp. 13, 17.
48. *Ibid*., p. 10.
49. See Cain's introduction to *October*, in Spenser, *Shepheardes Calender*, p. 167.

Bibliography

PRIMARY SOURCES

Anon., *A Knack to Know a Knave* [1594] ed., G. R. Proudfoot (Oxford University Press, 1964)

Anon., *Cyvile and Uncyvile Life* in *Inedited Tracts: Illustrating the Manners, Opinions, and Occupations of Englishmen during the Sixteenth and Seventeenth Centuries*, ed., W. C. Hazlitt 1868 (New York: Burt Franklin, 1964)

Aristotle, *The Nicomachean Ethics*, trans. H. Rackham (London: William Heinemann; New York: G. P. Putnam's Sons, 1926)

Ascham, Roger, *Toxophilus, the Schole of Shootinge* (1545) (Menston: Scolar Press, 1971)

Ascham, Roger, *The Schoolmaster (1570)*, ed., Lawrence V. Ryan (Charlottesville: University Press of Virginia, 1967)

Ascham, Roger, *The English Works of Roger Ascham*, ed., James Bennet (London: White, Cochrane, and Co., 1815)

Bretan, Nicholas, *The Court and Country, or a Briefe Discourse betweene the Courtier and the Country-Man* (1618)

Bryskett, Lodowick, *Literary Works*, ed., J. H. P. Pafford (Gregg International Publishers Ltd, England, 1972)

Casa, Giovanni della, *Galateo of Master John Della Casa* (London, 1576)

Castiglione, Baldassare, *Il libro del cortegiano*, ed., Vittorio Cian (Firenze, 1947)

Castiglione, Baldassare, *The Book of the Courtier*, trans. Thomas Hoby, ed., Virginia Cox (London: Everyman, 1994)

Cheke, John, *The Hurt of Sedition* (London, 1549)

Cheke, John, trans., *The Gospel according to Saint Matthew and Part of the First Chapter of the Gospel according to Saint Mark*, ed., James Goodwin (London: William Pickering; Cambridge: J. J. and J. Deighton, 1843)

Cicero, Marcus Tullius, *The thre bookes of Tullyes offyces, bothe in latyn tonge & in englysshe, lately translated by Robert Whytington* (London, 1534)

Cicero, Marcus Tullius, *Marcus Tullius Ciceroes thre bokes of duties, turned oute of latine into english, by Nicholas Grimalde* (London, 1558)

Cicero, Marcus Tullius, *Tusculan Disputations*, trans. J. E. King (London: William Heinemann; New York, G. P. Putnam's Sons, 1927)

Cicero, Marcus Tullius, *De officiis*, trans. Walter Miller (London: William Heinemann; Cambridge, MA: Harvard University Press, 1956)
Cicero, Marcus Tullius, *De oratore*, 2 vols., trans. E. W. Sutton and H. Rackham (London: William Heinemann; Cambridge, MA: Harvard University Press, 1988)
Cicero, Marcus Tullius, *De senectute, De amicitia, De divinatione*, trans. William Armistead Falconer (London: William Heinemann; New York: G. P. Putnam's Sons, 1923)
Cinthio, Giovanni Battista Giraldi, *De gli Hecatommithi di M. Giovanni Battista Giraldi Cinthio, nobile Ferrese. Nella quale si contengono tre Dialoghi della vita Civile* (Vinegia, 1566)
Cleland, James, *The Institution of a Young Noble Man* [facsimile of the 1612 edition], ed., Max Molyneaux (New York: Scholar's Facsimiles and Reprints, 1948)
Cooper, Thomas, *Thesaurus linguae Romanae & Britannicae* (London 1565)
Crowley, Robert, *The Way to Wealth, wherein is plainly taught a most present remedye for Sedition* (London, 1550)
Crowley, Robert, *Philargyrie of greate Britayne* (London 1551)
Edwards, Richard, *The Paradyse of daynty devises, aptly furnished, with sundry pithie learned inventions* (London, 1576)
Edwards, Richard, *Paradyse of daynty devises* (London 1578)
Edwards, Richard, *The Works of Richard Edwards: Politics, Poetry and Performance in Sixteenth-Century England*, ed., Ros King (Manchester University Press, 2001)
Elyot, Thomas, *The Boke Named the Governour* (London, 1531), ed., Foster Watson (London: J. M. Dent; New York: E. P. Dutton and Co., 1907)
Elyot, Thomas, *The Dictionary of syr Thomas Eliot knight* (London, 1538)
Erasmus, Desiderius, *De Ratione Studii* ('On the Method of Study'), trans. Brian McGregor in Desiderius Erasmus, *Collected Works of Erasmus. De Copia and De Ratione Studii*, vol. XXIV, ed., Craig R. Thompson (Toronto University Press, 1978)
Foxe, John, *Acts and Monuments*, ed., Reverend George Townsend, 8 vols. (New York: AMS Press Inc., 1965), vol. VII
Furnivall, F. J., ed., *Manners and Meals in Olden Times* (London: N. Trübner and Co., 1868)
Gardiner, Stephen, *The Letters of Stephen Gardiner*, ed., James Arthur Miller (Cambridge University Press, 1933)
Gascoigne, George, *The Steele Glas* (London, 1576)
Gascoigne, George, *Certaine Notes of Instruction in Inglyshe Verse* (1575) ed., Edward Arber (London 1868)
Gascoigne, George, *A Hundreth Sundrie Flowres*, ed., G. W. Pigman III (Oxford: Clarendon Press, 2000)
Googe, Barnabe, *Eclogues, Epitaphs, and Sonnets*, ed., Judith M. Kennedy (Toronto University Press, 1989)
Guazzo, Stefano, *The Civile Conversation of M. Steeven Guazzo*, books 1–3 translated by George Pettie (1581), book 4 by Bartholomew Young (1586),

ed., Edward Sullivan (London: Constable and Co. Ltd; New York, Alfred A. Knopf, 1925)

Guevara, Antonio de, *A Dispraise of the life of a Courtier, and a Commendacion of the life of the labouryng man*, trans. Sir Francis Bryant (London, 1548)

Hart, John, *An Orthographie* 1569, ed., R. C. Alston (Menston: Scolar Press, 1969)

Hartley, T. E., ed., *Proceedings in the Parliaments of Elizabeth I, 1558–1581*, 3 vols. (Leicester University Press, 1981)

Harvey, Gabriel, *Letter-Book of Gabriel Harvey AD 1573–1580*, ed., Edward John Long Scott (London: Nichols and Sons, 1884)

Harvey, Gabriel, *Pierces Supererogation, or A New Prayse of The Old Asse* (1593), in *The Works of Gabriel Harvey*, 3 vols., ed., Alexander B. Grosart (London, 1884), vol. II

Harvey, Gabriel, and Edmund Spenser, *Three Proper, and wittie, familiar letters; lately passed betwene two Universitie men. Two Other very commendable Letters, of the same mens writing: both touching the foresaid Artificiall Versifying, and certain other Particulars* (London, 1580)

Harvey, Gabriel, *Gabriel Harvey's Marginalia*, ed., G. C. Moore Smith (Stratford upon Avon: Shakespeare's Head Press, 1913)

Harvey, Gabriel, *Foure Letters and certaine Sonnets, especially touching Robert Greene, and other parties, by him abused* (1592)

Heresbach, Conrad, *Foure Bookes of Husbandry*, trans. Barnabe Googe (London, 1577) (Amsterdam: De Capo Press, 1971)

Humphrey, Gilbert, *Queene Elizabethes Achademy*, ed., F. J. Furnivall (London: N. Trübner & Co., 1869)

Latimer, Hugh, *A notable Sermon of the reverende father Maister Hughe Latemer, whiche he preached in the Shrouds at paules churche in London on the xviii. daye of Januarye* (London, 1548)

Latimer, Hugh, *Sermons and Remains (Sermons 1552–1555, and Letters)*, ed., G. E. Corrie, (Cambridge University Press, 1845)

Mantuan, Baptista Spagnuoli, *The Eglogs of the Poet B. Mantuan Carmelitan, Turned into English Verse, and set forth with the Argument to everye Egloge by George Turbevile Gent* (London, 1567)

Mulcaster, Richard, *The First Part of the Elementarie which Entreateh Chefelie of the Right Writing of our English Tung* (London, 1582) (Menston: Scolar Press, 1970)

Nashe, Thomas, *The Works of Thomas Nashe*, ed., Ronald B. McKerrow, 5 vols. (Oxford: Basil Blackwell, 1958)

Philibert de Vienne, *The Philosopher of the Court*, trans. George North (London, 1575)

Pritchard, Thomas, *The schoole of honest and vertuous lyfe* (London, 1579)

Quintilian, *Institutio Oratoria*, 4 vols., trans. H. E. Butler (London: William Heinemann; New York: G. P. Putnam's Sons, 1921)

Rich, Barnaby, *The honestie of this age* (London, 1614)

Robson, Simon, *A new yeeres gift. The courte of civill courtesie: assembled in the behalfe of all younge gentlemen, to frame their behaviour in all companies* (London, 1577)

Sidney, Philip, *The Countess of Pembroke's Arcadia (The Old Arcadia)*, ed., Katherine Duncan-Jones (Oxford University Press, 1999)
Smith, Thomas, *Literary and Linguistic Works. Part 3. De Recta et Emendata Linguae Anglicae Scriptione, Dialogus* (Paris 1568), trans. Bror Danielsson (Uppsala: Almquist & Wiksell, 1983)
Smith, Thomas, *Literary and Linguistic Works. Part 2. A Critical Edition of De Recta et Emendata Linguae Graecae Pronuntiatione* (*Lutetiae* 1568), ed. and trans. Bror Danielsson (Stockholm: Almquist and Wiksell International, 1978)
Smith, Thomas, *De Republica Anglorum* (1583) (Menston: Scolar Press, 1970)
[Smith, Thomas] *A Compendious or brief examination of certayne ordinary complaints of divers of our country men in these our dayes: which although they are in some parte unjuste & frivolous, yet are they all by way of dialogues throughly debated and discussed* (London, 1581)
[Smith, Thomas], *A Discourse of the Commonweal of This Realm of England*, ed., Mary Dewar (Charlottesville: University Press of Virginia, 1969)
Spenser, Edmund, *The Shepherd's Calender*, ed., W. L. Renwick (London: Scholartis Press, 1930)
Spenser, Edmund, *A View of the Present State of Ireland*, ed., W. L. Renwick (Oxford: Clarendon Press, 1970)
Spenser, Edmund, *The Yale Edition of the Shorter Poems of Edmund Spenser*, eds., William A. Oram, Einar Bjorvand, Ronald Bond, Thomas H. Cain, Alexander Dunlop and Richard Schell (New Haven, CT: Yale University Press, 1989)
Tawney, R. H. and Eileen Power, eds., *Tudor Economic Documents* (London: Longmans, 1924)
Turbeville, George, *Epitaphes, Epigrams, Songs and Sonets* (London, 1567)
Tuvill, Daniel, *Essays Politic and Moral and Essays Moral and Theological*, ed., John L. Lievsay (Charlottesville: University Press of Virginia, 1971)
Virgil, *Eclogues, Georgics, Aenied I–VI*, trans. H. Rushton Fairclough (Cambridge, MA: Harvard University Press, 1999)
Wilson, Thomas, *Arte of Rhetorique*, ed., Thomas J. Derrick (New York: Garland Publishing Inc., 1982)
Xenophon, *Xenophons treatise of house holde*, trans. Gentian Hervet (London, 1532)
Xenophon, *Oeconomicus: a Social and Historical Commentary*, trans. Sarah B. Pomeroy (Oxford: Clarendon Press, 1994)

SECONDARY SOURCES

Agnew, Jean-Christophe, *Worlds Apart: the Market and the Theater in Anglo-American Thought, 1550–1750* (Cambridge University Press, 1986)
Arendt, Hannah, 'Truth and Politics' in *Between Past and Future: Eight Exercises in Political Thought* (Harmondsworth: Penguin, 1954, rpt 1968), pp. 227–64
Armstrong, C. J. R., 'The Dialectical Road to Truth: the Dialogue' in Peter Sharratt, ed., *French Renaissance Studies 1540–1570: Humanism and the Encyclopedia* (Edinburgh University Press, 1976)

Attridge, Derek, *Well-Weighed Syllables: Elizabethan Verse in Classical Metres* (Cambridge University Press, 1974, rpt. 1979)
Baron, Hans, *The Crisis of the Early Italian Renaissance: Civic Humanism and Republican Liberty in the Age of Classicism and Tyranny* (Princeton University Press, 1955, rpt. 1967)
Barry, Jonathan, 'Civility and Civic Culture in Early Modern England: The Meanings of Urban Freedom' in Burke et al., eds., *Civil Histories*, pp. 181–96
Beers Quinn, David, 'Sir Thomas Smith (1513–1577) and the Beginnings of English Colonial Theory', *Proceedings of the American Philosophical Society* 89 (1945): 543–60
Blank, Paula, *Broken English: Dialects and the Politics of Language in Renaissance Writings* (London: Routledge, 1996)
Blank, Paula, '"niu ureiting": the Prose of Language Reform in the English Renaissance', in Elizabeth Fowler and Roland Greene, eds., *The Project of Prose in Early Modern Europe and the New World* (Cambridge University Press, 1997), pp. 31–47
Brady, Ciaran, 'Spenser's Irish Crisis: Humanism and Experience in the 1590s', *Past and Present* 111 (1986): 17–49
Bray, Alan, 'Homosexuality and the Signs of Male Friendship in Elizabethan England', in Jonathan Goldberg, ed., *Queering the Renaissance* (Durham, NC: Duke University Press, 1994), pp. 40–61
Bray, Alan, *Homosexuality in Renaissance England* (New York: Columbia University Press, 1982, rpt 1995)
Brennan, Michael, *Literary Patronage in the English Renaissance: the Pembroke Family* (London: Routledge, 1988)
Brooks, Christopher, 'Apprenticeship, Social Mobility and the Middling Sort, 1550–1800' in Jonathan Barry and Christopher Brooks, eds., *The Middling Sort of People: Culture, Society and Politics in England, 1550–1800* (Basingstoke: Macmillan, 1994), pp. 52–83
Brooks, Christopher, 'Professions, Ideology and the Middling Sort in the Late Sixteenth and Early Seventeenth Centuries' in Jonathan Barry and Christopher Brooks, eds., *The Middling Sort of People: Culture, Society and Politics in England, 1550–1800* (Basingstoke: Macmillan, 1994), pp. 113–40
Brown, Penelope and Stephen C. Levinson, *Politeness: Some Universals in Language Usage* (Cambridge University Press, 1978, rpt. 1987)
Bryson, Anna, *From Courtesy to Civility: Changing Codes of Conduct in Early Modern England* (Oxford: Clarendon Press, 1998)
Burke, Peter, 'The Renaissance Dialogue', *Renaissance Studies* 3 (1989): 1–12.
Burke, Peter, *The Art of Conversation* (Cambridge: Polity Press, 1993)
Burke, Peter, *The Fortunes of the* Courtier: *the European Reception of Castiglione's* Cortegiano (Cambridge: Polity Press, 1995)
Burke, Peter, Brian Harrison and Paul Slack, eds., *Civil Histories: Essays Presented to Sir Keith Thomas* (Oxford University Press, 2000)
Burke, Peter, 'A Civil Tongue: Language and Politeness in Early Modern Europe' in Burke, Harrison and Slack, eds., *Civil Histories*, pp. 31–48

Bushnell, Rebecca W., *A Culture of Teaching: Early Modern Humanism in Theory and Practice* (Ithaca: Cornell University Press, 1996)
Cameron, Euan, '"Civilized Religion" from Renaissance to Reformation and Counter-Reformation' in Burke, Harrison and Slack, eds., *Civil Histories*, pp. 49–66
Canny, Nicholas P., *The Elizabethan Conquest of Ireland: a Pattern Established, 1565–1576* (Hassocks: Harvester Press, 1976)
Caspari, Fritz, *Humanism and the Social Order in Tudor England* (University of Chicago Press, 1954)
Clarke, M. L., *Rhetoric at Rome: a Historical Survey* (London: Cohen and West Ltd, 1953)
Collinson, Patrick, *The Elizabethan Puritan Movement* (Oxford: Clarendon Press, 1967, rpt. 1990)
Collinson, Patrick, *De Republica Anglorum. Or, History with the Politics Put Back*, Inaugural Lecture 9 November 1989 (Cambridge University Press, 1990)
Cox, John D., *Shakespeare and the Dramaturgy of Power* (Princeton University Press, 1989)
Cox, Virginia, *The Renaissance Dialogue: Literary Dialogue in its Social and Political Contexts, Castiglione to Galileo* (Cambridge University Press, 1992)
Curtis, Mark H., *Oxford and Cambridge in Transition, 1558–1642: an Essay on Changing Relations between the English Universities and English Society* (Oxford: Clarendon Press, 1959)
Davies, Kathleen M., 'The Sacred Condition of Equality – How Original were Puritan Doctrines of Marriage?', *Social History* 5 (1977): 563–80
Deakins, Roger, 'The Tudor Prose Dialogue: Genre and Anti-Genre', *Studies in English Literature* 20 (1980): 5–23
Dewar, Mary, *Sir Thomas Smith: a Tudor Intellectual in Office* (London: Athlone Press, 1964)
Dewar, Mary, 'The Authorship of the "Discourse of the Commonweal"', *Economic History Review*, 2nd ser., 19 (1966): 388–400
Dyck, Andrew R., *A Commentary on Cicero, De officiis* (Ann Arbor: University of Michigan Press, 1996, rpt. 1999)
Eagleton, Terry, *The Idea of Culture* (Oxford: Blackwell, 2000)
Eccles, Mark, 'Barnabe Googe in England, Spain and Ireland', *English Literary Renaissance* 15 (1985): 353–70
Elias, Norbert, *The History of Manners: the Civilizing Process*, vol. I, trans. Edmund Jephcott (New York: Pantheon Books, 1978)
Elshstain, Jean Bethke, *Public Man, Private Woman: Women in Social and Political Thought* (Princeton University Press, 1981)
Elsky, Martin, *Authorizing Words: Speech, Writing, and Print in the English Renaissance* (Ithaca, NY: Cornell University Press, 1989)
Empson, William, *The Structure of English Words* (Harmondsworth: Penguin, 1995)
Fletcher, Anthony, *Tudor Rebellions* (Harlow: Longman, 1968, rpt. 1983)
Foucault, Michel, *The Use of Pleasure*, vol. II of *The History of Sexuality*, trans. Robert Hurley (Harmondsworth: Penguin, 1985)

Fox, Adam, *Oral and Literate Culture in England, 1500–1700* (Oxford: Clarendon Press, 2000)
Friedman, Alice T., *House and Household in Elizabethan England: Wollaton Hall and the Willoughby Family* (University of Chicago Press, 1989)
Freud, Sigmund, *The Standard Edition of the Complete Psychological Works of Sigmund Freud, vol. XXI (1927–1931): The Future of an Illusion, Civilization and its Discontents and Other Works*, trans. James Strachey in collaboration with Anna Freud (London: Vintage, 2001)
Frow, John, *Time and Commodity Culture: Essays in Cultural Theory and Postmodernity* (Oxford: Clarendon Press, 1997)
Gallagher, Catherine and Stephen Greenblatt, *Practicing New Historicism* (University of Chicago Press, 2000)
Garin, Eugenio, *Italian Humanism: Philosophy and Civic Life in the Renaissance*, trans. Peter Munz (Oxford: Basil Blackwell, 1965)
Goldberg, Jonathan, *Sodometries: Renaissance Texts, Modern Sexualities* (Stanford University Press, 1992)
Graham, Kenneth J. E., *The Performance of Conviction: Plainness and Rhetoric in the Early English Renaissance* (Ithaca, NY: Cornell University Press, 1994)
Gray, Hanna, 'Renaissance Humanism: the Pursuit of Eloquence', *Journal of the History of Ideas* 24 (1963): 497–514
Greenblatt, Stephen, *Renaissance Self-Fashioning: from More to Shakespeare* (University of Chicago Press, 1980, rpt. 1984)
Greenblatt, Stephen, *Shakespearean Negotiations: the Circulation of Social Energy in Renaissance England* (Oxford: Clarendon Press, 1988, rpt. 1992)
Greene, Thomas, M., '*Il Cortegiano* and the Choice of a Game' in Robert W. Hanning and David Rosand, eds., *Castiglione: The Ideal and the Real in Renaissance Culture* (New Haven: Yale University Press, 1983), pp. 1–15
Grennan, Eamon, 'Language and Politics: a Note on some Metaphors in Spenser's *A View of the Present State of Ireland*', *Spenser Studies* 3 (1982): 99–110
Hackett, Helen, 'Courtly writing by women', in Helen Wilcox, ed., *Women and Literature in Britain, 1500–1700* (Cambridge University Press, 1996), pp. 169–89
Haigh, Christopher, ed., *The English Reformation Revised* (Cambridge University Press, 1987)
Halasz, Alexandra, *The Marketplace of Print: Pamphlets and the Public Sphere in Early Modern England* (Cambridge University Press, 1997)
Hall, Vernon, *Renaissance Literary Criticism: a Study of its Social Contexts* (New York: Columbia University Press, 1945)
Halpern, Richard, *The Poetics of Primitive Accumulation: English Renaissance Culture and the Genealogy of Capital* (Ithaca, NY: Cornell University Press, 1991)
Hammond, Paul, *Love between Men in English Literature* (Basingstoke: Macmillan, 1996)
Hanning, Robert W. and David Rosand, eds., *Castiglione: the Ideal and the Real in Renaissance Culture* (Cambridge, MA: Harvard University Press, 1983)
Hardison, Jr., O. B., *Prosody and Purpose in the English Renaissance* (Baltimore, MD: Johns Hopkins University Press, 1989)

Heal, Felicity, 'The Idea of Hospitality in Early Modern England', *Past and Present* 102 (1984): 66–93
Heal, Felicity, *Hospitality in Early Modern England* (Oxford: Clarendon Press, 1990)
Helgerson, Richard, *Forms of Nationhood: the Elizabethan Writing of England* (University of Chicago Press, 1992)
Hirschman, Albert O., *The Passions and Interests: Political Arguments for Capitalism before its Triumph* (Princeton University Press, 1977)
Hoffman, Nancy Jo, *Spenser's Pastorals: The Shepheardes Calender and 'Colin Clout'* (Baltimore, MD: Johns Hopkins University Press, 1977)
Hudson, Winthrop S., *The Cambridge Connection and the Elizabethan Settlement of 1559* (Durham, NC: Duke University Press, 1980)
Hunter, G. K., *John Lyly: from Courtier to Humanist* (London: Routledge and Kegan Paul, 1962)
Hutson, Lorna, *Thomas Nashe in Context* (Oxford: Clarendon Press, 1989)
Hutson, Lorna, *The Usurer's Daughter: Male Friendship and Fictions of Women in Sixteenth-Century England* (London: Routledge, 1994)
Hutson, Lorna, 'Chivalry for Merchants; or, Knights of Temperance in the Realms of Gold', *Journal of Medieval and Early Modern Studies* 26 (1996): 29–59
James, Mervyn, *Family, Lineage and Civil Society: a Study of Society, Politics and Mentality in the Durham Region 1500–1640* (Oxford: Clarendon Press, 1974)
James, Mervyn, 'English Politics and the Concept of Honour 1485–1642', *Past and Present* supplement 3 (1978)
Jardine, Lisa, 'Mastering the Uncouth: Gabriel Harvey, Edmund Spenser and the English Experience in Ireland', in John Henry and Sarah Hutton, eds., *New Perspectives on Renaissance Thought: Essays in the History of Science, Education and Philosophy in Memory of Charles B. Schmitt* (London: Duckworth, 1990), pp. 68–82
Jardine, Lisa, *Erasmus, Man of Letters: the Construction of Charisma in Print* (Princeton University Press, 1993)
Jardine, Lisa and Anthony Grafton, '"Studied for action": How Gabriel Harvey read his Livy',' *Past and Present* 129 (1990): 30–78
Javitch, Daniel, '*The Philosopher of the Court*: a French Satire Misunderstood', *Comparative Literature* 23 (1971): 97–124
Javitch, Daniel, *Poetry and Courtliness in Renaissance England* (Princeton University Press, 1978)
Johnson, Reverend A. H., ed., *The History of the Worshipful Company of the Drapers of London* (Oxford: Clarendon Press, 1914)
Jones, Howard, *Master Tully Cicero in Tudor England* (Nieuwkoop: De Graaf Publishers, 1998)
Jones, Norman L., *Faith by Statute: Parliament and the Settlement of Religion 1559* (London: Swift Printers Ltd; Atlantic Highlands: Humanities Press Inc., 1982)
Jones, Richard Foster, 'The Moral Sense of Simplicity', *Studies in Honor of Frederick W. Shipley* (St Louis: Washington University Studies, 1942), pp. 265–87

Bibliography

Kahn, Victoria, *Rhetoric, Prudence and Skepticism in the Renaissance* (Ithaca, NY: Cornell University Press, 1985)

Kearney, Hugh, *Scholars and Gentlemen: Universities and Society in Pre-Industrial Britain 1500–1700* (London: Faber and Faber, 1970)

Kelly, Joan, 'Did Women have a Renaissance?' in *Women, History and Theory: the Essays of Joan Kelly* (University of Chicago Press, 1984), pp. 19–50

Kennedy, George, *The Art of Rhetoric in the Roman World, 300 BC–AD 300* (Princeton University Press, 1972)

King, John N., *English Reformation Literature: the Tudor Origins of the Protestant Tradition* (Princeton University Press, 1982)

King, John N., *Spenser's Poetry and the Reformation Tradition* (Princeton University Press, 1990)

Klein, Lawrence E., *Shaftesbury and the Culture of Politeness* (Cambridge University Press, 1994)

Kristeller, P. O., *The Classic and Renaissance Thought* (Cambridge, MA: Harvard University Press, 1955)

Kristeller, P. O., 'Humanism and Scholasticism', in *Studies in Renaissance Thought and Letters* (Rome, Edizioni di storia e letteratura, 1956–96), vol. III, pp. 553–83

Langford, Paul, *A Polite and Commercial People* (Oxford University Press, 1989)

Lawson, John and Harold Silver, *A Social History of Education in England* (London: Methuen and Co. Ltd, 1973)

Leinwand, Theodore B., 'Negotiation and New Historicism', *Publications of the Modern Language Association of America* 105 (1990): 477–90

Lievsay, John, *Stefano Guazzo and the English Renaissance 1575–1675* (Chapel Hill: University of North Carolina Press, 1961)

Levack, Brian P., *The Civil Lawyers in England 1603–1641: a Political Study* (Oxford: Clarendon Press, 1973)

McCabe, Mary Margaret, *Plato and his Predecessors: the Dramatisation of Reason* (Cambridge University Press, 2000)

McConica, James, 'Scholars and Commoners in Renaissance Oxford' in Lawrence Stone, ed., *The University in Society*, vol. I (London: Oxford University Press, 1975), pp. 51–81

McKitterick, David, Review of Virginia Stern's *Gabriel Harvey*, *The Library* 6 (1981): 348–53

McRae, Andrew, 'Husbandry Manuals and the Language of Agrarian Improvement', in Michael Leslie and Timothy Raylor, eds., *Culture and Cultivation in Early Modern England: Writing and the Land* (Leicester University Press, 1992), pp. 35–62

McRae, Andrew, *God Speed the Plough: the Representation of Agrarian England, 1500–1600* (Cambridge University Press, 1996)

Mack, Peter, 'The Dialogue in English Education in the Sixteenth Century' in M. T. Jones-Davies, ed., *Le Dialogue au temps de la Renaissance* (Paris: J. Touzot, 1984), pp. 189–212

Magnusson, Lynne, *Shakespeare and Social Dialogue: Dramatic Language and Elizabethan Letters* (Cambridge University Press, 1999)

Major, John, *Sir Thomas Elyot and Renaissance Humanism* (Lincoln: University of Nebraska Press, 1964)
Manley, Lawrence, *Convention, 1500–1700* (Cambridge, MA: Harvard University Press, 1980)
Marsh, David, *The Quattrocento Dialogue: Classical Tradition and Humanist Innovation* (Cambridge, MA: Harvard University Press, 1980)
Martines, Lauro, *Power and Imagination: City-States in Renaissance Italy* (New York: Vintage Books, 1979, rpt. 1980)
Maslen, R. W., *Elizabethan Fictions: Espionage, Counter-Espionage, and the Duplicity of Fiction in Early Elizabethan Prose Narratives* (Oxford: Clarendon Press, 1997)
Mauss, Marcel, *The Gift: the Form and Reason for Exchange in Archaic Societies* (London: Routledge, 1989)
May, Steven W., *The Elizabethan Courtier Poets: The Poems and their Contexts* (Asheville, NC: Pegasus Press, 1991 rpt. 1999)
Mennell, Stephen, *Norbert Elias: Civilization and the Human Self-Image* (Oxford: Basil Blackwell, 1989)
Mohl, Ruth, *The Three Estates in Medieval and Renaissance Literature* (New York: Columbia University Press, 1933)
Mohrmann, Gerald P., 'The Civile Conversation: Communication in the Renaissance', *Speech Monographs* 39 (1972): 193–204
Morgan, Marjorie, *Manners, Morals and Class in England, 1774–1858* (Basingstoke: Macmillan; New York: St Martin's Press, 1994)
Mueller, Janel M., *The Native Tongue and the Word: Developments in English Prose Style 1380–1580* (University of Chicago Press, 1984)
Muldrew, Craig, 'Interpreting the market: the ethics of credit and community relations in early modern England', *Social History* 18 (1993): 163–83
Muldrew, Craig, *The Economy of Obligation: the Culture of Credit and Social Relations in Early Modern England* (Basingstoke: Macmillan, 1998)
Nielson, James, 'Reading between the Lines: Manuscript Personality and Gabriel Harvey's Drafts', *Studies in English Literature 1500–1900* 33 (1993): 43–82
Norbrook, David, *Poetry and Politics in the English Renaissance* (London, Boston: Routledge and Kegan Paul, 1984)
Norbrook, David, *Writing the English Republic: Poetry, Rhetoric and Politics, 1627–1660* (Cambridge University Press, 1999)
North, Helen F., *Sophrosyne: Self-Knowledge and Self-Restraint in Greek Literature* (Ithaca, NY: Cornell University Press, 1966)
North, Helen F., *From Myth to Icon: Reflections of Greek Ethical Doctrine in Literature and Art* (Ithaca, NY: Cornell University Press, 1979)
O'Callaghan, Michelle, *The 'shepheards nation': Jacobean Spenserians and Early Stuart Political Culture, 1612–1625* (Oxford: Clarendon Press, 2000)
O'Neill, Onora, *A Question of Trust: the BBC Reith Lectures 2002* (Cambridge University Press, 2002)
Orlin, Lena Cowen, *Private Matters and Public Culture in Post-Reformation England* (Ithaca, NY: Cornell University Press, 1994)

Palmer, Patricia, *Language and Conquest in Early Modern Ireland: English Renaissance Literature and Elizabethan Imperial Expansion* (Cambridge University Press, 2001)

Pelney, Sandy, *Speech Acts and Literary Theory* (London: Routledge, 1990)

Peltonen, Markku, *Classical Humanism and Republicanism in English Political Thought, 1570–1640* (Cambridge University Press, 1995)

Pincombe, Mike, *Elizabethan Humanism: Literature and Learning in the Later Sixteenth Century* (Harlow: Longman, 2001)

Poggioli, Renato, *The Oaten Flute: Essays on Pastoral Poetry and the Pastoral Ideal* (Cambridge, MA: Harvard University Press, 1975)

Plomer, Henry R. and Tom Peete Cross, *The Life and Correspondence of Lodowick Bryskett* (University of Chicago Press, 1927)

Pocock, J. G. A., 'Virtues, Rights, and Manners', in *Virtue, Commerce and History: Essays in Political Thought and History, Chiefly in the Eighteenth Century* (Cambridge University Press, 1985), pp. 35–50

Posner, David M., *The Performance of Nobility in Early Modern European Literature* (Cambridge University Press, 1999)

Prest, Wilfrid R., *The Inns of Court under Elizabeth I and the Early Stuarts 1590–1640* (Harlow: Longman, 1972)

Rambuss, Richard, *Spenser's Secret Career* (Cambridge University Press, 1993)

Roberts-Roddham, Alison J., *Fairs in England 1580–1680* (Bristol: Stuart Press, 1999)

Ruutz-Rees, Caroline, 'Some Notes of Gabriel Harvey's in Hoby's Translation of Castiglione's *Il cortegiano* (1561)', *Publications of the Modern Language Association of America* 25 (1910): 608–39.

Saccone, Eduardo, '*Grazia, Sprezzatura, Affettazione* in the *Courtier*', in Hanning and Rosand, eds., *Castiglione: The Ideal and the Real*, pp. 45–67

Schleiner, Louise, 'Spenser and Sidney on the *Vaticinium*', *Spenser Studies* 6 (1988): 129–45

Schleiner, Louise, 'Spenser's "E.K" as Edmund Kent (Kenned/of Kent): Kyth (Couth), Kissed, and Kunning-Conning', *English Literary Renaissance* 20 (1990): 374–407

Schoenfeldt, Michael C., *Bodies and Selves in Early Modern England: Physiology and Inwardness in Spenser, Shakespeare, Herbert and Milton* (Cambridge University Press, 1999)

Searle, John R. et al., *(On) Searle on Conversation*, intro. Herman Parret and Jef Verschueren (Amsterdam, Philadelphia: John Benjamins Publishing Co., 1992)

Sedgwick, Eve Kosofsky, *Between Men: English Literature and Male Homosocial Desire* (New York: Columbia University Press, 1995)

Seigel, Jerrold E., '"Civic Humanism" or Ciceronian Rhetoric? The Culture of Petrarch and Bruni', *Past and Present* 34 (1966): 3–48

Shapin, Steven, *A Social History of Truth: Civility and Science in Seventeenth-Century England* (University of Chicago Press, 1994)

Shepard, Alexander and Phil Withington, eds., *Communities in Early Modern England: Networks, Place, Rhetoric* (Manchester University Press, 2000)

Shrank, Cathy, 'Rhetorical Constructions of a National Community: the Role of English in mid-Tudor writing', in Shepard and Withington, eds., *Communities*, pp. 180–98

Shuger, Debora, 'Irishmen, Aristocrats, and Other White Barbarians', *Renaissance Quarterly* 50 (1997): 494–525

Sider, Gerald M., 'The Ties that Bind: Culture and Agriculture, Property and Propriety in the Newfoundland Village Fishery', *Social History* 5 (1980): 1–39

Simms, Katherine, 'Guesting and Feasting in Gaelic Ireland', *Journal of the Royal Society of Antiquaries of Ireland* 108 (1978): 67–100

Skinner, Quentin, *The Foundations of Modern Political Thought. Vol I: The Renaissance* (Cambridge University Press, 1978, rpt. 1996)

Snyder, Jon R., *Writing the Scene of Speaking: Theories of Dialogue in the Late Italian Renaissance* (Stanford University Press, 1989)

Spens, Janet, *Spenser's Faerie Queene: an Interpretation* (London: Edward Arnold and Co., 1934)

Stern, Virginia, *Gabriel Harvey: his Life, Marginalia and Library* (Oxford: Clarendon Press, 1979)

Stewart, Alan, *Close Readers: Humanism and Sodomy in Early Modern England* (Princeton University Press, 1997)

Stone, Lawrence, *The Crisis of the Aristocracy, 1558–1641* (Oxford: Clarendon Press, 1966)

Stone, Lawrence, 'Social Mobility in England, 1500–1700', *Past and Present* 33 (1966): 16–55

Strype, John, *The Life of the Learned Sir Thomas Smith* (Oxford: Clarendon Press, 1820)

Strype, John, *The Life of the Learned Sir John Cheke, Kt. First Instructor, Afterwards Secretary of State to King Edward VI* (Oxford: Clarendon Press, 1821)

Sullivan, Ceri, *The Rhetoric of Credit: Merchants in the Early Modern World* (London: Associated University Presses, 2002)

Thirsk, Joan, ed., *The Agrarian History of England and Wales, vol. IV 1500–1640* (Cambridge University Press, 1967)

Thirsk, Joan, *Economic Policy and Projects: The Development of a Consumer Society in Early Modern England* (Oxford: Clarendon Press, 1978)

Thirsk, Joan, 'Making a Fresh Start: Sixteenth-Century Agriculture and the Classical Inspiration' in Michael Leslie and Timothy Raylor, eds., *Culture and Cultivation in Early Modern England: Writing and the Land* (Leicester University Press, 1992), pp. 15–34

Tylus, Jane, 'Spenser's Virgil, and the Politics of Poetic Labor', *English Literary History* 55 (1988): 53–77

Veyne, Paul, 'Homosexuality in Ancient Rome', in Philippe Ariès and André Béjin eds., *Western Sexuality* (Oxford: Blackwell, 1985), pp. 26–35

Vickers, Brian, *In Defence of Rhetoric* (Oxford University Press, 1988)

Vos, Alvin, 'The Formation of Roger Ascham's Prose Style', *Studies in Philology* 71 (1974): 344–70

Whigham, Frank, *Ambition and Privilege: the Social Tropes of Elizabethan Courtesy Theory* (Berkeley: University of California Press, 1984)
Wilson, Katherine, 'The Revenge of the Angel Gabriel: Harvey's "A Nobleman's Suit to a Country Maid"', in Mike Pincombe, ed., *The Anatomy of Tudor Literature: Proceedings of the First International Conference of the Tudor Symposium (1998)* (Aldershot: Ashgate, 2001), pp. 79–89
Williams, Joseph M., '"O! when Degree is Shak'd": Sixteenth-Century Anticipations of some Modern Attitudes towards Usage', in Tim William Machan and Charles T. Scott, eds., *English in its Social Contexts: Essays in Historical Sociolinguistics* (Oxford University Press, 1992), pp. 69–101
Wood, Neal, 'Foundations of political economy: the new moral philosophy of Sir Thomas Smith', in Paul A. Fideler and T. F. Mayer, eds., *Political Thought and the Tudor Commonwealth: Deep Structure, Discourse and Disguise* (London: Routledge, 1992), pp. 140–68
Wrightson, Keith, 'Estates, Degrees and Sorts: Changing Perceptions of Society in Tudor and Stuart England' in Penelope J. Corfield, ed., *Language, History and Class* (Oxford: Basil Blackwell, 1991), pp. 30–52
Wrightson, Keith, *Earthly Necessities: Economic Lives in Early Modern Britain* (New Haven: Yale University Press, 2000)
Zim, Rivkah, 'Dialogue and Discretion: Thomas Sackville, Catherine de Medici and the Anjou Marriage Proposal, 1571', *Historical Journal* 40 (1977): 287–310

Index

agrarian improvement, 91, 96–97, 107, 169
Althusser, Louis, 113
anti-court satire, 10, 73, 96–97, 119, 169
Arendt, Hannah, 10
Ariosto, *Orlando Furioso*, 132
Aristotle, 78, 111
   Nicomachean Ethics, 57, 58, 60
Arte of Rhetorique, see Thomas Wilson
Ascham, Roger, 3–4, 17, 19, 47, 64, 66–67, 114, 121, 123, 124, 134
   familiar letters, 78
   Harvey's criticism of, 131
   Schoolmaster, 16, 17, 45–46, 78, 113, 120, 123, 125–130, 137, 153
   Toxophilus, 67, 71–72, 85, 91, 122, 136
Athenian tribe, 16, 17, 45, 47, 68, 140–143, 148
Attridge, Derek, 123, 130
Augustine, 68

Bacon, Nicholas, 84
Bamfield, Hugh, 163
Barclay, Alexander, 141
Barry, Jonathan, 15
Barston, John, 16
Bible, translation of, 70
Blundeston, Laurence, 156–157
Boccaccio, Giovanni, 75
Boke named the Governour, see Elyot, Thomas
Book of the Courtier, see Castiglione, Baldassare
Brennan, Michael, 157
Brook, Christopher, 72
Brown, Penelope, 23, 24–25
Bryant, Francis, 10
Bryskett, Lodowick, *Discourse of Civill Life*, 5, 106–112
   translation of Cinthio, 107–111
Bryson, Anna, 1, 12, 20
Burke, Peter, 23, 63

Cain, Thomas H., 162, 166
Cameron, Euan, 46

Capel, Arthur, 17, 46
Carafa, Diomede, 57
Casa, Giovanni della, *Galateo*, 12, 20, 63
Caspari, Fritz, 66
Castiglione, Baldassare, *Book of the Courtier* 1, 5, 7, 8, 15, 29–33, 34, 35, 39, 42, 43–48, 51–64, 66–67, 73, 128–129; translation of 44–47, 63, 64; reception of 44–47, 63–64; Harvey's copy of 63
Cecil, William, 79, 90, 126–128, 146, 157
Chaucer, Geoffrey, 149, 166
Cheke, John, 3, 16, 47, 64, 65–67, 70–72, 75, 78–86, 105, 107, 113, 122, 124, 129
   Letter to Hoby, 45, 46
   hurt of sedition, 68, 71–72
Cicero, 2, 6, 41, 47, 112
   De amicitia, 3–4, 15, 28, 78, 121, 126, 127, 147–148
   Pro Archia Poeta, 49
   De inventione, 50
   De officiis 3, 8–10, 16, 22, 24–28, 29, 36, 40, 47, 50, 56, 74, 75, 85, 88, 89, 93–101, 123, 147; translation of 92–93; compared with Xenophon's *Oeconomicus* 36–38, 112
   De oratore 10, 16, 23, 26, 47–51, 77–78, 84, 126, 130, 150–160; Castiglione's imitation of 51–55, 56, 134–136; Ascham's imitation of 127, 128
Cicero on Socrates, 10
Ciceronian dialogue, 5, 25
Cinthio, Giovanni Battista Giraldi 107–112; see Bryskett, Lodowick
Civile Conversation, see Stefano Guazzo
civilising process, 6–12
civility, 2, 4, 15, 18, 27, 37, 39, 104–105, 116, 169
Cleaver, Robert, 35
Cleland, James, *Institution of a Noble Man*, 30, 33, 69
Clerke, Bartholomew, 45, 46
closet, 21–22, 42
Collinson, Patrick, 19

Index

colonisation, 4, 56, 105–112
community, ideas of, 4, 14–15, 17, 19, 88, 140
conversation 23–29; see also rhetoric
    and commerce, 88–89, 101–105
    and sexual intercourse, 35, 40
    civil, 29–33
    domestical, 33–42
    rules of, 23–27
Cooper, Thomas, 27, 66
Court of civill courtesie, see Robson, Simon
courtly aesthetics, 56, 60, 66
Cowen Orlin, Lena, 37
Cox, John D., 68, 70, 74
Cox, Virginia, 25, 34
Coynie, 108–109
courtier
    and the citizen, 43
    see also husbandman
Cranmer, Thomas, 67
Cromwell, Thomas, 44
Crowley, Robert, 70, 71, 75, 87, 140, 141
    edition of *Piers Plowman*, 67–68
    Philargyrie, 95
    Voice of the Last Trumpet, 68
    Way to Wealth, 67, 68
custom, linguistic, 80, 84–86, 125
Cyvile and Uncyvile Life, 5, 7, 13–14, 90, 93–101, 103, 104, 107, 111, 112
    Gabriel Harvey's transcription of, 17

Damon and Pythias, see Edwards, Richard
Davies, Kathleen M., 35–36
decorum, see also *honestas*
    Augustinian, 68
    Horation, 141
    in *Shepheardes Calender*
Dee, John, 21
Dewar, Mary, 105
Discourse of Civill Life, see Bryskett, Lodowick
A Dispraise of the life of the Courtier, see Guevara, Antonio
dissimulatio, 26, 51, 52–53, 149–150
Dod, John, 35
double translation
    and Ascham, 127–128
    and Harvey, 131
Drant, Thomas, 123
Drapers, Company of, 72
Dudley, Robert, Earl of Leicester, 18, 45
Dyer, Edward, 125

Eagleton, Terry, 11
Edwards, Richard, 141, 142
    Damon and Pythias, 140, 147–148, 152–153
    Paradyse of daynty devises, 146–147

E.K., unreliability 142; see also Harvey, Gabriel
Elias, Norbert, 1, 6
Elizabethan settlement, 45, 79
Elshstain, Jean Bethke, 42
Elsky, Martin, 86
Elyot, Thomas
    Boke named the Governour, 44, 66, 69–70, 74–76, 84
    Dictionary, 27
    Pasquil the Playne, 75
Empson, William, 27
enclosure, 87, 94, 101, 102–103, 168, 169
Erasmus, Desiderius, 46, 47, 132, 153
estates satire, 62–63, 67–68, 75, 120, 144, 145–146, 153, 154

Faerie Queene, see Spenser, Edmund
Feckenham, Abbot of Westminster, 79
Fitzherbert, John, *Boke of Husbandry*, 96, 99
Fitzwilliam, William, 97, 110
Fleming, Abraham, 66
Foucault, Michel, 57, 113
Foure Bookes of Husbandry, see Heresbach, Conrad
Foxe, John, 80
Freud, Sigmund, 6
    Civilization and its Discontents, 6–7, 11
    Future of an Illusion, 11–12
Friedman, Alice T., 21
friendship, 7, 15, 17, 28, 75, 78–85, 118, 122–123, 125–134, 139, 143, 148
    and quantification, 122
    at the Inns of Court, 146–148
    between courtier and prince, 56, 62–63, 75
    between Spenser and Harvey, 142–143, 158

Galateo, see Casa, Giovanni della
Gallagher, Catherine, 6–7, 8
Gardiner, Stephen, 80–85, 86, 105, 134
Garin, Eugenio, 43
Gascoigne, George, 140, 144, 146
    Harvey's comments on, 142–143
    Hundreth Sundrie Flowres, 144
    Poesies, 144
    Steele Glas, 145–146, 166
Gilbert, Humphrey, 85, 144
Goldberg, Jonathan, 152, 153
Googe, Barnabe, 17, 38, 110, 142, 143, 153, 162
    Eglogs, 140–141, 146, 159, 166
    translator of *Foure Bookes of Husbandry*, 96, 97
    translator of Palingenius, 153, 157
Gosson, Stephen, 136
Greenblatt, Stephen, 6–7, 8–10, 57, 106–107, 110, 169

Greene, Robert, 4
  Harvey's attack on, 114, 115–116
  Menaphon, 119
  Quip for an Upstart Courtier, 115, 120
Greene, Thomas, 43–44
Lord Grey of Wilton, 108, 109, 110, 145
Grimalde, Nicholas, 92
Guazzo, Stefano, *Civile Conversation* 5, 13, 16–17, 19, 21, 22–42, 71, 73, 88, 107, 108, 112, 118, 166, 169; Harvey's copy of 47
Guevara, Antonio *Dispraise of the life of the Courtier*, 10
Gouge, William, 35

Hackett, Helen, 35
Halpern, Richard, 113
Hammond, Paul, 152
Hart, John, 85
Harvey, Gabriel, 3, 6, 7, 14, 17–19, 46, 86, 112, 114–138, 153
  and E.K., 140, 143, 161
  Foure Letters, 114, 115–117, 119, 120, 138, 143
  Letter-book, 17, 63, 118, 121, 132, 134, 135–136
  Rhetor, 158
  Three Proper Letters, 114, 115, 117–121, 122–126, 130–138, 139–143, 160–161
Harvey, John, 115, 121, 131, 134, 137
Harvey, Richard, 115, 119
Hastings, Henry, 45, 64, 70
Heal, Felicity, 21, 93
Helgerson, Richard, 124, 125, 132, 135
Heresbach, Conrad *Foure Bookes of Husbandry*, 38, 96–97, 99, 110, 153
Hervet, Gentian, 36, 37, 38
Hirschman, Albert O., 65
Hoby, Thomas, 5, 15–16, 44, 45, 46, 53, 63–64, 79
Hoffman, Nancy Jo, 163
homosexuality, 151–153, 154, 155
honest rivalry, 14–15, 28, 56, 76–78, 79, 119, 122–123, 138
  among artisans, 71
  among the Athenian tribe, 79
honestas, 2, 26–28, 31, 38, 47, 48–51, 60, 66, 76, 77, 86, 90, 122, 149–151
  and justice, 92–93, 98–100, 168–169
  translated as simplicity, 69, 74
honestie of this age, see Rich, Barnabe
honesty, 5, 7, 8, 10, 23, 38–39, 89–90, 107, 122–123, 149
  as liberality, 86
  for men, 27–29
  for women, 35, 40
  in *Book of the Courtier*, 61, 62
  in *Civile Conversation*, 30–31, 32, 40
  in *Cyvile and Uncyvile Life*, 90, 91, 92–101

  in commerce, 89–90, 103
  in *Discourse of Civill Life*, 107–108, 111
  in *Damon and Pythias*, 148
  in *honestie of this age*, 73
  in *Shepheardes Calender*
  in *Toxophilus*, 67, 72, 122, 149
  in *Oeconomicus*, 35
hospitality, 86, 90, 92–100, 107, 108, 155, 163, 166, 169
Hudson, Winthrop, 79, 146
humanism
  Italian, 43, 46, 49
  Tudor, 65–86
humanist
  and the courtier, 66–67, 105–112
Hunter, G. K., 66
hurt of sedition, see Cheke, John
husbandman
  and the courtier, 4–5, 10, 38, 91, 92–101
husbandry books, 4
Hutson, Lorna, 36–37, 57, 101

incorporation, 16–17
Inns of Court, 17, 140
Institution of a Noble Man, see Cleland, James
Ireland, 4, 7, 73, 86, 87, 91–93, 105–112, 145, 168

Jacobean Spenserians, 140
Jardine, Lisa, 132
Javitch, Daniel, 9

Kalos, 38
Kett's rebellion, 67–68, 72
King, John N., 67, 149
King, Ros, 146, 152–153
A Knack to Know a Knave, 72
Kosofsky Sedgwick, Eve, 152
Kristellor, P. O., 49

Langland, William, *Piers Plowman*, 67, 149, 166–167
Latimer, Hugh, 7, 75, 87, 93–96, 99, 103, 140, 149, 156
Levinson, Stephen, 23, 24–25
Lovelace, William, 156
Lydgate, John, *Stans puer ad mensam*, 20, 28
Lyly, John, 115

McCabe, Mary Margaret, 25
McRae, Andrew, 88, 96
Magnusson, Lynne, 23, 24–25
Mantuan, 140, 141, 163–165, 166
  see also Turbeville, George; see also Virgil
Marot, Clémont, 141
Martines, Lauro, 44

Index

Maslen, Robert, 144
Mauss, Marcel, 153
May, Steven, 66
Miller, James Arthur, 80
Mohl, Ruth, 68
More, Thomas, 132
More, William, 21
Mother Hubberds Tale, see Spenser, Edmund
Mulcaster, Richard, 85–86, 124–125, 134, 135
Muldrew, Craig, 88–89

Nashe, Thomas, 4, 131, 133
  Have With You to Saffron-Walden, 114–115, 119–120
  Pierce Penilesse, 115, 119
  Nashe-Harvey quarrel, 115–120
  Strange Newes, 117–118, 119, 120
negotiation, 3, 14–15, 28, 42, 65, 90, 91, 102, 103
Neville, Alexander, 153, 156, 157
Neville, Thomas, 18–19, 153
nobility debate, 32–33, 41, 53–55, 64, 150–151, 155
Norbrook, David, 45
Norris, Thomas, 107
North, George, 9
North, Helen F., 38, 57, 61
Norton, Thomas, 45

O'Callaghan, Michelle, 140
Oeconomicus, see Xenophon
  translation of, see Hervet, Gentian

Palmer, Patricia, 85
pastoral, 141
Patrizi, Francesco, 57
Peltonen, Markku, 16–17
Pettie, George, 5, 16, 71, 111
Philibert de Vienne
  Philosopher of the Court, 8–10, 45
Pigman, G. W., 144
Pincombe, Mike, 66, 160
plainness 67–72; plain style 71, 76–77
Plato, *Phaedrus*, 49, 78
politeness, 2, 23, 25
Pomeroy, Sarah B., 36
Ponet, John, 82
Pritchard, Richard, *schoole of honest and vertuous lyfe*, 29–30, 37
pronunciation, 19, 80–86, 124–125, 130

Quantification, 114, 122, 123–125, 126, 130–131, 136, 142, 160

Reformation, 5, 16–17, 47, 77, 79–80, 89
rhetoric
  argument *in utramque partem*, 49–50
  and conversation 43–55
Rhodes, Hugh, *Boke of Nurture*, 20–21, 22, 29
Rich, Barnabe, *Honestie of this age*, 73, 74
Robson, Simon, *Court of Civill Courtesie*, 13, 108
Russell, John, *Boke of Nurture*, 20

Sackville, Richard, 45, 126
Sackville, Thomas, 45, 126
Schoenfeldt, Michael C., 60
schoole of honest and vertuous lyfe, see Pritchard, Thomas
Schoolmaster, see Ascham, Roger
Shakespeare, William, 114
Shapin, Steven, 27
Shepard, Alex, 14, 73
Shepheardes Calender, see Spenser, Edmund
Shepheardes Hunting, 140
Shepheardes Pipe, 140
Shuger, Debora, 106
Sider, Gerald M., 14
Sidney, Henry, 45, 91, 105, 106, 109, 123
Sidney, Philip, 115, 123, 140, 149
  and the *areopagus*, 125
  Arcadia, 72
Simms, Katherine, 107
simplicity, 23, 69, 74, 75, 76
Skelton, John, 149
Skinner, Quentin, 57–58
Smith, Thomas, 3–4, 16, 17, 19, 45, 47, 65, 66–67, 75–76, 78–86, 107, 113, 115, 121, 122, 124, 125, 132–134, 140, 159
  De Republica Anglorum, 83–84, 158
  Discourse of the Commonweal of This Realm of England, 87–88, 90–91, 100–106, 138
  interests in Ireland
  on English spelling, 82–83, 133
  on Greek pronunciation, 79–82, 83
Socratic dialogue, 4, 5, 25–27, 29, 34, 50, 78, 91, 103–105, 112, 122–123, 149, 159
Spenser, Edmund, 3–4, 7, 17, 86, 112, 114–138
  in *Discourse of Civill Life*, 108
  Faerie Queene, 57, 132, 138, 160
  Mother Hubberds Tale, 119, 143
  Teares of the Muses [*Nine Muses*], 132, 138, 160
  Shepheardes Calender 5, 17, 122, 124, 137, 138, 139–167; *Januarie* 143, 151–153, 157–159, 161; *Februarie* 141–142, 159; *Aprill* 157; *Maye* 149; *June* 143, 159–162; *Julye* 149; *September* 149; *October* 143–144, 149, 162–167; *November* 143, 167; *December* 139, 151–161, 167
  Three Proper Letters, see Harvey

Spenser, Edmund (*cont.*)
  View of the Present State of Ireland, 4,
    106–107, 110, 112
sprezzatura, 8–9, 14, 31, 48, 98, 111, 118, 134, 160
  in *Book of the Courtier*, 51, 53–55, 106
  in *Shepheardes Calender*, 149–150, 160, 161
  in *Three Proper Letters*, 125
Stanyhurst, Richard, 123
Stewart, Alan, 21–22, 152–157
Stone, Lawrence, 12

temperance, 56, 84
  and continence, 57, 58
  in Aristotle, 57, 58, 60
  in Castiglione, 44, 48, 55–64
  in Cicero 9, 26, 56, 60–61; see also *honestas*
Thirsk, Joan, 87, 96
Toxophilus, see Ascham, Roger
Turbeville, George, translation of Mantuan, 17,
    140–141, 142, 143
  Eglogs, Songs and Sonets, 146, 162, 166
Tylus, Jane, 162

Urbanitatis, 20
uncivil conversation, 82, 115–121

Virgil, 140, 152, 153, 154, 157, 160
  and Mantuan, 163
Vives, Juan Luis, 47, 132

Walsingham, Francis, 57, 90, 109–110
Watson, Thomas, 123, 124, 129–130, 131, 134, 161
Whigham, Frank, 12
Whitney, John, 78, 127–128, 130, 131
Whytforde, Richard, 35
Whytington, Robert, 92–93
Wilson, Katherine, 118
Wilson, Thomas, *Arte of Rhetorique*, 69–70, 76
Williams, Joseph M., 69
Withington, Phil, 14, 73
women 7; see also conversation, domestic
Wood, Neal, 88
Wrightson, Keith, 69

Xenophon, 109
  Oeconomicus, 29, 35, 36–39, 40, 86, 95–97,
    105
  compared with *De officiis*, 36–38, 112

Young, Bartholomew, 5
Young, John, 17, 18–19

DISCARDED